LOVETT'S
LIGHTS
on
JOHN

LOVETT'S
LIGHTS
on
JOHN

WITH REPHRASED TEXT BY

C. S. Lovett

M.A., B.D., D.D.

author of
DEALING WITH THE DEVIL
JESUS WANTS YOU WELL!
SOUL-WINNING MADE EASY

director of Personal Christianity

Published by

PERSONAL CHRISTIANITY
Baldwin Park, California 91706

"THAT YOU MAY BELIEVE" CHRIST IS GOD!

THE APOSTLE JOHN

ILLUSTRATED by LINDA LOVETT

PRINTED IN THE UNITED STATES OF AMERICA
by
**EL CAMINO PRESS
LA VERNE, CA 91750**

BROTHER JOHN!

. . . Do you realize what people are saying?

Of course John knew. But writing a document to counteract rising public opinion isn't easy, especially when you are 90 years old. And he was just about that age when he began this Gospel. If ever there was a citizen of the First Century, it was John. His tombstone could have read:

JOHN—SON OF ZEBEDEE AND SALOME

BORN . . . A.D. 1
DIED . . . A.D. 100

Do we know that for certain? No, but it isn't far off. He was the youngest of the Lord's disciples, about 25 when John the Baptist introduced him to Jesus. And he stayed with the Lord right up to the Ascension and then served the Jerusalem church for a time as an elder. After that he drops out of the New Testament.

Years later, according to well established tradition, we find him serving the seven churches of Asia Minor as pastor. He assumed the leadership after the deaths of Peter, Paul and Timothy. Persecutions had taken their toll of the disciples. And now John is the last. His students are worried. They ask if he knows what people are saying, and rightly so. When John dies, not only would the last of the Apostles be gone, but with him the final, authoritative voice of the church. Who else had his first hand knowledge, his experience? And with the enemies of the church making good headway with their false teaching, John's disciples come to him:

> "John, everywhere people are saying that Jesus was not God. That He was merely a unique prophet who never really claimed to be God in the flesh. Don't you think you'd better get the facts in writing so as to preserve the truth for those who come after us! You are the last person alive who actually heard what Jesus said!"

Indeed. Who else would have the settling word for succeeding generations? John alone could now record what Jesus actually said.

ENEMIES?

A horrible system of false teaching arose less than fifty years after our Lord ascended into heaven. It had numerous forms but essentially it denied the Deity of the Lord Jesus. Scholars give it the high sounding name of Gnosticism. These false teachers allowed that Christ was a unique personage, perhaps even "A" son of God, but that He was "equal with God," was vigorously and viciously denied. Of course this isn't too surprising when you consider there is so much about our Lord Jesus which is a stumbling block for natural man.

Outwardly He was just an ordinary Person. He came from a peasant family, arriving in this world amid the most crude and humble circumstances. He grew to manhood in obscurity, working at a carpenter's bench. There was nothing about Him to suggest He was the Lord of Glory. When He began His ministry it was not with the pomp and fanfare of the great of this world. Instead, He was meek and lowly. Why, even His companions were unlettered fishermen. Beyond that, what He had to say was utterly rejected by the religious leaders of that day. Little wonder some choked on the idea this Carpenter was "equal with God." It's too much for many today.

So the suggestion that John counter these false charges in writing was inspired. No doubt about it, there was an urgent need for an authoritative, systematic presentation of Jesus' claim to be God in the flesh. Everything hinges on what He said of Himself. For if He is not what He claimed, Christianity crumbles. The enemies of the truth believed the Deity of Christ to be the most vulnerable point in Christianity. Their subtle attacks were gathering momentum in John's day. This heresy was rising fast in every place where the Gospel had been preached.

SO JOHN WRITES.

And who is better qualified? He was the one who knew Jesus best. His spiritual discernment was the keenest. He had the privilege of leaning on the Master's bosom. Yes, John is the one to restate Jesus' claim to Deity. And this was the perfect time in history.

As did the Apostle Paul before him, he dictates, using flawless Greek. His readers were Gentiles, for Christianity was now flourishing among them. This accounts for his numerous explanations of Jewish customs which would be familiar to any Jew. As his secretary prepares to scribe the letters, John goes over his notes. Before him are references he has collected over the years. All of Paul's letters are there, plus the three Gospels written at least 35 years earlier.

Paul wrote letters to people and churches. The other Apostles addressed themselves to problems within the church. Matthew, Mark and Luke (the synoptics) gave the history of our Lord, desiring to preserve the record of what He did, where He went, etc. But John writes to set forth the Lord's **claim** to Deity. This is why He presents Jesus as the WORD OF GOD, drawing our attention to WHAT HE SAID, as distinct from what He did.

The Gospels are narratives reporting how Jesus went here and there, doing this and that. But John selects only certain events from the life of the Lord and those as a means of presenting the long discourses which followed them. He is far more interested in reporting what Jesus SAID **after a miracle,** than the supernatural event itself. If Jesus is the WORD OF GOD, then the chief thing to come from Him is . . . WORDS! Jesus worked with words. He spoke and a storm subsided. A word from Him and the blind saw, the lame walked, and demons fled. He called and Lazarus came forth from the grave.

John therefore confronts us with the WORDS of Jesus and particularly His claim to Deity. Before him is a great body of evidence. He has only to start dictating. But how will he start? He needs a provocative opener for his Gospel. And then John is struck with a great idea!

JOHN'S IDEA.

You know how good writers try to select fascinating items from their times as a kickoff for their articles. They do this to grab a reader's interest from the very first line. Well, John did precisely that. In his day there was a philosophical term which was popular with religious thinkers. The True God, they said, the Absolute God, was unknowable. But there were evidences of His workings and interventions within space and time. Further, it was agreed that God personally revealed Himself through certain writings (Moses) and manifestations (Angel of the Lord). Over the centuries a great deal of information on God's workings in the affairs of men had been gathered and it had become a rather unwieldy mass of data.

About A.D. 50, some forty years before John wrote his Gospel, Philo, a Jew of Alexandria, began to use a word that lumped all the knowable things of God into a single package. That word was LOGOS. In this word "LOGOS" was compressed all that the Jews and Greeks knew of the reasonings and manifestations of God. It was a useful term and people soon began to refer to the "Logos" rather than go into detail about the way God worked in human affairs.

By the time John was ready to start his Gospel, the term LOGOS was the common way of referring to God's revelation of Himself. Of course it was an abstract, impersonal reference. No one ever thought of ascribing it to an individual. That is, no one until John was casting about for a way to begin his Gospel. Then the Holy Spirit struck him with the thought . . .

"Why not use this term which everyone knows and then let what I want to say, prove that JESUS is the LOGOS!"

After all, there was precedent for such a thing. The Apostle Paul had done just that when he reached Athens and found the altar dedicated to the "Unknown God." He took that popular fact, you recall, and used it for the introduction to his famous sermon on Mars hill . . .

"Men of Athens, I see that you are very religious. When I came into your city I saw your altar to the Unknown God. He Whom you worship in ignorance, I am now going to explain and present to you!" (Acts 17:23).

In John's time, the thinking world was using the term LOGOS to indicate the revelation of the "Unknown God." So he seized it as a terrific way to present the truth of Christ. It is as though he were saying . . .

> "This LOGOS of Whom you speak in ignorance, I will now declare unto you. He is none other than Jesus Christ of Nazareth!"

And that is what John does in the first fourteen verses of his Gospel. It is commonly called the PROLOGUE, but it is helpful also to think of it as a writer's device for capturing readers. You can be sure these words really "grabbed" the people of John's day. And the meaning was clear, too.

THE LOGOS.

Without any apology John states bluntly, "This Logos people are referring to is a PERSON. He is a specific Person, and I am going to identify Him for you. He is none other than Jesus, the Christ of God." Thus the Gospel of John is a careful selection of a few scenes from the life of the Lord which prove that He is the Logos. John has but one purpose, proving that Jesus is the LOGOS, Who claimed to be God in Person.

But Logos, what does it mean?

Logos is a Greek term for WORD. It does not mean "word" as a part of speech, something you find in a sentence. It has an altogether different meaning, yet it is one not unfamiliar to you.

You and I communicate with each other by means of WORDS. That is, an idea can be transferred from my mind to yours by means of a word. If I say "dog," at once a picture forms in your imagination. If I add the word, "Collie," likely you see the same thing in your mind, I see in mine. Thus the image I behold is transferred to your mind by means of a WORD from me. It is in this sense that John uses the term WORD (Logos), for that is exactly how it was employed by the religious thinkers of his day. It meant the **communication** of ideas from God to man.

So John takes this term WORD and says a particular Person is the LOGOS. That this PERSON is the means by which ideas are transferred from the mind of God to man. He says that the image God wishes to create in the imaginations of men is that of HIMSELF, the divine image. As a result, men could behold Jesus and visualize the character of the UNKNOWABLE GOD, even the very **nature** of His personality. Jesus is what God SAYS (the Word) which causes us to **picture** the Deity. Jesus is the WORD God **"speaks"** to trigger the divine image in our imaginations. Imaginations, you see, are designed to hold images.

It follows then, that when Jesus speaks, ideas are passing from the mind of God to those who hear. But please observe, even though an idea is transmitted from the mind of a person, the original idea NEVER LEAVES. Even as I cause you to visualize a "Collie" with a word, the original "Collie" is still in my mind. Thus, while Jesus is the WORD which causes the divine image to blossom in our minds, He is nonetheless as fully "in the bosom of the Father," as He is on earth (John 1:18). If that seems unfathomable now, it will get clearer as you read the Gospel.

When John began with his LOGOS (Word) idea, it was a writer's gimmick—but a fabulous one. Everybody knew at once what he was saying. Today, of course, people are not speculating about a WORD from God. No one is going around using the term LOGOS as a synonym for divine revelation. Consequently we have to explain it. What was a remarkable device for a writer in John's day, can be a clumsy, awkward phrase for us. Even so, when properly understood, it is packed with truth. And we must understand it before John's opening words make sense. That's why I have taken this space to comment on the Logos truth.

AS YOU READ THE GOSPEL.

The fact that John begins with the LOGOS (Word) truth, tells us what to expect in the chapters ahead. We will be meeting the **words** of Jesus. They will cause the Glory of God to appear on the screen of our imaginations. Profound things will surface in our minds. They will be mystical, reflective, as something of the Mind of God unfolds within us. Wondrous images will be triggered by Jesus' words, for

His are like no other's. Once He said, "Let there be light!" And there was light. Who but God can speak and have worlds appear (Col. 1:16)!

When Jesus speaks, God is speaking. This must be so or else His claims are ridiculous. Even more, He has said to us . . . "The words that I speak unto you, they are spirit and they are life" (John 6:63). As those spirit-words penetrate our souls via this Gospel, miracles happen and our faith rises to heights of worship. Yes, John did well to call Him the Word of God, for . . .

"Never spake a man like this man!"

—C.S.L.

JOHN

1 1. In the beginning, the Word was already existing. And the Word was fully and completely intimate with the Father. Therefore what God was, the Word was also— absolute Deity.

BEGINNING. Sounds like Genesis? It's supposed to. However the book of Genesis refers to the beginning of things. Since Jesus already existed, it is a reference to His supernatural pre-existence. He was BEFORE any beginning, therefore eternal. John opens with a declaration of Jesus' eternal history, whereas Matthew and Luke begin with His human history. See that His **intimacy** with the Father requires the same essence—Deity. John's Gospel is not a narrative, but a selection of events from Jesus' earthly life to prove He is God. In calling Him the WORD, John means to emphasize what Jesus said, as well as what is revealed by His Person. People communicate by words, even God with man. But God's Word is a Person. What an ingenious communication!

"If the Father and the Word were the same in essence, did they do things together and make plans together for the coming world?"

2. This same Word, the God/Word, was actively participating with God in eternity.

PARTICIPATING. In John's day, false teachers were claiming that a series of gods ranged between the unseen God of heaven and the physical universe. God was too holy, they said, to have any contact with sinful man. And since Jesus made the actual contact with sinners, He was the farthest removed from the Father. Not only was He the lowest in rank of these gods, they said, but He was Himself a created being and not the Creator. John does not write his Gospel to deal with this error, he nonetheless strikes hard at such a notion with these opening verses. His real purpose in writing is to show that Jesus is God incarnate and that people can have eternal life by depositing their complete trust in His Name.

"What was the connection then, between the Word and the physical world!"

3. The entire creation came into existence through Him, so that nothing which exists can remain in existence apart from His presence.

EXISTENCE. John says everything that exists owes its being to Christ, which at once covers unseen things too. Thus he consents with Paul who said that even the "principalities and powers in the heavenlies" owed their existence to Jesus. The Greek hints at still more. Not only did Jesus make this world, but He is also holding it together. He is its Sustainer. It is one thing to create the sun, quite another to maintain its daily orbit and atomic fire. Were Jesus to withdraw His presence from the visible world, it would disappear! (Col. 1:16). Scientists have speculated as to what holds the atom together or makes natural laws valid from one day to the next. A Person does—Jesus! It is a manifestation of His power (Heb. 1:3). One day He will convert the world back into energy and when He does—BANG! (2 Peter 3:10).

"Then He is also the source of life. Man's too!"

4. In Him was life. Every living thing owes its being to Him. However the life He gave to men was different. It set them apart from all other living things, for in them it was light—reason and recognition.

LIGHT. Light is for seeing. Physical light reveals a man's surroundings. Spiritual light illuminates a man inside and is called insight. This light is spiritual perception permitting a man to see WHO and WHAT he is. Today it shines in man revealing him a sinner. It brings guilt-consciousness even as it did with Adam who hid from God because of what he saw. Man can't cover his sin. And since the light reveals God in the things about him, it is painful. So man attempts to hide in the world. He now knows "good and evil" (a conscience) and he sees himself a sinner, deserving death.

The light that is in man condemns him. He doesn't like it. When it reveals the truth of God it terrifies him. So man turns his head away from God.

"Then sin and the fall really didn't damage the light in man! It damaged only the man. So now the damage is revealed by it!"

5. The light continues to shine in man and the darkness has not been able to extinguish it.

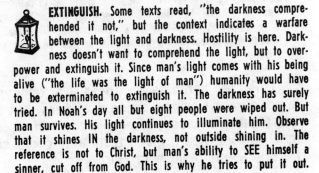

EXTINGUISH. Some texts read, "the darkness comprehended it not," but the context indicates a warfare between the light and darkness. Hostility is here. Darkness doesn't want to comprehend the light, but to overpower and extinguish it. Since man's light comes with his being alive ("the life was the light of man") humanity would have to be exterminated to extinguish it. The darkness has surely tried. In Noah's day all but eight people were wiped out. But man survives. His light continues to illuminate him. Observe that it shines IN the darkness, not outside shining in. The reference is not to Christ, but man's ability to SEE himself a sinner, cut off from God. This is why he tries to put it out.

DARKNESS. This darkness is not the absence of light, but the world man now sees. Once he was in fellowship with God. The spiritual bond was Adam's real world. But the fall ended that. Adam was spiritually removed from God and the physical, fleshly world became his real world. Darkness is this world with God excluded—banned. It is a preference for the world of the senses, rather than the one of spiritual reality. Man no longer sees himself the image of God destined for eternity with His Creator, but as belonging to the physical world only. He may consider himself a bug or a god. **Refusing to SEE God in His own creation, man worships created things—himself, money or objects. Today, man would use the light that is in him to prove there is no God, claiming "God is dead."**

"With man in that condition, wouldn't it take something special to get him to acknowledge his Creator!"

6. Suddenly a man appeared on the scene. He was sent as a special ambassador from God. His name? John.

JOHN. The Carpenter of Galilee didn't choose a day and then announce, "Hey world! Here I am, your Messiah, your Creator!" Who'd believe that? So God prepared a special introducer, a publicity agent named John the Baptist. It was his task to present the Saviour to the world. He was the final O.T. prophet, for now God Himself was entering the world. The former prophets said . . . "A Messiah is coming." But John announced, "God's Lamb has arrived! There He is!" How shocking! This Carpenter who had grown up in their midst was the awaited Messiah. More staggering, He did not come as a delivering King, but as a sacrificial Lamb. Indeed an introducer was needed to get people to look on Jesus as a sacrifice.

7. This man came as a witness. Not only was his appearance on the scene a witness, but he went about witnessing to people concerning the Light. Anyone hearing His testimony could see The Light and believe in Him.

WITNESS. John's witness was twofold. His birth was miraculous, his parents were past child-bearing. So unusual was his naming that word spread throughout the land. People wondered, "What manner of child shall this be?" (Luke 1:66). His father announced his mission, "He shall go before the Lord to prepare His way; to give His people the knowledge of salvation by the forgiveness of sins!" (Luke 1:77). The Greek makes a play on words: John, a man, became a messenger of God. Whereas Jesus (The Logos), the Message of God, became a Man. John the writer has this in mind when he says . . . "There was a man sent from God."

BELIEVE. John asked people to look at Jesus and see Him for what He was—God's Lamb! His words shed light on Jesus. Because of that light they could see Him as Saviour and respond in faith. The world was dark in that day. No prophet had spoken for 400 years. John the Baptist was a flash bulb exploding in pitch blackness! His ministry was spectacular. To men, seeing was believing. So John gives them something to SEE. "There you are, you Israelites, that PERSON you see there is your Messiah."

"Then John the Baptist was himself a spectacular blaze in the world showing people the way to God!"

8. John (the Baptist) was not The Light. He came only to bear witness to The Light.

 NOT JOHN. What a testimony to John's brightness! At the close of the first century it is necessary for John the writer to say, "John was not THE Light." Jesus spoke of his glory too, ". . . there hath not risen a greater than John the Baptist" (Matt. 11:11). How remarkable that a brilliant flash was needed for men to behold the True Light. What a testimony to the darkness and its true nature— blindness. Inasmuch as Jesus comes into the world as "spiritual illumination," He can be referred to as The Light. By Him, man will see not only himself as he is, but God too. By the True Light, man sees his true condition, and God's only remedy for it.

"Then Jesus was coming into the world to provide spiritual illumination!"

9. Yes, the True Light, the One Who enlightens every man, was even then coming into the world.

 TRUE LIGHT. See again how Jesus is called the True Light for it is by Him that men SEE things TRULY. Men can look upon Jesus and SEE what God is TRULY like. They can behold Him and SEE what man is TRULY supposed to be. He supplies INSIGHT, thereby coinciding with our definition of spiritual light. Uniquely this Insight walks about on two legs and speaks. He Himself is the only correct information about man and God. Sin has so damaged the creation, this clear word or insight is not found anyplace else. Since Jesus is God, man can see God's true nature. Since He is also man, men can behold the truth of their own natures. That's why John calls Him the Word. He sheds light on God and man. True information reaches mankind via a Person, The Word Himself, the Logos.

 EVERY MAN. Every baby arrives factory equipped with the vital capacities of self-consciousness and spiritual perception. This is the LIGHT that Jesus puts in each man He creates. Of course it needs to be developed. But soon every child sins wilfully. Adam saw to that. So man's advance is not toward the spiritual realm. He focuses on physical things only. The verse is saying "Even though sin has frustrated its usefulness, the One Who installed man's light in the first place, is Himself coming into the world to remedy the situation."

"With every man so enlightened, surely people ought to be able to recognize the hand of the Creator in the creation!"

10.   The Light has always been in the world for it requires His presence to exist. But sinful man, in whom He placed the lamp of recognition, didn't even know him. And this is in spite of the fact that His presence may be discerned everywhere in creation.

IN THE WORLD. "The fool hath said in his heart, there is no God!" (Psa. 53:1). Why? Because he says this in his heart, the very place his Creator installed man's light. In each person there is a permanent witness that the creation did not make itself. And while Satan has managed to isolate man from God with sin, there is still sufficient light in man to perceive the Creator's hand in the universe about him. Of course it is painful for a sinner to behold this, for there is no mercy in the creation. A fierce God is revealed in the sinful earth. On the other hand there is NOT ENOUGH light in man to CONVINCE anyone who elects to doubt what he sees. In the Spirit, Jesus has always been touching consciences of men, so that they are without excuse (Rom. 1:20; 2:15). Because the knowledge of God is painful to sinners does not excuse their trading it for their own ideas.

"What if He came in Person! Surely then people would have to recognize Him!"

JOHN
1

21

11. He did come—and to His very own things. But His own people wouldn't even let Him in the house.

 HIS OWN. Centuries before Jesus' appearance, God made a covenant with one nation. They were to be His very own people. He assigned them real estate (Israel) on which they were to build Him a temple to which He would one day come and take His place. Well, He came, and to the very property set aside for Him. But the people who were pledged to serve Him, spurned His presence and refused to listen to Him. The nation Israel was His scheduled earthly inheritance, but as a nation, she wanted nothing to do with Him.

"Even if the nation didn't want Him, what about those individuals who did!"

12. But to those individuals who did receive Him, He gave the power and legal right to become the natural children of God. How? By placing their complete trust in His name.

RECEIVE. Whereas the nation of Israel barred Christ from His own land and house, some individuals welcomed Him into their hearts. Consequently they became His possession, their hearts His temple. And John tells how they did this. They deposited their complete trust in His Name. This Greek word "Name" sums up all that Jesus is and said, as well as the revelation of God concentrated in Him. This is a faith in His PERSON, not in FACTS ABOUT Him. No intellectual assent to His words, but a commitment to Jesus Himself. It so involves the surrender of one's will, that Christ finds in a man what Israel refused Him . . . a place to dwell and someone to be His very own!

CHILDREN. The Greek word denotes a relationship based on having the same nature. John doesn't use the word "sons" to describe our relationship with God, for that is a legal term applying to adoptees. Our sonship is based on a supernatural event, the receiving of a new life. Observe that we BECOME by REGENERATION the children of God, whereas Jesus ALWAYS WAS the eternal Son of God. The legal aspect applies to Gentiles. The Jews were the legal heirs of this experience, on the basis of God's covenant, but with their refusal of Christ, the privilege passes to all who place their trust in His PERSON.

"You mean we become sons as though we were naturally born to God!"

13. This new sonship, being spiritual, is in no wise connected with human descent. Religious tradition has nothing to do with it, so it is not theologically acquired. Neither can man perform such a thing. It is wholly supernatural for God Himself produces it.

BIRTH. John declares the new birth to be supernatural, offering a 3-fold denial of any human source. It is not sexual, not theological, nor accomplished by human determination. Why? The SEED of this conception is not found in man, but God. We become pregnant with a new life—His! The Greek phrase, "Begotten of God," clearly makes Him the Sire. Humans cannot sire God-children. Why? The Seed comes from above (John 3:3), making the experience supernatural and spiritual. See how the righteousness of faith is present . . . "to those who place their trust in His Name!"

"Then, when The Word came, He really was recognizable for what He was."

14. So the Word came to dwell among us by taking on a new kind of existence. He became flesh, living as we do in a human tent. Once He was fully human, we who are only human, could behold His glory. We perceived that His glory was precisely that of the Father—for He was from the Father—God's uniquely begotten Son.

What was His glory? We beheld the most gracious individual anyone could know, Who was in His Person, the fully revealed truth of God and man.

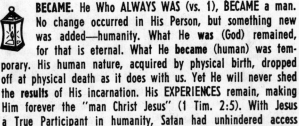

BECAME. He Who ALWAYS WAS (vs. 1), BECAME a man. No change occurred in His Person, but something new was added—humanity. What He **was** (God) remained, for that is eternal. What He **became** (human) was temporary. His human nature, acquired by physical birth, dropped off at physical death as it does with us. Yet He will never shed the **results** of His incarnation. His EXPERIENCES remain, making Him forever the "man Christ Jesus" (1 Tim. 2:5). With Jesus a True Participant in humanity, Satan had unhindered access to Him. Observe His two natures. He arrived with the **divine,** acquiring the **human** by **physical** birth. We arrive with the human, acquiring the second by a **spiritual birth.** He didn't need to be born again, we do. He already had the divine nature, we don't.

GLORY. To man glory means miracles and might. To God, glory is character. With God dressed in humanity and living among men, it was possible to discern the divine nature. Jesus was an understandable projection of the Father's character. In Him we behold the NICEST, SWEETEST and most SELFLESS Person this world has ever known. His limitless mercy, absolute graciousness and total giving of self for others, is the real glory of God. Only those who hunger after righteousness see Him this way. Even He is a parable.

BEGOTTEN. Jesus arrived in this world in the EMPTIEST FORM possible (Phil. 2:6-8), as the SEED of God. No one can be reduced to anything smaller, physically. Mary became pregnant by this Seed (Luke 1:31-35). Today we know the SEED of man contains the personality traits and character determinations, so that one's nature is shaped in the instant of conception. Our Lord arrived with the divine nature as the SEED, acquiring the human nature from Mary. In that our Lord was born, coming FROM the Father, He is called the ONLY begotten. None other was begotten in this fashion for we are spiritually begotten GOING TO the Father.

15.   Here is John's testimony to Him: "I told you," he exclaimed, "there was One coming after me Who was ahead of me, for He existed before I was born."

AHEAD. Strange words? John the Baptist is saying, "My Successor (in time) is my Predecessor (in rank), for He was before me (in existence)." Humanly and officially, Jesus came after John. He was born six months later than the Baptist. Yet, as the Eternal Word, He existed before John had any being. John is heralding the Saviour's pre-existence with these words. He is saying, "I became a man, but He always was, though He became a man after me!" Amazing statements about Jesus show the Baptist's insight by the Spirit, i.e., "baptizes with the Holy Spirit," "Bridegroom of the church," "from Heaven," the "only begotten Son." Remarkable, since he is an O.T. prophet.

"Sir, was all that John the Baptist declared about
Christ really accurate!"

16.   We have all sampled His fullness. Grace after grace has brought each of us the awareness of Who Christ really is!

GRACE. With Jesus the Truth of God IN PERSON, Grace now becomes the N.T. word indicating God's favor toward man in advancing the fullness of HIS revelation. In successive generations God has graciously and gradually exposed Himself, but now that revelation comes to its climax in Christ's Person. Paul affirms "the fulness of the Godhead dwelleth in Him bodily" (Col. 2:9, 10). Again John the writer speaks, "To this we agree, for we have seen and sampled this fullness as we lived with Jesus and walked with Him. By the grace of God we know Him for Who He really is!" Then John explains further:

17. For while the Law was administered through Moses' Law Office, Grace and Truth arrived in the world in Person, in Jesus Christ!

 MOSES. John the writer continues. Moses was a lawyer, handling God's Law for Him. But since the Law condemned sinners, pronouncing death on us all, it was powerless to help man. So God's Grace was needed to rescue sinful man. Yet His Grace didn't come through an agent, but in Person. Jesus is God's Grace with legs. You don't see Him, for example, **dispensing** forgiveness—HE FORGIVES! He is the Forgiver. At the same time He **is** the Truth of God, for He **is** God. The Truth of God also walks around. John finally names the Person he has had in mind from verse one . . . JESUS CHRIST! At last we have the specific identity of the Word.

"Are you saying then, that since you were with Jesus you actually saw God the Creator, God the Father!"

18. No one has ever seen God in His absolute essence. Yet the only begotten God/Son, Who even now abides in the bosom of the Father, He is an accurate translation of Him!

TRANSLATION. You are reading English words which advance truths from a language you do not know. By this rephrasing, the meanings of the Greek become known to you. God, as a Spirit (John 4:24) is also unknown to us. Like another language, He cannot be understood apart from some translation or **interpretation.** Jesus is an accurate translation of an otherwise unknowable essence. We can see and hear Jesus. He is a communication we can grasp. This is why John calls Him the Word. For the Word translates what is unknowable and brings an understanding to our minds. Yet, only that which we can see and hear of Christ is the translation. Part of Him remains unseen. Since He is God, begotten as a man, that unseen part is the invisible essence of God!

BOSOM. This word explains how that works. The invisible part of Jesus is the OMNIPRESENT GOD. Thus He can appear among men and be in the BOSOM of the Father SIMULTANEOUSLY. The term indicates more than intimacy. It shouts the fact that the ONE GOD is present to the incarnate Christ. Yet it also indicates the Son's conscious existence distinct from the Father. Thus one could say the Father and the Son were IMMEDIATELY PRESENT to each other. Some choice Mss. read, "God only begotten," and others, "Only begotten Son," but the meaning remains the same. I have called Him the God/Son. Only such a Person could accurately translate the Father to us (Heb. 1:3).

"Could you tell us more about John the Baptist and what he said! How did he answer when people asked about his ministry!"

19. Here is the recorded testimony of John when the Jews of Jerusalem sent a delegation of priests and Levites to find out who he was. "Who are you?" they asked.

JEWS. This is a special word for John, used over 70 times in this Gospel. It is not found a dozen times in the Synoptics or Paul. It represents the narrowest sect of Judaism, the rulers and leaders who opposed Christ, not the majority of residents of Palestine. The "Jerusalem Jews," were the Sanhedrin who had charge of public teaching of religion. Word of John's ministry had reached them. They dispatched a committee of temple officers (priests and Levites) to investigate. This interview occurs after Jesus' baptism, yet near the time when He is returning from His wilderness testing. John answers with certainty. He has seen the divine attestation to Christ. He makes fascinating replies to the investigating committee.

20. He was open and honest with his answers, denying neither himself nor the Christ. "As for myself," he replied candidly, "I am not the Christ."

CANDIDLY. John knew the mood of the nation. Israel ached for the Messiah to come and cast out the Romans. John's amazing appearance and startling message made many wonder if he were not the Messiah. Having baptized Jesus and received heaven's witness to Him, John owned the greatest secret in Israel. He knew the precise identity of Messiah. But it had to remain locked inside him until Jesus returned from the wilderness testing. See how careful he is not to let them think him greater than he is. They didn't ask if he were Messiah, but knowing their motives, he wouldn't even let them think such a thing. See now how the delegation's questions indicate Israelite confusion in Messianic expectations.

21. "Who then are you," they asked. "Are you Elijah?"

"No," he returned, "I'm not."

ELIJAH. They ask this, half-inferring he is Elijah the Tishbite, returning in person rather than someone coming in the spirit of Elijah. It reveals their superstition. They felt anyone coming with such pretentions, if not the Messiah, at least must be the Elijah who was to precede Him (Mal. 4:5). John was an ideal Elijah. Jesus called him that (Matt. 11:14). John says, "No, I'm not Elijah the Tishbite whom you mean." His denials become successively shorter.

"Are you the Prophet?"

"No."

PROPHET. The theology of John's inquirers moves systematically. They are going through a descending list of expected people. Thus, "The Prophet" here is NOT the One Moses mentioned (Deut. 18:15), for that is clearly Messiah. The Jews anticipated someone even before Elijah who might represent the sufferings of Isaiah 53. In their confusion they believed that possibly Jeremiah would return as a wailing forerunner (Matt. 16:14). They are asking John if he is that prophet. His answer is an emphatic no. He desires no reputation for himself at all, choosing only to exalt Christ. His humility is amazing. Of course, this accounts for his great success and Jesus' later honoring of him.

22. "Well then," they demanded, "you tell us who you are. We have to take back some kind of an answer to the people who sent us. What do you call yourself, what is this that you are doing?"

WHO! This is an official demand. The priests of the delegation have ecclesiastical authority. The Levites (temple police) put teeth into the committee. Yet they avoid calling him an unauthorized teacher. He bears too many signs as being from God. His arrival on the scene has been explosive, his effect on the people startling. Rumors flooded the land. They ask for his credentials. Like some today, they were more concerned with his degrees than his message. When they ask about his person, he refers them to his work. "I'm nobody, just a voice. It's what I am saying that is important, not who I am." He could have said, "My cousin is the awaited Messiah!"

23. "I am a voice," said John, answering in the words of Isaiah the Prophet, "shouting in the desert—'Make way! Clear a path for the Lord!' "

VOICE. John does a remarkable thing here. Taking a passage from Isaiah Forty, as yet uncorrupted by the Jewish theologians, he applies it to himself! By the Spirit, John understands the reference is specifically to him. He considers himself that prophesied figure of Scripture. The investigating committee is baffled. It appears the Pharisees had no exegetical tradition for this passage, so his claim confuses them. They shift their questioning. Apparently they don't wish to challenge his authority, so they ask about his work.

24. Now these people sent to John were Pharisees. **25.** And they then asked, "If you are not the Messiah, not Elijah, neither the Prophet, how is it you are baptizing?"

BAPTIZING. John's baptizing puzzled them. Jewish tradition held that three persons would come baptizing—the Messiah and the two forerunners they had scheduled to appear before Him. They knew of no fourth person. When John denied he was of the expected three, they naturally began to question why he was using their method and gathering a following. Thus his method and message staggered them, for he was clearly ministering in the Messianic tradition. You can imagine their shock when he claimed to be the fulfillment of a Scripture announcing a forerunner of the Lord, which was apparently one the Pharisees had overlooked.

26. "I baptize in water only. But there is One standing in your midst of Whom you know nothing. 27. He is the One Who is to come after me, as I said. Yet I am not good enough to untie the strap of His sandals."

WATER. This had long been the Jewish symbol of spiritual purification. People were washed with it, objects were sprinkled. But the Messiah, the True Prophet, was to come baptizing in the Spirit making men totally clean—inside. John's baptism, a submersing of people in water, pictured total cleansing. Yet his words are a rebuke. "My baptizing," he says, "is but preparation for Spirit baptism. It only symbolizes total cleansing, picturing the baptism to come." They should have known that. Then his thought breaks. He sees something, apparently the Lord (across the river?)—"Standing in your midst," suggests this. "I may look like a prophet to you," John says, "but compared to Him I am a slave!" Eastern slaves unloosed their master's sandals, standard footwear in that day.

28. Now this took place at Bethany, which is beyond Jordan, where John was baptizing.

BETHANY. Not the Bethany of the Mt. of Olives, but a place of the same name—probably opposite Jericho. John's answer hints that Jesus is in the vicinity. He is likely to pass through the delegation's midst on their return trip to Jerusalem. The Baptist perceives by the Spirit that Jesus' temptation has ended and the Messianic ministry is about to begin. John's temptation is also ending. Possessed of the knowledge of Messiah's identity he could have made himself a religious big shot, but he remained just a voice. He could have impressed the committee with his knowledge. Think how he felt when he spied Jesus returning. How glad then he was he didn't exalt himself.

"Did John the Baptist know that Jesus was coming as a sacrifice for sin?"

30

29.   The next day he saw Jesus coming toward him and said, "Look! There is the Lamb of God Who takes away the sin of the world!"

LAMB. John's first exclamation upon seeing Jesus after His testing . . . "Behold the Lamb!" Was the solemnity of Jesus' mission in His face? The strain of testing too? Under inspiration, the Baptist announces the Lord's mission—to die. Amazing! He understood the system of sacrifice for sin clear back to the Paschal Lamb. If Isaiah understood the germ form (Ch. 53), why not John who was called to introduce the Sin-Bearer? The word SIN (not sins) shows he understood Christ would bear a single burden. The sins of man are compressed into one awful fact. John begins to keep track of days, they are important. Between verses 28 and 29 we have the end of Jesus' testing and the beginning of His ministry.

30.   "This is the One I meant when I said, 'After me comes a man Who outranks me, because He existed before I was born.'   31.   I didn't know exactly Who He would be myself, although the reason I came baptizing with water was to make Him known to Israel."

DIDN'T KNOW. John was never sure of Messiah's identity before he baptized Jesus. Likely he had a hunch Who it was, but all he knew for certain was that he was called to announce Him. He tells HOW he was supposed to recognize Him—he would baptize Him. Jewish tradition held Messiah would remain unknown until anointed by Elijah. This was made known to John who in turn introduced Him to Israel. John's baptism of Jesus did not exclude the tributary idea of preparing a people for the Lord. Since John was to make an "official" presentation of Christ, he needed an "official" revelation. He describes it.

32.   Then John testified further saying, "I saw the Spirit coming down from heaven in a dove-like shape and it came to rest on Him. 33.   Until then I wasn't certain who Messiah was. But you see I had been told by God when He sent me to baptize in water . . . 'You will see the Spirit descend and come to rest upon a man. He is the One Who baptizes with the Holy Spirit!' "

DESCEND. John had been told in advance HOW he would officially recognize Messiah. The Trinity certified it to him. His hands held Jesus, his eyes saw the Spirit manifested, and his ears heard the voice of God. This is not a vision only, for the Greek word for "saw" requires both inward and outward vision. Besides, it was a sign, and signs are outward. Observe the two baptisms; John's is in water, Jesus' in the Spirit; one is outward, the other inward; one is symbolical, the other real; one is preparatory, the other fulfilling.

34.   "I saw this," said John. "So I have been bearing witness to something I have seen. I tell you . . . HE is the Son of God!"

HE. The Messianic prophecies of the centuries converge at last, like an index finger. John is pointing to a man when he says this—JESUS! The secret is out. Israel's Messiah is formally identified. All who stand around John at this moment may look upon their Saviour. John's ministry has climaxed, he has just fulfilled his call. Jesus is on the scene ready to begin His walk toward a death which will take away the sin of the world. From this moment on, John's glory must subside. Men will turn from following him to the One he has just introduced to the world.

"Did John's disciples immediately leave him to follow Jesus!"

35.   The next day John was standing there, along with two of his disciples,   36.   and he saw Jesus walking by. After eyeing Him carefully, he called, "Look! There is the Lamb of God!"

LAMB. A remarkable shift in John's announcement occurs. He has been giving testimony to the pre-existence and glory of Christ, heralding Him as the Spirit-baptizer. Now John points to a man walking past the group. His heart almost burst as he cries . . . "Behold the Lamb!" He was pointing to the One of Whom all the O.T. sacrifices had foretold. For 1400 years, the Levitical system had slain millions of lambs to dramatize the coming Sin-bearer. It was the biggest fact in Judaism . . . and here He was! Had John said, "There is our King!" the crowds would have seized Jesus and lifted Him over their heads. But a sobering thing happens instead.

37.   And the two disciples heard him say this and they began to tag along behind Jesus. 38.   When Jesus looked back and saw them following Him, He asked, "What do you want?" They replied, "Rabbi (meaning teacher), where are You staying?"

FOLLOWED. Christianity begins here, with two men following Jesus. John's crowd was huge, all Israel was tingling with his announcements. Yet only two (not priests either) caught his "Lamb" message. Their hearts were ready to be drawn to the Lamb. The Greek indicates they follow Jesus with an eye to becoming His disciples. With reverence and awe they hear the Messiah's first words . . . "What do you want?" It was a test of their motives and intentions, but they scored well. "We don't want anything, we want You! Where are You staying so that we might get to know You as we should?" Jesus replies with His warm invitation.

39.   "Come," He said to them, "and you will see." So they went and saw where He had taken lodging and stayed with Him the rest of the day. This occurred about four in the afternoon.

LODGING. The implication is that Jesus had either camped or taken quarters not far from where John was baptizing. Perhaps with relatives or at an inn. Jesus has returned from the wilderness testing, having been away from home over a month and a half. His mother hasn't heard from Him. He is making a bee line for Nazareth. But John and Andrew have left the crowd to seek Him, so He must stop. The cry of faith always gets His full attention. So He gives the opportunity to come and satisfy themselves by first hand experience. They believed in Him and John even records the hour . . . "I was saved at 4 p.m. the day after Jesus was introduced to the world!" Nobody paid any attention to Him the first day.

40. One of the two who heard John's announcement and followed Jesus, was Andrew, Simon Peter's brother. 41. He was the first to locate his brother Simon and say to him, "We have found the Messiah!" (Interpreted, this word means Christ or Anointed One.)

FOUND. The movement is now animated, things happen fast. Excitement fills the disciples. Jesus really is the Christ. Andrew slips out for a bit to find his brother. He must have been close by, possibly at their camp. The word "first" intimates that John, not long thereafter also found his brother James and brought him to Jesus. John writes with delicate reserve, never speaking directly of himself or his kindred. After all the years of waiting and expecting, you can imagine the feverish joy that moved them to action. See how only the seekers found Christ, while the rest of John the Baptist's audience ceremoniously awaited its king.

42. He then brought him to Jesus who looked upon him intently and said, "You are Simon the son of John, but your name shall be Cephas!" (Translated this means Peter, or rock.)

PETER. Andrew is labeled the "brother of Simon Peter," because of the later distinction of Peter. This was written 70 years afterwards. This penetrating look introduces us to a mental miracle, the Lord's ability to read men. The "Knower of hearts," here displays His ability to discern character. Simon is convinced Jesus is Messiah. Names meant much to Israelites for persons were commonly dubbed by their personality traits. The Lord quite obviously read Simon and then prophesies what he is to become, for the title "Peter" (or rock) is just the opposite of Simon's present temperament. He will soon be manifesting a wild, unstable, vacillating disposition which does not change until after Pentecost.

43. The next day as Jesus was intending to set out for Galilee, He found Philip. And He said to him, "Follow Me." 44. As in the case of Andrew and Peter, Philip was also from Bethsaida.

PHILIP. This is the first soul Jesus won by Himself. We're not even told what it took to convince Philip Jesus was the Messiah, but it probably wasn't much. And there was surely something in Philip Jesus saw or He wouldn't have let the winning of Philip interfere with His plans to get back to His mother. John the Baptist is to be credited with his part in preparing Philip for the appearance of Messiah. Now the band numbers six and they are all from Galilee and can travel together. But Philip has someone he cares about and the entourage is delayed while Philip goes after him.

45. Philip found Nathanael and told him, "Hey! We have found the One of Whom Moses wrote in the Law and the Prophets too! It is Jesus the Son of Joseph, from Nazareth!" 46. "From Nazareth!" exclaimed Nathanael, "Can any good thing come out of Nazareth?" "Come and see!" said Philip.

NAZARETH. He is astonished that Nazareth should be the origin of Messiah. It was an insignificant place, lacking entirely in eminence. Not only that, it was an immoral town. How unlikely that a celebrity should come from there. But Philip repeats the formula for Christian satisfaction, "Come and see!" As customary among the Jews, Jesus is first identified by His father, then by His residence. You can tell by Nathanael's reaction it is going to take some convincing. But Jesus will have the right answer for him.

47. When Jesus saw Nathanael coming, He said, "Here comes a true Israelite, a man without deception."

NATHANAEL. Watch how rude and uncivil he is. He doesn't address the Lord as "Rabbi." He blurts out his prejudices. But this is what the Saviour likes about him, his non-subtlety. He is guileless, that is, not treacherous as those who use deceit. He is unlike his patriarch Jacob (the supplanter) who was full of tricks until God changed him to Israel. He is a real descendant of Israel, open and honest. He corresponds to what we would call a "real Christian" today. Notice that he doesn't deny Jesus reading of his character, but reacts, "How come you know me?" Then Jesus speaks words which satisfy his heart completely.

48. "How come you know me?" said Nathanael. "Before Philip called you," answered Jesus, "when you were there under the fig tree, I saw you." 49. Nathanael exclaims, "Master, You are the Son of God, the King of Israel!"

MASTER. Nathanael gets polite fast. All he needed was some evidence and his heart is ready to believe. No doubt he is also one conditioned by John the Baptist. His theology is sufficient too. He sees that the King of Israel is also the Son of God. He is obviously a deep student of the Scriptures. According to Jewish tradition, rabbis often resorted to the shade of a fig tree to meditate on the teachings of Moses. Nathanael was doing that before Philip called him and Jesus, by a mental miracle, tells him so. More than that, Jesus is about to tell him what he was thinking as he meditated under the fig tree.

50. "Do you believe in me," replied Jesus, "because I said I saw you under the fig tree? Well, you are going to see greater things than this! 51. In all truth I say to you, you will see heaven opened and God's angels ascending and descending upon the Son of Man."

SEE. Nathanael's outburst of faith, his remarkable acknowledgment of Jesus' divinity and rank, is rewarded with a second miracle. The Lord tells him that He not only saw his location under the fig tree, but beheld his thoughts as well. Nathanael was meditating upon Jacob's dream (Gen. 28:10-17), where God spoke from ATOP a ladder which rested on the earth. Jesus says it is no dream. Heaven is open and the angels are communicating with Him. God is now speaking from the BOTTOM of the ladder. Jesus is God speaking.

Whereas the prophets had cried, "Thus saith the Lord," Jesus says, "Truly I say unto you!" Nathanael was looking at God's Ladder, Christ—the only way up and out of this world! This would correspond to John 10:9 where He calls Himself the DOOR to heaven.

2 1. Two days later a wedding was taking place in the Galilean village of Cana and the mother of Jesus was there.

WEDDING. It takes at least two days to get to Nazareth on foot from the Jordan crossing, traveling the regular route. Jesus is anxious to see His mother and allay her fears caused by His extended absence. Also she is to learn that He is no longer subject to her as a son, but is in fact, her Messiah and God. A difficult moment is ahead and He would face it as quickly as possible. But she has gone to Cana where some friends of the family are getting married. Word is left for Jesus. Consequently He and His disciples have 4½ more miles to go.

2. And Jesus and His disciples were made welcome at the wedding, invited to stay as guests. 3. Then it happened that the wine gave out. So the mother of Jesus said to Him, "They have no more wine."

MOTHER. This is very embarrassing, as Eastern pride suffers when something like this happens. Mary is used to bringing problems to Jesus. He had taken over family responsibility after Joseph had died (indicated by her presence there alone). She was confident He would offer a solution. This was a private moment, such as Jesus needed to advise her of the new status which existed between her and Him. Will He come out and say, "I am no longer your son, but your God and Maker?" He doesn't do that to anyone. Instead, he selects a Hebrew idiom that does the job very well. He adds a comment which requires her faith to rise. Like any of His disciples, she too has to believe in Him.

4. "Nay, woman, what have I to do with you?" replied Jesus, "My hour has not yet come."

 WOMAN. Literally the idiom reads, "What to Me and to you?" It appears often in the O.T. and in Matthew 8:29, where the demons say this to Jesus. It is a gentle reproof, but it is explained. When He says, "Mine hour has not yet come," she understands. Had not the angel said 30 years before that the "Holy Thing" conceived in her would "save His people from their sins?" (Matt. 1:21). A godly Jewess, she knew it took God's Lamb to deliver from sin. She had pondered those lines all these years. Now they pierced her soul afresh. Seven times in John, reference is made to this "hour." Each time it refers to His death. She gets the message. She understands she is facing her Messiah. The next words indicate she passes the test of faith.

5. With that His mother said to the servants, "No matter what He says to you, do it."

 DO IT. See, she does expect Him to do something. And He does. The miracle which is about to occur is not for the guests, but for Mary. This sign to Mary indicates that she has indeed given birth to Messiah and provides more ground for her faith. From now on Mary fades into the crowds. She is never again present at any of the miracles. Yet her glory remains, for multitudes today call her "blessed." All that the angel had said to her was true. It is now certified that the hope of all Israelitish women was fulfilled in her.

6. Now there were six stone waterpots standing there for use in the Jewish ceremonial washings. Each held around 20 to 30 gallons. 7. And when Jesus said, "Fill up those water pots," they filled them to the brim. 8. Then He said to them, "Now draw some out and take it to the headwaiter." They did, and gave him some.

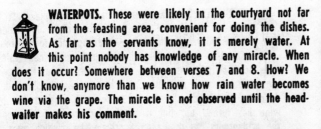 **WATERPOTS.** These were likely in the courtyard not far from the feasting area, convenient for doing the dishes. As far as the servants know, it is merely water. At this point nobody has knowledge of any miracle. When does it occur? Somewhere between verses 7 and 8. How? We don't know, anymore than we know how rain water becomes wine via the grape. The miracle is not observed until the head-waiter makes his comment.

9. The headwaiter tasted the water now turned into wine, but with no clue as to where it had come from. Only the servants who had drawn the water knew that. So he called to the bride-groom, 10. "Hey, you've reversed the cus-tom! Usually we serve the good wine first and wait until the people are really happy before we slip in the poorer wine."

SERVANTS. Once the miracle is exposed, only those who worked closely with the Lord knew of it. The same is true today. Spectators see what appears to be routine Christian activity, yet the results are divine. Watchers have no knowledge as to how it comes about, but those working intimately with the Holy Spirit know. See how shocked, yet delighted the headwaiter is? He is not only pleased that more wine has turned up, but it is of good quality. He supposes the bridegroom has drawn on a private stock which must now be used rather than dampen the festive spirit of the wedding. Custom called for the wedding to be held at the home of the bridegroom.

11. So it was in Cana of Galilee that Jesus **began** performing His signs. By these He manifested His glory enabling His disciples to believe in Him.

BELIEVED. Did not His disciples believe in Him from the first? Yes. But faith is a living thing and must grow. All living things either grow or die. Consequently this verse speaks of a higher faith than the introductory or initial faith they first evidenced. They will be continually strengthened in their belief by startling evidences of Jesus' Messianic power and dignity. Stories of miracles performed by Jesus in earlier years must now be dismissed as false.

"Once Jesus dissolved the mother-son relationship, did He continue to live with His earthly family?"

12. After this He went down to Capernaum accompanied by His mother, His brothers and His disciples. But they didn't stay there very long.

CAPERNAUM. This village, whose exact location is unknown today, was situated on the Western shore of the Lake of Galilee. Jesus has come with His entourage expecting to join a caravan as it heads for the festive days at Jerusalem. This is in anticipation of the Passover which He plans to attend with His disciples. See how His brothers are distinguished from His disciples. As yet His natural relatives do not believe in Him as we deduce from John 7:5. The Holy Spirit shows us this transition scene in Jesus' life that we might observe the different categories. The brothers are either elder sons from a former marriage of Joseph or younger children of Joseph and Mary, and if so, half-brothers of Jesus. Some of His brothers become disciples later on.

13.   Inasmuch as the Jewish Passover was at hand, Jesus went up to Jerusalem.

 PASSOVER. Without this report by John, it could never be positively stated that Jesus visited Jerusalem until the Feast of Tabernacles, 7 mos. prior to His arrest and crucifixion. John alone mentions this **first cleansing,** the other Gospels reporting only the second cleansing (Matt. 21:12-17). Thus, this account is vital, for it is by the number of His Passover appearances that scholars establish the duration of His earthly ministry. The first and last PUBLIC acts of Jesus are purifications of the fountainhead of Israel's spiritual life, her temple. It was foretold by Malachi (3:1ff.) that immediately after the appearance of the fore-runner (John the Baptist), the Messiah Himself "shall suddenly come to His temple" for the purpose of cleansing it.

14.   And He found seated in the outer-court those in the business of selling oxen, sheep and doves as well as the money changers at their tables.

SELLING. It is not known when this practice started, but it began as a convenience for those who came with animals and foreign money. For the purpose of paying the temple tax, Roman money or live-stock had to be converted into the sacred shekel or double drachma. In time avaricious motives cloaked this convenience. Jesus found the fore-court, the court of the Gentiles, turned into a bustling market. The spirit of the Law was violated, God's house was now being exploited as a merchandising gimmick. Pilgrims were at the mercy of these profiteers.

"How did Jesus react to this monstrous desecration of the temple!"

15. He made a crude rope of twisted rushes and using it as a whip against the sheep and oxen, drove the cattlemen out of the temple area. He next brushed off the money tables scattering the coins and overturning the tables.

 WHIP. This was a symbol of divine wrath. But it was not used against the men, for that was not His design. It was raised against the secularizing of God's house, the idea of using God as a money-making gimmick. Church cake sales, bazaars, and lotteries of today are of this same order, where the din of such things destroys the place of prayer. Worship was hindered as people emerged from the temple into the shouts and touts of bargaining cattlemen. Everyone knew it wrong, but none had the boldness to do anything about it. History's most striking example is the peddling of indulgences where the forgiveness of sin was made an article of merchandise.

16. Then, speaking to the dove-dealers, He said, "Get these things out of here! Stop using My Father's house for a market place!"

 DOVES. Cattle could be driven and later collected, so nothing is lost, neither is there any hurt. Money thrown to the ground could be regathered. But loosed doves would fly away, so He merely orders them taken away. Even in anger, Christ acts prudently. He rebukes all, yet none is injured, nothing is lost. What an example! It was prophesied, "Behold my servant shall deal wisely!" (Isa. 52:13). Observe Jesus' identification with the temple, terming it, "My Father's house." By this He claims divine sonship. No prophet dared to call the temple or tabernacle HIS Father's house! A startling expression of Deity.

"What did Jesus' disciples think when they saw Him do this?"

17. His disciples then recalled the Scripture which says, "Passion for Your house, O God, burns within Me, eating like a fire."

RECALLED. See how the Word of God is brought to mind AFTER some act of Jesus. The Scripture looms to confirm what He has done, even more, confirming He is truly Messiah (Psa. 69:9). Put yourself in their place. How would you feel to see the One you were following suddenly pit Himself against the entire religious system of your land? You'd wonder, "If He does things like this, what will become of me if I follow Him?" Thus it was a test for the disciples. His first public act was a showdown with the secular spirit in Israel. It is clear that Jesus has not embarked on a popular course. What now would the future hold for His disciples?

"Surely His actions didn't go unchallenged!"

18. Then the Jews began to respond to His actions. "What sign," they demanded, "can you give us as a warrant for doing these things?"

SIGN. Jesus' actions here were themselves fulfillment of the prophetic Word. He did precisely what was expected of Messiah (Mal. 3:1). Observe they did not dispute the rightness of what He did, all knew it should be done. But they wanted His credentials for doing it. The opposition comes from the Pharisaic and Judaistic Jews. They are the ones meant here. Failing to see that His act was itself a remarkable sign, fulfilling Malachi's prophecy, they ask for an attesting miracle. The ancient prophets usually supported their zealous acts with miraculous signs. They want to be convinced that heaven has authorized His purification of the temple. From now on these Jews will be His dogged enemies.

19. Jesus answered right back, "Destroy this temple and in three days I will raise it up again."

TEMPLE. Likely He was pointing to His own body as He said these words. But men blind enough to desecrate God's house, are also blind to spiritual truth. So now it begins, Jesus' parabolic double-talk in addressing vulgar crowds. To His disciples He would manifest His glory (Cana), to the crowds His ZEAL for God's house. To His own He speaks with directness and simplicity, to the unbelieving with riddles and ambiguities. This will be His pattern from now on. He is referring to His body as God's temple. They can think only of the literal temple. When asked for a sign He replies with the ONLY sign given to unbelievers, the sign of the resurrection (Matt. 12:39, 40). Since "God was in Christ," He is mysteriously referring to His own body as the abode (Gk.: sanctuary) of God, predicting His death and resurrection.

20.   "You mean you could rebuild this temple in three days?" they challenged. "Why it has taken forty-six years to build this temple."

 FORTY-SIX. The Jews persist in their blindness. They are thinking of the renovating of the temple of Zerubbabel which began some 46 years before and wasn't yet completed. Their vision is restricted to the symbolical temple on Zion, whereas the body of Christ was the true dwelling of God. The shekinah glory which formerly graced the most holy place of the tabernacle, now had two legs and walked among them. His glory was wonderfully manifested by this act of cleansing the temple, but they didn't get it. Inasmuch as they are spiritually blind, such language is unintelligible to them. So as to remove all doubt in any reader's mind, the Spirit inserts the following:

21.   But the temple of which He was speaking was His own body.

"Didn't anyone understand what He meant by those words?"

22.   When He was raised from the dead, His disciples remembered that He had said this and it caused them to believe both the Scriptures and the words which Jesus had spoken.

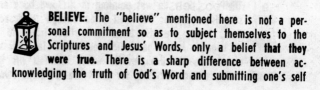 **BELIEVE.** The "believe" mentioned here is not a personal commitment so as to subject themselves to the Scriptures and Jesus' Words, only a belief that they were true. There is a sharp difference between acknowledging the truth of God's Word and submitting one's self

to it. Even "the devils believe (the Scriptures are true) and
tremble," but they do not humble themselves before them. The
precise Greek can make this distinction, but the English cannot.
The verse above shows Jesus' Words were for the future. When
He was risen, the resurrection validated all that He had said.
Words from His mouth have the force of Scripture, for He was
God speaking.

**"Did Jesus leave Jerusalem right after this, or did He stay
for the Passover!"**

23.   All during the time Jesus was in Jerusalem for the Passover festivities, there were
many who came to believe in His Name after
seeing all the miracles which He did.

 BELIEVE.   Again, this is not the faith that saves. This
was a belief in the fact that He was from God. The
signs convinced them He had a right to purify the
temple and might even be the Messiah, though He
never said so. These "believers" were like those who today
affirm Jesus was from God, but refuse to receive Him as their
own Saviour. While they accept the FACT of God, they don't
want to get involved with Him. Such faith is mere OPINION
only. It contains no commitment, appropriation or submission.
Given their way, these "believers" would have seized Him
and paraded Him as their king. But Jesus spurns such faith.
The world is full of those who say, "Seeing is believing."
Jesus wants those who find that "believing is seeing."

"Didn't Jesus want a crowd of followers!"

24.   But as far as Jesus was concerned, He
wasn't about to commit Himself to them. He
knew men too well to do such a thing. Within
Himself He possessed the ability to read one's
character and faith.   25.   So complete was
His understanding of human nature, it was
impossible that anyone should teach Him about
people.

READ. Jesus discerned men's hearts. By means of prophetic illumination and His penetrating spiritual insight, the God-Man discerned the faith of those who would join with Him. He performed many miracles after His appearance in the temple, mostly healings. Healing meetings draw crowds. Everyone has hurts. Just as He read Peter and Nathanael, so did He behold the faith of those wanting a Miracle Man in their midst. But this kind of faith comes to GET, not GIVE their lives to Him. Even Jesus' miracles require faith to see and understand what they really mean. There are those today, pleased to identify with the glory of Christ as a Miracle Worker, but unwilling to suffer the indignity of becoming His bondslave.

"You mean no one in Jerusalem responded with the kind of faith Jesus longed to see!"

3 1. Well, there was one man, a Pharisee called Nicodemus, a very outstanding ruler of the Jews.

NICODEMUS. He was an honest, circumcised, orthodox, high-ranking member of the Supreme Council, the Sanhedrin. A man favorably disposed to the Messiah, but belonging to the Pharisees. This sect was hostile to the idea of spiritual regeneration since their religion consisted of outward rules and self-made holiness. When Nic. beheld the attesting miracles of Jesus, something within him responded. He saw something the crowds missed, but he wasn't sure what it was. Spiritual hunger and curiosity cause him to seek out Jesus. Yet, even as he comes, he has no reason to suspect himself spiritually inadequate in any way. He is comfortable in his Jewishness, owning circumcision, rank and legal perfection.

2. This man paid a night-time visit to Jesus and said to Him, "Rabbi, we know you have come to us as a Teacher from God; for no man can constantly perform the miracles you do unless God is with Him."

TEACHER. Nic. approaches Jesus respectfully. He comes inquiring. He wants to know what is **behind the miracles,** acknowledging He is indeed FROM God. This faith is in germ form only, but it was enough to separate him from the crowd. He has to defy his high station and Pharisaical prejudice to come like this. Much is at stake. So he comes wisely at night. Weak in faith, perhaps, but no coward. Cowardice would have kept him home. No one else came, day or night. As soon as he speaks, his Pharisee pride shows . . . **"WE KNOW."** The "we" hints a few other rulers likely shared his opinion of Christ. Nic. feels secure in his religion, yet this "Teacher from God," makes him feel there is more to be had. After all the country is alive with rumors of the Messiah's coming.

3.   "In all truth," answered Jesus, "I tell you that unless a person is born from above he cannot see the Kingdom of God."

ABOVE. Nic. thought he belonged to the Kingdom of God, now "The Teacher" says it can't be seen without regeneration. But the Greek word Jesus used has two meanings: "born again" (or afresh) or, "from above." This is a test for Nic. Depending on his spiritual understanding he will select one meaning or the other. But Nic. can think only in natural terms. A Pharisee would. Jesus' statement is calculated to humble Nic. He has come with his proud, "WE KNOW," now the untitled Teacher says, "You think I am from God because of what you see. You haven't seen anything yet. In fact, you can't SEE the Kingdom of God until you start life over with another birth." When Jesus used the word "another," He meant from "above," but in his carnality, Nic. can only render the word to mean "again," or another beginning to this life.

"Surely Nic. couldn't grasp the idea of spiritual regeneration, could he!"

4.   "How is it possible," asked Nicodemus, "for a man to be born once he is already an adult? Can he enter into his mother's womb to be born again and start life over a second time?"

POSSIBLE? What Nic. is thinking isn't possible. Even if it were, a thousand such births wouldn't accomplish what Jesus is saying. The Lord is speaking of a supernatural birth, a spiritual rebirth, one which has a different source, (heaven). Jesus is speaking of a new life with a DIFFERENT beginning. Nic. is thinking another run through the old life with the SAME kind of beginning. In fairness we note that Nic. was probably ready to make any kind of an OUTWARD reformation Jesus might ask, once satisfied Who Jesus really was. That's what he came for. His heart is tender. But the Lord must shift his thinking from natural to spiritual things. A supernatural experience is needed for him to become a child of God and true disciple.

"Won't Jesus have to explain what He means before Nic. can understand 'born from above!' "

5. "Believe Me," replied Jesus, "for I tell you in all truth that unless a man is born of water and the Spirit he cannot enter the Kingdom of God."

WATER-SPIRIT. Israel was alive with these two words. John the Baptist was vigorously declaring, "I baptize with water . . . He with the Spirit!" A water-baptizer was on the scene, a Spirit-baptizer was coming. One was getting the nation ready for the other. Nic. understood what water meant—any Israelite leader did—ceremonial cleansing. It had meant that for 1400 years. John (using water baptism) challenged the nation to repent in preparation for her King. The water baptism was an outward act indicating inner repentance. While Nic. may not have been baptized by John, he was satisfied he qualified in all it stood for. He was confident of this as he faced Jesus. Now he finds he lacks the urgent fundamental . . . "birth by the Spirit." He has preparation by water (repentance), but he yet needs birth by the Spirit (regeneration). These two are not the same. And one precedes the other.

6. "Natural birth can only produce things of nature. It requires a spiritual birth to produce anything of the Spirit. 7. You really

shouldn't be surprised at my telling all of you that you have to be born from above."

 NATURAL-SPIRIT. Here are the two realms. Natural birth makes one a member of the human family. Spiritual birth makes one a member of God's family. Both families are entered by a birth. This is what was missing from Nic.'s qualifications. And yet, there was in rabbinical theology a superficial conception of the new birth, though it was largely confined to the external ceremony of bringing Gentiles into Judaism. What is obvious, is that Nic. being a circumcised Jew, didn't feel the need of any such radical or dramatic change in himself. This is why his mind refuses to embrace the idea of beginning a whole new life with a supernatural birth. He thought he was qualified. Now he hears he can't get into the kingdom without an experience he doesn't comprehend. He is deflated. His mind struggles to think how this might be. "All" those listening to the conversation likely wonder the same. The plural "you" shows this is not a private interview.

8. "Consider the wind," continues Jesus. "It blows as it pleases. You hear its sound, but you can't tell where it comes from or where it is going. It is like that with everyone who is born of the Spirit."

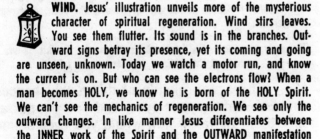 **WIND.** Jesus' illustration unveils more of the mysterious character of spiritual regeneration. Wind stirs leaves. You see them flutter. Its sound is in the branches. Outward signs betray its presence, yet its coming and going are unseen, unknown. Today we watch a motor run, and know the current is on. But who can see the electrons flow? When a man becomes HOLY, we know he is born of the HOLY Spirit. We can't see the mechanics of regeneration. We see only the outward changes. In like manner Jesus differentiates between the INNER work of the Spirit and the OUTWARD manifestation in the changed life.

9. Perplexed, Nicodemus answers the Lord, "How is such a thing possible?" 10. "What!" replied Jesus, "You, the teacher of Israel, and you find this strange!"

STRANGE. Nic.'s request is humble, he is not contradicting the Lord. Yet he is rebuked. Not for failure to understand Who Jesus is or the mechanics of the new birth, but for his lack of faith in the power of the Holy Spirit. As a teacher of the things of the Spirit he should know that nothing is impossible for God's Spirit. Besides the O.T. is full of the Spirit's mighty works. "The teacher" (likely indicating an official post) should be the first to know of the Spirit's anointing, both from the Scriptures and by EXPERIENCE.

11. "Believe me when I tell you," said Jesus, "When we say we know something, we really know it. For we are speaking of that we have actually seen, and yet all of you reject our testimony."

WE—YOU. Here is a further rebuke. The "we know," of Jesus is set against the "we know" of Nic. when he first came into the room. The "we" must include all who possess a knowledge of Jesus' real identity, i.e., John who witnessed His anointing from heaven (Matt. 3:13-17), His disciples who satisfied themselves, first by talking to Him and then seeing water turned into wine. It also includes the idea that Jesus is no more standing alone, but has friends. He is proud of the "we." It is set against the "you," which includes the Sanhedrin with its refusal of John the Baptist's testimony and finally Nic. himself who acknowledges only the prophet in Christ, having now objected to the doctrine of regeneration.

"Precisely how does the Lord rebuke Nicodemus for his failure to apprehend the truth of regeneration by faith!"

12. "If I speak plainly of things which occur on earth before your eyes, and you cannot accept them by faith, how would you ever believe if I were to speak of heaven's mysteries which occur in the spirit?"

EARTH-HEAVEN. Obviously the Lord considers regeneration (just explained by an earthly illustration) as something easily embraced by faith. With the "heavens opened" to Him since His baptism, He could speak of more profound things. The realities of the spirit are before Him now. If Nic. resists the basic Christian truth, he is likely to be more obtuse to what the Master says next. Jesus classes Nic. as one of "the Jews," allowing this is what makes it hard for him to believe. Even so He is going to drop a mystical bomb of heaven-truth, uttering remarkable statements first about His **PERSON** and then His **WORK**.

"What is meant by heavenly mysteries! Could we have an example
of something occurring in the spirit!"

13.   "No man has ever gone up so as to enter into heaven. But there is One Who has come down from heaven—the Son of Man—Who is in heaven.

 UP-DOWN. Jesus is not merely citing the obvious in saying no one has ever entered into heaven. He has stated a spiritual birth is the requirement for entering in. That applies to the O.T. saints as well. Access to heaven is a remarkable matter, but more astonishing is some-one's descent from there! Jesus claims He has, again titling Himself the "Son of Man." Recall He promised Nathanael and the disciples they would see the heavens opened with the angels "ascending and descending on the Son of Man." But then the bomb . . . "Who dwells in heaven!" How is this possible? Only by omnipresenc . Hence it is a remarkable claim of Deity. Only the Omnipresent God can be on earth and in heaven simultaneously. Jesus obviously knows now Who He really is . . . GOD!

14.   And this same Son of Man must be lifted up as the brazen serpent was lifted up by Moses in the wilderness.

 LIFTED UP. This is for Nicodemus. It is an earthly illustration of the heavenly truth of Christ's sacrifice. Nic., "the teacher," surely had taught this story often. A world of truth must have exploded in his mind as he now understood the mystery of the serpents in the wilderness (Num. 21:8). As men beheld the "dead" serpent and lived, now will they behold one taken from the "serpent family" (though not a sinner Himself) and slain for the healing of men. Jesus not only knew His personal identity (God), He also knew of His work from the beginning of His ministry. Thus the cross is predicted and the results.

"What does that have to do with Nicodemus!"

15. So that all those who believe in Him might not perish but have eternal life."

 NOT PERISH. Jesus has obviously read Nic.'s mind and using an O.T. illustration which has baffled Nic. for years, explains Himself by it. Nic. can make the application. Many perished in the wilderness, but those beholding the lifted serpent were healed. Jesus says He must similarly be lifted up, bringing eternal life to those who behold Him as slain for them. This is universal, not for Jews only, but for "all those who believe." The believe here is set against the "believe" of vss. 11, 12. Some Mss. omit "not perish," but the context demands it. **Nic. is being warned.** He will perish in unbelief if he does not abandon his trust in Jewish ceremonial righteousness and place his faith in Jesus.

"But why would anyone care to leave heaven and enter this sin-sick, perishing world!"

16. "God's love for mankind was so great He sent His uniquely begotten Son, that everyone who puts his trust in Him, might not perish but have eternal life.

 LOVE. This is the only explanation for the divine behavior. God is in love with man. Yet He hates the worldliness which estranges Him from man. So consuming is His love, no price is too great to pay in recovering His beloved. He will bear anything, humiliation, rejection, death, to salvage man for Himself. These are John's words here, telling us how it was done. God, as the Incarnate Son, enters the human stream via the virgin birth. See how the perishing idea is maintained. The consequences of rejection are always present to the invitation to salvation.

17. "When God sent His Son into the world He did not come as the world's Judge, but as its Saviour. God wanted the world saved.

 JUDGE. Jesus is indeed the Judge of this world, duly qualified since He is also a Man (John 5:27). But that was not His object in coming. God's passion for men was so desperate that He SENT Jesus from heaven. Why? So that men could see what God is really like AS A PERSON! This way they could respond to Him for WHO HE IS, not what they can get out of Him. Those who like Him and want Him are saved. Those who do not, must be excluded from heaven. God practices discrimination. Jesus is heaven's discriminator, the divider of men. But the damnatory judgment of men is a by-product of His coming. He first came to save, not to condemn.

"If a man doesn't believe in Jesus is he as good as in hell right now!"

18. "The one who believes in Him has no condemnation whatsoever. But he who does not believe is condemned already. Why? Because he has not believed in the Name of the uniquely-begotten Son of God.

 CONDEMNED. Ever see the tract, "What one must do to be lost!" When you open it the pages are blank. The answer is—nothing! All men are headed for hell, "for all have sinned . . ." (Rom. 3:23). Mankind is destined to share Satan's fate, belonging to him by virtue of Adam's capitulation. To avoid going to hell, people must therefore DO SOMETHING. What? Put their complete trust in the ONLY ONE who can save them from that awful fate. How does He do this? By providing sinners with the righteousness needed to live in the presence of a Holy God. Consequently the destiny of every man depends on what he DOES with Christ.

 UNIQUELY. Faith by itself does not save, it must have the proper object. It is not a matter of "only believe," for John declares a precise faith is required in a specific Person, and he furnishes precise details concerning Jesus as the object of faith. Thus the basis for doing business with Christ is a matter of trusting in the NAME (the person) of Jesus as the UNIQUELY-BEGOTTEN (unique meaning only one of its kind, referring to His virgin-birth) SON OF GOD (that is, God incarnate). "Uniquely-begotten" is to be preferred over "only begotten," since we too are the "begotten" sons of God (1 Peter 1:3). Jesus is uniquely virgin-born, while we are born of the Spirit. He needed a human nature, whereas we need the divine nature.

"Can people truly understand the seriousness of receiving Christ, that He is their only hope of escaping perdition!"

19.   "Man's condemnation is based on this fact: that light has come into this world, but men have preferred darkness because their deeds were evil.   20.   Obviously, one who does evil hates the light. He knows his shameful acts will be exposed if he comes to the light.

EXPOSED. Patients going to a psychiatrist must bare their souls to a man. The more that is revealed, the more likelihood of healing. But some would rather be sick than suffer exposure. It's like that in coming to Christ (The Light of the World). Our unholiness is fully exposed. Even so we confess the whole sordid mess and receive our spiritual healing. But he who prefers the darkness so that he may continue to delight in his evil ways, forfeits spiritual healing. He dreds exposure, not interested in forgiveness, and doesn't really want to be healed. He makes this decision for himself, thus the consequences rest on him. Man's condemnation is based on the fact that some prefer darkness and evil, while others prefer exposure and healing.

"But those who really want Christ, how do they feel about this exposure!"

21.   "On the other hand, he who does the truth will come to the light. There is a working of God which takes place in such a man, so that he doesn't mind having his deeds seen for what they are."

DOES. See the words, "does the truth?" In Greek this signifies a once-and-for-all act. Once a man comes to Christ (The True Light), acting on the truth, a CHANGE occurs in him. He finds he prefers holiness to evil. This is a supernatural event. But note it is a shift in his **preference**, not a sudden revamping of his life. It is this new desire for holiness that makes a man willing to have his sins exposed and forgiven. He is on God's side, judging the evil in himself. He doesn't like it any better than God does. Whereas the man who will not act on the truth of Christ, does not undergo this change. By his own choice he is condemned to remain in darkness and his hatred of the light continues.

"What was John the Baptist doing while Jesus' Messianic ministry was getting under way?"

22.   After these things, Jesus and His disciples moved into the Judean countryside and He stayed with them, baptizing.   23.   John continued baptizing, but in Aenon close to Salim, because there was an abundance of water in the region. Even so, people continued coming to him for baptism,   24.   for as yet, John had not been thrown into prison.

 BAPTIZING. Jesus and John were now baptizing concurrrently. Having finished everything in connection with His Jerusalem stay, He moved toward the Jordan, probably Northeasterly, with His disciples. John, on the other hand, retired to a watery place in Samaria, removed from the Jordan, so as to give Jesus the prominent baptismal grounds. Yet John didn't stop his work because the Messiah had arrived. Aware that he was appointed to die in his calling, he wished to give way to the Lord **voluntarily**, decreasing by His side. This withdrawal was an act of humility.

"Wasn't it a little confusing with Jesus and John baptizing in the same vicinity?"

25. Then some of John's disciples got into a dispute with a Jew about the matter of ceremonial washings for cleansing.

 DISPUTE. Here we have the beginnings of sacramental controversy. Not a few have raged since. Please note that **any** baptism occurring before the completion of Christ's work, can only be **preparatory.** Hence the baptism performed by Jesus' disciples was essentially the preparation-baptism of John. It was not Christian baptism, for that was not inaugurated until after the resurrection (Matt. 28:19) and first performed on the church's birthday (Acts 2:41). Yet John's baptism had a prophetic character which was completed by the Pentecostal baptism of the Spirit when thousands entered in on the day of Pentecost. The mentioned Jew was obviously seeking to provoke John's disciples by extolling Jesus' baptism. He thought, perhaps, to get John to come out against Jesus.

"Surely John wouldn't walk into such a trap as that!"

26. And they came to John and told him, "Rabbi, remember that Man Who was with you when you were baptizing on the other side of the Jordan, the One to Whom you bore witness? Did you know He is now baptizing and everybody is going over to Him!"

 EVERYBODY. Jealousy is at the bottom of this remark. They imply that Jesus is now overshadowing the one who got Him started, and it isn't right. Irritated, they want John to view Jesus now as an **unauthorized rival.** But John had purposely withdrawn to this more remote region. His disciples, recalling the better baptizing days, are bitter about it. Eventually they split into two camps, one friendly and the other hostile. This shows Satan's power to use one vicious tongue to kindle jealousy and division among God's people.

27. John's answer to that was: "A man cannot invest himself with a heavenly call, it must come from God. 28. You yourselves can witness to the fact that I said I am not the Messiah, but was merely sent ahead to announce Him.

CALL. "I have my work," says John, "And Jesus has His. We both are doing as God has appointed." This is what demands humility in us all. Our gifts and tasks come by way of free grace and investiture of God Himself. No one selects his own function in the Body of Christ. John is commenting on the two baptismal programs going on not more than 30 miles apart. John's words are a subhead for what he is about to say, for he is going to explain his relationship to Jesus in detail. He employs a common figure in O.T. prophecy to picture his role with respect to Jesus.

29. "The bridegroom is the one with the bride, but the bridegroom's friend also has a joy of his own. He stands by, thrilled as he listens to the bridegroom's voice. That joy is mine and it is as full as can be.

JOY. The figure is that of a bridegroom, escorted by his friend, to his bride's house. Where, for the first time (or at least to bring her back for the wedding), according to Jewish custom, he speaks to his bride. The friend is like a male chaperon. He is charged with making all the arrangements. And is privileged to stand and hear the words of delight from the lips of the groom as he greets his intended. John applies this to Christ and himself. Jesus (the Bridegroom) has been escorted by John (the friend) to the bride (Israel) and John is able to rejoice upon being present at the meeting and seeing her response to Christ. Many of these Israelites will be among those who will later be baptized into the Body of Christ (the true Bride of Christ) on the day of Pentecost. The figure is not to be pressed as far as the wedding, only the VOICE of the bridegroom is in view here, his happiness. John answers his disciples this way: "I am thrilled to see Jesus prosper, for I was used to introduce Him to the Bride of Jehovah" (Isa. 54:5; Hos. 2:19).

30. "He must increase, but I must decrease."

DECREASE. The relationship between John and Jesus, is like that of Judaism and Christianity. One gives way to the other. This is John's admonition to his disciples, "Everything is going according to plan, this is the way it is supposed to be." In authority and disciples John must decrease as Christ's ministry unfolds and becomes the important one. What humility is here. This grand disciple announces that his joy comes as the by-product of pleasing Christ. What a lesson. Humility is not something acquired by direct cultivation. It is the by-product of exalting Christ at the expense of yourself!

"WOW! What a statement of humility! Surely such words as these move John the Evangelist also to extoll the greatness of Christ!"

31. "Anyone who originates from above of necessity outranks everyone else. Whereas he who originates in the earth, is earth-bound and must speak from an earthly point of view. Yet, when the One Who is from above and above all, 32. testifies to what He has seen and heard, people simply will not accept His words.

SEEN-HEARD. At His baptism, Jesus was so fully anointed He owned by direct revelation the full realization of WHO He was in both worlds. All creation and the divine plan, including His pre-existence, were before Him as an open book. He knew that ". . . in Him dwelleth all the fulness of the Godhead bodily!" (Col. 2:9). If Paul knew this, surely Jesus did. It must be understood that the Omnipresent God was PRESENT TO the Incarnate Christ. (Weigh that statement carefully.) Jesus was fully God and His baptism permitted Him to behold what was laid aside when He entered the human stream as a SEED in Mary's womb (Luke 1:31). When Jesus speaks, men are listening to an EYE WITNESS of heaven's operations. They can believe Him if they want to, or treat Him as a fictitious man from Mars.

33. "Anyone who accepts Jesus' words, is at the same time certifying that God speaks the truth. 34. For He, Whom God has sent, not only speaks with the authority of heaven, but utters the very words of God Himself. For God has given Him the fulness of the Spirit.

FULNESS. John the Evangelist rejoices in John the Baptist's words, "He must increase, but I must decrease." And immediately he begins to assert that Christ is God. He says that Jesus has been so fully anointed (without measure), that when He speaks, God is talking. And anyone who accepts the Lord's message, is not merely affirming the words of a heavenly messenger, but of God Himself! That is how completely Christ is filled with the Spirit—**so full that He is God.** When Jesus speaks it is **instant-communication** from heaven, not a relayed broadcast. Never did any prophet say, "Verily I say unto you." Always it was "Thus saith the Lord." Clearly they spoke FOR God. Jesus speaks AS GOD. Next, John tells us why this has to be.

35.   "The Father loves the Son and has put everything in His hand.

EVERYTHING. Such a thing is not possible unless Jesus is God. The Greek not only implies Jesus' possession of "everything," but the **power of disposal.** From here on, throughout the Gospel of John, it will be necessary for the reader to think of Jesus as fully aware of events taking place both in heaven and in earth and completely in charge of all that has to do with earth, man and the spirit-world. True, there are things Jesus must yet **accomplish,** but nothing is lacking either in authority or power. What comes in the following chapters will be easier to understand if the reader simply considers, "Jesus is God."

"No wonder it is so serious to ignore Christ! Shunning Him is the same as spurning God!"

36.   "He who places his trust in the Son has eternal life. He who refuses to obey the Son by faith, will not see that life, but God's wrath remains on Him."

WRATH. Coming to Christ is more than a "life or death" matter. The choice is actually LIFE or WRATH, with death but the usher. With hell created to satisfy the wrath of God, it is not a nice alterative. The same genius which designed the flawless snowflake, of which no two are alike, also conceived perdition. It was not prepared for man, "but for the the devil and his angels" (Matt. 25:41). Yet, all without Christ must share Satan's fate. Let none think a good God would not send men there. Our God is vengeful and says so, "Vengeance is mine," saith the Lord, "I will repay!" (Rom. 12:19). Sinful man is already headed there, needing Christ to escape. Those without Jesus OWN God's wrath now, for they are as good as in hell until they receive Christ as Saviour. On the other hand, the one who receives Christ, begins the same life he will have in heaven.

"Did Jesus have to keep moving for fear of arousing the opposition of the Jews!"

4 1. And now it became known to the Lord that the Pharisees had received word, "Jesus is winning and baptizing more disciples than John!" 2. Yet the fact was, only the disciples of Jesus were doing this baptizing, not Jesus Himself. 3. So He left Judea and again withdrew Himself toward Galilee.

WITHDREW. By spiritual insight, Jesus perceives that opposition to His ministry on the part of the Pharisees is stirring. His teachings naturally condemned their practices, but He doesn't want open conflict with them this early in His mission. They could tolerate John, he was the son of a priest. But Jesus was just a Carpenter, and from Nazareth at that. That He should eclipse John was unthinkable. So their jealousy against Him, as head of a new movement, was easily aroused. No doubt they sponsored the quarrel of 3:25. Since it is not God's timing for a showdown, Jesus moves out of the area. Observe that He did not personally baptize. Confusion would result should the One Who baptizes with the Spirit, be found baptizing with water! His disciples continued to minister the **baptism of preparation** (for the kingdom), while He reserved to Himself, the baptism of the Holy Spirit (into the Church which is His Body) 1 Cor. 12:13.

4. And He was obliged to go by way of Samaria.

 OBLIGED. There were two routes from Judea to Galilee. The more direct lay through Samaria; the other, more circuitous, crossing the Jordan and passing through Perea, ended at the southern shores of Gennesaret. The stricter Jews preferred traveling the longer route to avoid intercourse with the Samaritans, whom they hated. The natural route for Jesus was through Samaria. Not only was it more direct, but the Galilean Jews didn't have such fierce prejudice. But there was a higher reason. Heaven's timetable called for an appointment. He was to meet someone there. And when He does, we have the first instance of turning from the Jews to reach Gentiles with the Gospel!

5. Thus He came to a Samaritan city called Sychar, close by the plot of ground which Jacob gave to his son Joseph.

SYCHAR. The name means drunken or lying town. Commonly identified with Shechem of the O.T., it lies about 34 miles north of Jerusalem. It is now called "Nablous." Observe that the parcel was a gift. It contained a flowing spring which was 105 feet below ground. That depth was reached by cutting through rock, which formed the sides of a well, known as "Jacob's well." It was regarded as sacred by the Samaritans. These people accepted the five books of Moses as divine, but refused the historical books of the Jews whom they regarded as their worst enemies. The Jews and the Samaritans hated each other more than the idolatrous nations which surrounded them. Religious hatred is most intense.

6. The spring called Jacob's well was there. It was just about noon and Jesus, wearied from His journey, sat there by the well exhausted.

WEARIED. Here is a very human scene of our Lord. By means of the historical present tense of the Greek language, we're going to be permitted to overhear what took place. His disciples had gone into the village to buy food. He stayed behind, more tired than they. He had a strain they knew nothing about. An "hour" awaited Him, the cross was before Him. He lived in "death row," and that takes a lot out of a man. He is seen here truly as a man upon the earth. Yes He was perfect God, tasting fully of our humanity. The One Who made the worlds (Col. 1:16), sits wearily by a well . . . alone . . . waiting for His appointment to show up. Here she comes now.

7.   Presently a Samaritan woman came to draw water. Jesus said to her, "Give Me a drink of water," 8.   for His disciples had gone into town to buy food.

WOMAN. This woman had no thought save to draw water without being seen. That's why she came at noon, in midday heat. She was the town harlot. She didn't want to meet anyone. She was shunned by the other women who usually came to draw water in the cool of the evening. But God's grace reached out to her when Jesus said, "Give Me a drink." It was no accident that the disciples were some two miles away in town. (Galileans could buy food of the Samaritans.) God in the flesh wanted this poor soul alone with Himself. So He asks of her to provoke her to inquire of Him.

9.   "What!" replied the woman, "You a Jew, asking a drink of me, a Samaritan woman?" (It should be noted that the Jews refuse to have any dealings with the Samaritans whatsoever.)

A JEW. She instantly recognized His Jewish dress and Aramaic dialect and Rabbi garb. Several things shocked her. Not only was this a Jew speaking to her, but a distinguished Jew stooped to ask of her. More than that,

He was ready to defile Himself on her bucket. Women were always regarded as less than men. The gap between Jesus and this woman was so great she could only feel that what He had asked was the greatest kind of free condescension. Notice that the woman does not refuse, but only expresses her surprise at Jesus' request. The observation that Jews have no dealing with Samaritans must belong to the woman's reply, even though it is in parenthesis.

"Well, He got her attention all right. Did her reply make it possible for Him to say what He wanted!"

10.   "If you only knew the gift of God," replied Jesus, "and Who it is that is asking you for a drink, you would be asking of Him and He would give you living water."

ONLY KNEW. She can't know the spiritual meaning of Jesus' words. But she is disarmed by His extreme humility and listens. Like Nicodemus, she is met with words having a double meaning, spiritual and natural. "Gift of God," is an Eastern expression for water. Water boys sell it in the streets, calling out, "The gift of God!" But Jesus, of course, means Himself when He offers her "living water." To her that means the spring water at the bottom of the well, where it bubbles and flows. "Living water" meant then what "running water" means to us. This too had spiritual meaning, referring to the satisfaction of soul-thirst, which only Jesus can give. On these double meanings rests the turn of the conversation from earthly to heavenly matters. The woman is curious, baited—ready to inquire further of this humble Rabbi.

11.   "Sir," said the woman, "how can you reach down to the living water? This well is very deep. Besides, you don't have anything to draw with.   12.   Do you consider yourself greater than our father Jacob who gave us this well and drank here himself, along with his family and cattle?"

DEEP. It was deep all right. The water level was about 90 feet below ground and reached by means of a lowered skin bucket. That is not the same as her waterpot (vs. 28). The "living water" or spring at the bottom pushed the water upwards about 15 feet. She wonders just how He can reach the spring water 105 feet below with no bucket. Only a supernatural person could do such a thing, and her mind begins to move that way. But then she checks herself. Why that would make this Rabbi even greater than the revered patriarch. It is possible she resents the notion. This is a Jew speaking. She challenges Him on it.

GREATER! Indeed, but she couldn't know it—yet. When Jesus offers "living water," she suspects He is hinting at spiritual power, perhaps akin to that of Moses, in whom she believed. He once produced a gushing fountain by miracle. But if that is the case, then the noble Jacob is being downgraded by this Teacher. Digging a well through rock to bring forth a well that supplied an entire community was no small thing. It was the finest gift the ancient nomad could grant his heirs. But now this Teacher expects to do better and He hasn't a thing in His hand. She doesn't know whether to get insulted or ask further. In a way she is now like Nicodemus in allowing herself to be blinded by tradition. Yet she is more open than Nic. "If you can do such a thing, I'd like to see it!" That is really her attitude.

"But isn't she thinking only in terms of physical water, even if she thinks He might produce a fountain by miracle!"

13. "Anyone drinking this water will surely thirst again," said Jesus, 14. "but whoever drinks of the water that I shall give him, shall thirst no more. For the water I give becomes inside that person a spring which wells up into eternal life."

 THIRST AGAIN. She knew about that. The poor woman had drunk often at the well of lust and repeated draughts served only to increase her thirst. She was thirsty for something more than the vanity of earthly pleasures.

And Jesus' insight to her need allowed Him to hear and touch the cry of her soul. Jesus, of course, speaks of the overflowing satisfaction of the Christ-life, where the infinite appetite of man is slaked by the Infinite God Himself. But she only knows that her thirst brings her to this well often, and that her need for water is akin to the thirst of her empty spirit. Jesus' words sound appealing. Even if her mind cannot grasp the full import of what He is saying, her spirit responds.

ETERNAL LIFE. How wonderfully this pictures the satisfying of man's hunger through the gift of eternal life in Christ. The image in the woman's mind is that of the spring at the bottom of Jacob's well suddenly gushing with such force and plentitude that the water-level rises up and over the top. The spiritual sense of Jesus' words are thus apparent. The gushing spring, He says, is not at the bottom of Jacob's well, but INSIDE A PERSON. He Himself is overfilled, His thirst ever slaked. This can only refer to the fulness of joy and peace in the filling of the Holy Spirit!

"What a profound statement! Surely she can't grasp the idea of an internal fountain of satisfaction!"

15. "Then Sir," replied the woman, "give me that water that I may not thirst again, and neither must I keep coming all this way to draw water."

GIVE ME. The positions are reversed. She is now willing to become indebted to a Jew. She buys the idea of super-water. True, she's in the dark as to the real meaning of His words, but her prejudice is overcome. She does ask. Also, religious feelings are awakening in her soul. There's a mixture of physical and spiritual in her reply. She knows what He has offered to do is physically impossible, yet she is moved to ask Him for the water anyway. Her faith in the Rabbi has risen. But the Lord has yet to reach her conscience, for conviction of sin MUST precede salvation. Confession is needed. One must taste guilt and personal wretchedness before he desires salvation. So the Lord answers her request with words calculated to prick her conscience. He discerns she is ready.

16.   Upon that, Jesus said to her, "Go call your husband and come back here to Me."

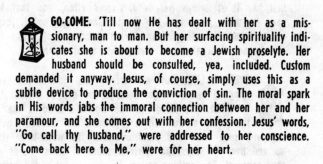

GO-COME. 'Till now He has dealt with her as a missionary, man to man. But her surfacing spirituality indicates she is about to become a Jewish proselyte. Her husband should be consulted, yea, included. Custom demanded it anyway. Jesus, of course, simply uses this as a subtle device to produce the conviction of sin. The moral spark in His words jabs the immoral connection between her and her paramour, and she comes out with her confession. Jesus' words, "Go call thy husband," were addressed to her conscience. "Come back here to Me," were for her heart.

17.   "I don't have a husband," answered the woman. To which Jesus replied: "True enough, you don't have a husband.   18.   In fact you have had five husbands and the man you are living with right now is not your husband. In saying this, you have told Me the truth."

FIVE HUSBANDS. She feels the effect of His words. The conversation turns. Her illicit relationship is before her and a frank confession is on her lips. That's what Jesus wanted. She is sincere, otherwise she could have gone away pretending to go call her husband. As Jesus knew Peter the second they met and beheld Nathanael under the fig tree, so now is the life of this woman before Him. This is not to teach that Jesus was strictly omniscient during His earthly ministry. He disclaimed certain knowledge (Mark 13:32). But when it was necessary for His mission and saving sinners, He could by virtue of His essential union with the Father (omnipresence), penetrate the secrets of the human heart to unlock their histories.

**"She must have felt that. Her estimate of Jesus seems
to have risen sharply."**

19. "Sir, I am fast coming to the conclusion that you are a Prophet," said the woman. 20. "Now our ancestors have always worshipped on this mountain, but you Jews say that Jerusalem is the only place for men to worship—"

PROPHET. She responds to this prophetic look into her life as coming from a Prophet of God. Unlike the Jews, who expected their Messiah to arrive as a King, the Samaritans believed He would appear as a Prophet (Deut. 18:15-19). There is nothing in her background to keep her from embracing this mysterious stranger as the Samaritan Messiah should that truth become apparent. Having confessed her sin, the need for atonement rises. But where should she go? This isn't clear to her. So she raises the old issue which raged so hotly between the Jews and the Samaritans. This Prophet might have the answer. Yes her conscience pinched. There is even pride in her holy mountain and the "our ancestors" is versus "you Jews," but the question is honest. She wants to know where to go for atonement now that a Prophet of God has put His finger on her sin.

21. "Believe Me woman," said Jesus, "the time is at hand when your worship of the Father will have nothing to do with a specific place, neither here nor yet at Jerusalem."

ME-YOUR. Again see Jesus' Deity. The woman made reference to Jewish insistence on Jerusalem as the ONLY place of worship. But Jesus says, "Believe ME (not us)." An ordinary prophet would have said, "WE shall worship . . . ," but Jesus said "ME," He is the One Who is worshipped. The woman learns the time is at hand when all controversies respecting PLACE of worship will be obsolete. The meaning is, that very soon now, worship of God will no longer be confined to any one place. The idea of INTERNAL worship is about to do away with the requirement to worship God in a **specific** place. Note, though, that even as Jesus says this, it is still the O.T. era and the temple at Jerusalem is still in business. He Himself, carefully observes the Passovers.

"Well, if the Samaritans didn't really know WHERE to worship, how could they rightly know WHOM to worship!"

22. "You Samaritans have no idea what you are worshipping, but we do, for salvation comes from the Jews."

NO IDEA. That's blunt enough. When it comes to salvation, says Jesus, the Jews are right and the Samaritans are wrong. He speaks plainly when it is called for. By this, Jesus sets His seal on the Jewish religion as divine revelation meant to prepare mankind for His coming. Thus, He set aside all other religions as false, or certainly in the dark as they grope after the "unknown God." This is one of the most convincing statements that Christianity is the final, perfect religion of mankind. Salvation here we take to mean the Messiah.

23. "But the time is coming and is already here when all genuine worshippers will worship the Father in spirit and in truth—in fact, this is exactly the kind of worshippers the Father wants, even seeks."

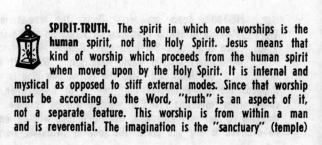

SPIRIT-TRUTH. The spirit in which one worships is the human spirit, not the Holy Spirit. Jesus means that kind of worship which proceeds from the human spirit when moved upon by the Holy Spirit. It is internal and mystical as opposed to stiff external modes. Since that worship must be according to the Word, "truth" is an aspect of it, not a separate feature. This worship is from within a man and is reverential. The imagination is the "sanctuary" (temple)

of the human spirit. God seeks people who will enjoy His presence as they behold His Person in their imaginations. This is the metaphysical side of Christianity. Jesus worshipped the Father that way, hence the time was "already here." His disciples would also learn this kind of worship (Matt. 6:9-13). The statement strikes hard against formalism and all outward substitutes for internal worship.

"Why would Jesus bring such deep teaching to this woman! Her soul was hungry, but was it necessary for her to understand the spiritual nature of true worship!"

24. "God is Spirit, and those who worship Him must worship Him in spirit and in truth."

 MUST. There is no alternative, this word is emphatic. It is now LAW that God can only be approached in the spirit according to truth. Any other approach is hereby outlawed. Some worship in the spirit, but have not the truth. Others have the truth, but worship not in their spirit. These words are not hard to understand. It means the kind of worship given must correspond to the nature of the god worshipped. Even an ignorant Samaritan woman can sufficiently understand this. Our God is Spirit, hence He cannot be approached in the flesh. Flesh cannot worship spirit. Sadly, much of what is called worship today is fleshly. God, being spiritual, can be worshipped anywhere by a spiritual person independently of any mountain or building.

"Surely those words heightened her spiritual expectations!"

25. The woman said to Him, "I know that Messiah is coming. You know, the One called Christ. When He gets here He will explain all these things to us."

 COMING. See her faith in the Messiah? Ah, but not just the Samaritan Messiah either. She adds the Jewish reference, "called Christ." She believes His statement, "Salvation is of the Jews." She says, "I KNOW He is coming!" Her reasonings have now brought her to the point of saying, "I want Messiah." Jesus' Words have reached deep. Her soul responds in spirit and in truth. Her head doesn't grasp it all, but her heart is ready. Illumination often comes via the heart. While she does not lay hold fully of Jesus' Words, they lay hold of her. Her heart is saying what her mind cannot totally grasp . . . **"I want Christ!"**

26. Then Jesus said to her, "I AM that is talking to you!"

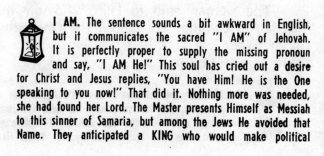

I AM. The sentence sounds a bit awkward in English, but it communicates the sacred "I AM" of Jehovah. It is perfectly proper to supply the missing pronoun and say, "I AM He!" This soul has cried out a desire for Christ and Jesus replies, "You have Him! He is the One speaking to you now!" That did it. Nothing more was needed, she had found her Lord. The Master presents Himself as Messiah to this sinner of Samaria, but among the Jews He avoided that Name. They anticipated a KING who would make political changes, not a Saviour to love. Inasmuch as the Samaritans expected a Prophet like Moses, Who would reveal the divine will, they would not be apt to abuse the revelation. A sinful woman, an outcast, was the first to hear it straight out from the Lord . . . "I AM HE!" What grace!

"What a moment for that woman! She knew she had found the Messiah! What did she say to that!"

27.   At precisely that moment His disciples returned and were shocked to find Him talking to a woman. Yet none dared question this action or ask, "What do you want of her?" or, "Why do you even speak with her?"

SHOCKED. Well might they be astonished, for oriental custom imposed rigid restrictions on public conversations with females. Rabbis, according to tradition, were forbidden to speak openly with any woman. And here was a low woman. But His disciples keep their questionings to themselves thinking He might now be establishing a new custom or enlarging human relationships. It was an act of respect for His authority.

28.   So the woman put down her waterpot and went back into the city where she spoke to the men there.   29.   "Come here! I want you to see a man who has told me everything I have ever done! Could this possibly be the Christ?" 30.   Whereupon many of those men streamed out of the city to go to Jesus.

THE CHRIST! She didn't forget her waterpot. She was coming back. It would only slow her down as she ran into the village. She's excited, even carried away in her female exuberance. She stretches Jesus' words to . . . "All things I ever did!" See her old nature! She knew Who this was, Jesus had told her. She is eager for the honor of discovering the Messiah. She asks, "Could this be the Christ?" meaning, "Have I found the Messiah?" Then note the disposition of these people. They RAN out to see Jesus. This was a Messiah-hungry city. They were ready. The disciples bought food here, yet never said a word about the Messiah being outside of town. So God used a harlot to bring the news. She not only gets the credit for winning a city, but reaps the joy. The disciples missed a great opportunity. No doubt prejudice sealed their lips.

"What did the disciples do when the woman left?"

31. In the meantime the disciples kept pressing the Lord to eat. "Please Master, take some food." 32. But He said to them, "I have food to eat you know nothing about." 33. This naturally prompted the disciples to inquire among themselves, "Do you suppose someone brought Him some food?" 34. "My food," said Jesus, "is doing the will of Him that sent Me and seeing that the job gets done."

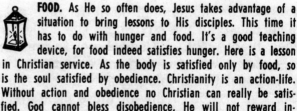

FOOD. As He so often does, Jesus takes advantage of a situation to bring lessons to His disciples. This time it has to do with hunger and food. It's a good teaching device, for food indeed satisfies hunger. Here is a lesson in Christian service. As the body is satisfied only by food, so is the soul satisfied by obedience. Christianity is an action-life. Without action and obedience no Christian can really be satisfied. God cannot bless disobedience, He will not reward indifference to His commands. James agrees, saying we are to be DOERS of the Word and not HEARERS only (James 1:22). Jesus sees the men of Samaria coming through the fields. A whole town is to be His food, His satisfaction.

"Didn't the disciples see all those people coming toward them from the city?"

35. "Have you not been saying, 'Four more months and then comes the harvest?' Well — take a look out there across the fields! I tell you they are harvest white already!"

HARVEST. Jesus intuitively knows of their conversations as they returned from the city. They had been commenting on the state of the crops. The fields were green, making His words (white) more striking. Jesus' spiritual stomach is full as He sees the men coming. He's stuffed with satisfaction. He directs their eyes to the approaching men. "That field is white right now," He says, "the harvest is ready." They saw green fields, He saw men. What a lesson! They considered Sychar a poor place to prospect for souls, but now a whole village is turning out. They went after food, but they could have returned with souls. Compare this reception with the one He received at Jerusalem where He performed many miracles. Here He simply spoke to one woman.

36. "Even the one who reaps is being rewarded while he gathers fruit into the granary of eternal life. And as you know, the sower and reaper share a common joy in the harvest. 37. And here, in this instance, we see fulfilled the old proverb, 'One sows and another reaps.' "

REAPS. This is connected with the preceding verses setting forth the whited fields. The woman has sown in the village, now a harvest is coming to Jesus. The disciples will have the joy of reaping. It must have been a shock to think they would reap a Samaritan harvest sown by an adulteress. Of course the sowing had been going on for centuries. These people had Moses and the Pentateuch. The prophets had sown in tears in this area, even as recently as John the Baptist. God's truth had been planted here long before Jesus and the disciples arrived. Now it comes to harvest. In the next life, the sowers and the reapers will jointly delight in what they have done for Christ where the fruit of their labors will be displayed forever! Jesus teaches that one work is no more important than another.

38. "For you see I have sent you to reap a harvest for which you did not work at all. Other people have labored and you have inherited the results of their toil."

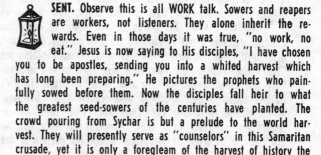

SENT. Observe this is all WORK talk. Sowers and reapers are workers, not listeners. They alone inherit the rewards. Even in those days it was true, "no work, no eat." Jesus is now saying to His disciples, "I have chosen you to be apostles, sending you into a whited harvest which has long been preparing." He pictures the prophets who painfully sowed before them. Now the disciples fall heir to what the greatest seed-sowers of the centuries have planted. The crowd pouring from Sychar is but a prelude to the world harvest. They will presently serve as "counselors" in this Samaritan crusade, yet it is only a foregleam of the harvest of history the church is to take.

"What happened when the Samaritans reached Jesus! Did they welcome Him as the Prophet! Did they harken to His Words!"

39. Now the many Samaritans who came out from the town believed in Jesus purely on the basis of the woman's testimony, "He told me everything I've ever done!" 40. So convinced were they, that when they reached Him, they begged Him to return to the village and stay with them. And He did, remaining with them two days.

BEGGED. What a contrast to His experiences in Judea. There they ordered Him away, taking up stones against Him, finally plotting His death. But look how these heretical Samaritans treat Him! They WANT Him! Observe that it is menfolk the woman contacted. Those who come running from the village are the ones who believe her and

act on her testimony. The woman testified to His PERSON.
"Could this be the Christ?" she asked. How wonderfully God's
power is manifest in weak vessels. It was not the clergy who
shook this town, but a harlot. And her testimony precipitated
a city-wide revival!

**41.   And many more believed because of what
He Himself said.**

HIMSELF. If Jesus had been like other men, His Words
would have no weight. A man's personal testimony to
himself is always discounted. But as the sun in the sky
proves its existence by the light and warmth it gives,
so Jesus, the SUN of Righteousness, proves Himself as His
words pierce the souls of men. By this operation (the Spirit's
witness) He takes possession of unprejudiced hearts. Laboring
for two days, apparently without any miracles, He makes more
converts among the Samaritans than in all His preceding time
in Judea. This episode is surely one of the brightest spots in
the earthly life of our Lord. Gentiles brought Him His joy this
day.

**42.   So they graciously informed the woman,
"Our faith in Him no longer rests solely on
what you said, for we have heard Him with our
own ears and know for certain that He really
is the Saviour of the world."**

WORLD. The woman testified to His PERSON, saying He
was the Christ. She told WHO He was. After feeling His
Word upon their souls, they become convinced as to
WHAT He was—the Saviour of the world! The Samaritans find that He is not just a JEWISH Messiah, but a Gentile
Saviour as well. And a SAVIOUR has to do with SIN. They
kindly inform the woman that their own experiences with Him
convince them He is more than the expected PROPHET, He is
the Saviour of mankind. After listening to Him, their faith ad-
vances. They know (as did John and Andrew), by personal
experience, that Jesus is Saviour of the world. Of course they

are grateful for the woman's testimony. It led them to the conviction that Jesus was also their OWN PERSONAL Saviour as well. How fortunate for them He was rejected in Jerusalem. They want Him. The Jews didn't.

"Did they resume their journey after the two days passed?"

43. Then after the two days had gone by, He returned to Galilee (by-passing His home town of Nazareth), 44. for Jesus Himself had said, "A prophet is never treated with honor in His own country."

HONOR. This is a disputed passage. It is handled easiest by saying He by-passed the place where He was raised and lived for thirty years. It would have been natural to stop and see the family and how things were at the shop, but He didn't. Some hold that since He had gained a reputation outside of Galilee, He could now expect a hero's welcome upon return. Another explanation divides Galilee into North and South, allowing He had no honor in S. Galilee (Nazareth is there), but found favor in N. Galilee (Capernaum is there). These views have plausibility. But this was a common proverb and seems to apply best to His hometown. He Himself applied the same proverb to Nazareth later on (Matt. 13:57).

45. And when He arrived the people welcomed Him with fanfare for they had seen all the things He had done at the Passover Feast in Jerusalem, having gone there themselves. 46. So once again He visited Cana of Galilee where He had previously turned the water into wine. It turned out that a government official was there who had a son lying gravely ill at Capernaum. 47. And hearing that Jesus had returned from Judea into Galilee, went to Him begging Him to come down

and heal his son, for he was at the point of death. 48. Jesus therefore answered, "Except you people see signs and wonders you just won't believe, will you!"

SIGNS-WONDERS. Jesus does answer the official, but His reply is addressed to the Galilean crowds. He is testing the official who apparently feels the Lord must be present to heal his son, exhibiting a rather weak faith. The Master would deepen that faith with a blunt reply, such as He gave to Nicodemus. Yet, He will honor the request of this official, but not until He gives a mild scolding to all present. He wants to move the man away from a faith which rests on miracles, to faith in **His Word.** When Jesus says, "wonders," He is reproving their miracle-mania, a craving for wonders, intimating there is a higher faith than that based on seeing miracles. In nowise does He reject the man's plea, but He seeks to hush the excitement of seeing signs, and turn his heart to the quiet voice of the Lord.

49. "Sir," pleaded the officer, "won't You come down before my boy dies?"

COME. The official's faith doesn't quite measure up to Jesus' challenge. He still wants the Lord to travel to Capernaum, "The lad is dying while we stand here talking. Won't You please come!" The distress of love for his child is about to make him a believer. He accepts the reproof of Christ, yet he does not feel wounded or rejected. Growing more urgent, he persists in his petition, "Signs or no signs, won't you come?" His real test is at hand. He will be required to put his faith in the Word of Jesus without the attesting help of miracles or signs.

50. "Go on back home," said Jesus, "your son will live!" The man believed the Word that Jesus spoke and immediately headed for home.

GO. Two things were necessary here: First, the man had to believe the Word of Jesus and then act on it (James 1:22). If he truly believed the Lord, he would GO. He passed the test. His faith rose past the sign-seeing kind, to trust in Jesus' Word alone. How was the miracle done! By the WILL of the Lord Whose will is ever in concert with the Father's (5:19). To restore health to a dying person at a distance and simultaneously have perfect knowledge of his recovery, is evidence of Jesus' power and omniscience. Distance is no hindrance to One Who sees "all things whatsoever the Father doeth" (5:19) . . . as He affirms in the next chapter.

"When did the man find out whether or not his son had been healed!"

51.   On his way back, his servants met him with word that his son had survived.   52.   So he asked what time it was when the lad began to recover. They answered, "His fever broke yesterday at one o'clock in the afternoon!" 53.   The father then realized it was precisely the moment when Jesus said to him, "Your son will live." Not only did he become a believer, but faith came to his entire household.

WHAT TIME! The father was not satisfied merely to hear that his boy was getting well. His spiritual interest has been aroused. It is for reasons of faith that he wants to know the exact time the condition changed. He would trace the event to its cause. He does, realizing the fever departed the moment Jesus spoke to him. The faith which was now sealed to him and subsequently came to his family, was belief in the WORD of God, not that which rests on seeing miracles. Surely the family had witnessed the recovery, but it wasn't until the officer reached home to tell about Jesus that this kind of faith was possible. Like the Samaritan woman, this man brought faith to his whole house by testifying to Jesus. This was perhaps the most important house in Capernaum.

54.   So for the second time Jesus immediately performed a sign after coming down from Judea into Galilee.

5 1. Long after these things occurred, Jesus went up to Jerusalem to attend a feast of the Jews.

AFTER. The gap between Chapter Four and Five covers a period of months, perhaps as much as two years depending on which feast this is. The passage is highly disputed, for on it rests whether Jesus' ministry was 2½ years or 3½ years. That it was a Passover seems to present the least difficulty and most researchers favor this view. If so, 18 to 20 months have gone by since the healing of the official's son in Chapter Four. If not, then no more than 8 months. John records three other Passovers (2:13; 6:4; 13:1), and this would be a fourth. Between these chapters, the Lord carried out His great Galilean ministry during which He called The Twelve and performed many miracles.

2. Now at Jerusalem, near the Sheep Gate, there is located a pool which is called in the Hebrew tongue, Bethesda. It is sheltered by five porches.

BETHESDA. This pool cannot be identified today, but is believed to have been a spring-fed reservoir just outside city walls where flocks of sheep, brought in for temple ritual, were watered. A section of it appears to have been set aside for the sick and enclosed with five sheltered walks or porches. It would be the closest thing to a hospital, Bethesda meaning "House of Mercy." The porches were no doubt provided with stalls or resting places for the patients. The Lord deliberately chose to enter the city by this gate, perhaps because He is God's Lamb.

3. In these lay crowds of sick people—those who were blind, the lame, even the disabled, all waiting for a peculiar disturbance of the water. 4. For at certain times an angel of the Lord would come down to the pool and

swish the waters. Then, the first person who stepped into the stirred waters would be healed of his particular ailment.

 WAITING. The words, "waiting for a disturbance of the water," and verse 4 are not found in the Revised Version, but are found in many ancient Mss. Apparently Jewish tradition held that an angelic stirring of the pool's waters produced miraculous healings. John makes mention of this tradition to explain the crowd gathered there. There must have been healings of some kind or people would not be there. Besides, had the tradition not been true, it would have been denied by multitudes of people who had knowledge of Jerusalem when this account was written. It is safer to assume John had good reasons for admitting the tradition into his narrative than to leave it out.

"Was there something special the Lord wanted to do at this pool!"

5.   Now there was a man there who had been disabled by his affliction for thirty-eight years.

 MAN. This man is Jesus' target. He singles out the most pitiable case. Everyone surely knew of his plight. He may have even been famous for his persistence in trying to get into the water. Jesus is going to heal this man and do it deliberately to cause trouble between Himself and the Jewish leaders. This man does not ask for help. John records this **unsolicited** miracle as the starting gun of open conflict between the Lord and the religious rulers. In past months He has avoided this, but now He is about to take them on in open controversy. It is by this means that He will get the hearing He seeks, for He is going to cause trouble at the very point where they were the most sensitive—the Sabbath. This is but one of six miraculous cures performed by Jesus on the Sabbath, all of which were **unsought**.

"You mean Jesus deliberately picked out a man and decided to heal him!"

6. When Jesus saw this man lying prostrate and knew that he had been sick like this for such a long time, He said to him, "Are you really serious about getting well?" 7. "Yes Sir," replied the man, "but I don't have anybody to put me in the pool while the water is moving, for while I am trying to get there, someone else always manages to reach the pool before me."

SERIOUS! A strange question to ask a sick person? No. Not everyone wants to get well. Some enjoy the pity and attention they get. Jesus read this man's heart. He saw the cause of his ailment (a particular sin). He knew how long he had been that way and was aware of the fame the man likely enjoyed due to his plight. He also knew how serious he was about getting well. We do too when we examine his reply, "Yes, but nobody will help me." He doesn't say, "Oh yes, please help me!" Besides, he can move . . . "While I am coming," indicates that. So he can't be too serious about it. The Lord will not heal this man against his will, his permission has to be secured. And it is. He is willing to be made well.

"Is this all Jesus wanted from him, just permission to heal him! And did He then heal him!"

8. "Rise," said Jesus, "take up your bed and walk." 9. All at once the man's full strength returned and he gathered up his pallet and began to walk. Note that this took place on a Sabbath.

PALLET. Jesus didn't have to say that, hence it is a key. When He says, "take up your bed," it is not merely to add proof to the miracle, but to cause trouble. He knows it is the Sabbath and that the legalistic Jews had strict prohibitions against such a thing. It called for the death penalty to break the Sabbath in this fashion. But the man doesn't stop to think. He slings that quilt (pallet) over his shoulder and goes skipping into the city to show off his healing. The instant transition from 38 years a cripple to a furniture mover in one second is indeed a miracle. The man is too excited to say, "Thank you." Now the Lord did this intentionally to stir up opposition. He knew the rulers would be seeking Him out. The time has come for them to hear from Him concerning His mission. This is Jesus' way of securing the right audience and proper attention for His claims.

10. Consequently the Jews challenged the man who was healed. They said to him, "Hey, it's the Sabbath! You know it is not legal for you to carry your bed like this!"

NOT LEGAL. Listen to that, would you. This man is carrying the very bed on which he has been suffering for years, demonstrating a miracle of God before their eyes. But it is a Sabbath and they see NOT the glorious work of God, but a violation of one of their ordinances. Informers were everywhere, so in due course, word reaches the Sanhedrin and the man is arrested. Now the healing was not illegal, but carrying a heavy quilt was. This was like citing a man for spitting on the sidewalk who had coughed up a toothpick that was choking him. The man is then taken before the leaders and charged with Sabbath-breaking. Jesus, of course, knew this would happen. This is why He healed the man in the first place.

11. But he defended himself by saying, "He Who made me well told me to do it. He said to me, 'Take up your bed and walk!'"
12. "Who is this man?" they asked, "You'd better tell us who it was that instructed you to take up your bed and walk."

WHO. The poor man is under their thumb, he has indeed broken one of their laws. His only defense is that his Healer told him to do it. So naturally they will turn their hypocritical guns in the direction of the Healer. The man is small fry, but they can use him to get their hands on the Person Who was teaching Sabbath-breaking, the One defying their regulations and backing His action with miracles. So they threaten the man with the death penalty in order to secure the name of his Healer.

"Did the man then explain about Jesus and identify Him!"

13.   But the cripple who had been healed didn't really know Who had healed him, for Jesus had eased Himself out of sight and into the crowd that quickly filled the place.

EASED. Not wishing to be identified at the pool, seeking also to avoid the miracle-hungry crowd, Jesus slipped out of sight. Neither did He wish a confrontation with lesser Jews. His plan was to smoke out the rulers and let them come seeking Him. The strategy of having the healed man carry his bed worked perfectly. The crime was sufficient to stir the Sanhedrin. Besides, anyone who could do such healings obviously could lay claim to great authority. It is the authority of Jesus that frightens and enrages the rulers. This is what brings the high-ranking Jews into open conflict with the Lord.

14.   Yet it wasn't long afterwards that Jesus found the man in the temple and said to him, "All right, you are well now. But you must not continue in that sin, for if you do, a worse thing is sure to come upon you."

FOUND. It was necessary for the man to secure Jesus' identity, so the Lord waited for him in the temple. Such a healing would stir his soul to bring a thank-offering, but also it would be a likely place to find the Man of God who had healed him. Jesus located the man and revealed Himself to him. See the severe injunction delivered to a man just healed? Note also this is a particular sin connected with a particular disease. This is not the general rule which connects sickness with sin, but a specific sin which was known only to the Lord and the man. See how it magnifies the penetrating knowledge of our Saviour. The man is warned that a continuation of this sin, which has already produced 38 years of infirmity, could bring greater disaster. Since this healing is NOT related to forgiveness, it is almost certain that the **cause** is still within the man.

15.   The man went back and told the Jews that it was Jesus Who had healed him.

 TOLD. He squealed to save his skin. It was a matter of supplying the name of his healer or bear the penalty for Sabbath-breaking himself. Nothing more is heard of the man, so he does get off the hook by informing. But again, this is why the Lord healed him. The man has been used by the Lord, but well paid for his trouble. He is healed of a terrible crippling and is cleared of the charges against him. It never hurts anyone to be used by the Lord.

"How did the ruling Jews react to the information that Jesus was the Healer!"

16.   It was on account of this that the Jews seriously began to persecute Jesus, and all because He did these things on the Sabbath.

 PERSECUTE. Jesus was no doubt hauled before some kind of a court for a hearing on the charge of Sabbath-breaking. But the case was shaky inasmuch as a merciful act was involved. Besides the Law allowed that "all danger or preservation of life removed the Sabbath restrictions." So the charge against the Lord was confused by the remarkable healing. The Greek terms express a continuance of the persecutions, indicating the trial was a failure. However this is without doubt the beginning point of their determined hatred of the Lord, seeking His death. Now Jesus deliberately brought this about. It was their vicious harrassment and plotting against Him that made it possible for Him to have their undivided attention. No doubt every word from Him, from now on, was copied down and reported to the Sanhedrin. They were looking for an excuse to execute Him.

 SABBATH. Man's sabbath is based on God's Sabbath. God did rest from His creative labors, but He didn't retire. He shifted to a new kind of work, that of maintaining—preserving—governing—helping—redeeming His creation. The point: **It is work.** Man's sabbath is a rest FROM the struggle to survive TO take up a different work—**God's work.** The O.T. idea of the Sabbath was "Thou shalt not," which insisted on a cessation of all work needed to make a living. The N.T. idea is positive telling us that which we SHOULD DO on the Sabbath. Man's sabbath, therefore, is a rest from self-labors to WORK for the Lord. And it is the CHANGE in the **kind of work** that provides the real refreshment. Consequently, the real Sabbath-breaker is one who leaves the work of the Sabbath UNDONE!

17. "My Father has never stopped working," replied Jesus. "The very fact that I, MYSELF, am working indicates that He is working, even this very moment."

 MYSELF. What a remarkable refutation of the charges. The "Myself," is forceful in the Greek. "If you are going to arrest Me, you'll have to arrest My Father too! If I am guilty of Sabbath-breaking, so is He!" That, of course, would find the Jews charging God with breaking His own Law! Jesus' words go beyond the idea of a son imitating his father or even cooperating with his father. He is saying, "My working is God at rest!" He avoids saying, "I am God," but they draw that inference, indeed they do. In fact, it becomes the basis of a new charge leveled against Him. See here how the Lord rescues us from the negative side of the Law, that slavery of the hypocritical sabbatarianism of the Pharisees? He shows us the positive side—working for the Father instead of ourselves. At least one day out of seven is to be set aside for helping, healing, and occupying with the things of God.

"WOW! That must have upset the Jews!"

18.   Because He said this, the Jews were even more determined to kill Him. Now it was no longer a matter of Sabbath-breaking, He had claimed God as His own Father in such a unique way, that it could only mean He was equating Himself with the Deity.

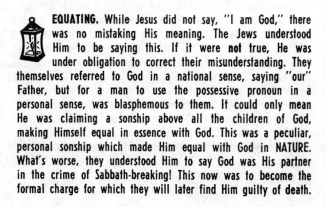

EQUATING. While Jesus did not say, "I am God," there was no mistaking His meaning. The Jews understood Him to be saying this. If it were **not** true, He was under obligation to correct their misunderstanding. They themselves referred to God in a national sense, saying "our" Father, but for a man to use the possessive pronoun in a personal sense, was blasphemous to them. It could only mean He was claiming a sonship above all the children of God, making Himself equal in essence with God. This was a peculiar, personal sonship which made Him equal with God in NATURE. What's worse, they understood Him to say God was His partner in the crime of Sabbath-breaking! This now was to become the formal charge for which they will later find Him guilty of death.

"How did Jesus react to this new charge of blasphemy?"

19.   In response to these new charges, Jesus replied, "Believe this, for in all truth I tell you the Son cannot do one thing independently of the Father. In fact, He doesn't do anything unless He sees the Father doing it. Then, whatever He sees the Father doing, the Son does likewise—and in precisely the same manner."

SEES. The "truly truly," of the common versions indicates a new truth is emerging. Having already declared equality with the Father in **nature,** He now claims equality in WILL. Jesus has His own will (John 6:38; Luke 22:42), but He is so fully in accord with the divine intention, it is impossible for Him to bring Himself to act independently of the Father. He says it is impossible to bring Himself to do any act at variance with the Father. And because He is UNWILLING to do so, He **cannot** do so. Thus there appears to be but ONE WILL between them. But how does Jesus know the Father's will? He SEES it. How? We could say because the omnipresent God is present to the incarnate Son, but that is too abstract. Better to think that by means of a closed circuit TV arrangement, the thoughts of the Father are displayed on the mind of the Son. "Same manner," indicates exactly as though the Father Himself were on earth doing this.

"You mean the Son can see the Father's WILL by virtue of being able to view the Father's thoughts!"

20. "On account of His deep affection for the Son, the Father shows Him everything that He Himself is doing. And if what has taken place so far has failed to impress you, you will be astonished at the greater works He has yet to show the Son!"

SHOWS. This tells us WHAT the Son sees. The Father is the Program Director, determining what appears on the screen (mind) of the Son. Though standing as a man on the earth, Jesus views the eternal and infinite workings of God. Now if a reader can grasp the idea of this spiritual video between Father and Son, He should next consider WHO Jesus has to be, in order to fathom and execute what He sees! He can be no less than God. Who but God can comprehend ALL the workings of God, grasping even the motives and intentions and then executing them as precisely as God Himself? What the Son sees He is impelled to carry out. Thus the healing of the man was as much the Father's doing as the Son's! It occurred in the mind of God even as the Son performed the act on earth. Everyone's act is FIRST performed in his mind, before being executed as a deed! The Son carries out what the Father is thinking.

 GREATER WORKS. The use of the Greek term "affection" here speaks of the family intimacy. Since they are "family," they have no secrets from each other. Because of this non-secretive arrangement, the Son is shown the "greater works" to come. The verses which follow tell what they are. He is saying to the Jews, "If what the Father and I have done in healing this man fails to impress you, you will be astonished when you learn what is to come!" While God cannot compel faith, He can compel astonishment. They will be shocked to discover that this "man," whom they are accusing will be the JUDGE in the day of their accusing. But now see again the Deity of our Lord as He looks forward to the future, citing works which only GOD can do!

"Just what are the 'greater works' which Jesus has in mind?"

21. "For as the Father raises the dead, restoring them to life, so does the Son give life to whomever He wishes. 22. And the same is true of the Judgment, for the Father is not going to judge a single person. The whole sequence of judging men has been placed in the hands of the Son. 23. Why? So that everybody might honor the Son just as they honor the Father. To deny the Son, you see, is the same thing as denying the Father Who sent Him."

LIFE-JUDGMENT. Jesus has unveiled the "greater works," but look! These are the most absolute divine prerogatives! Jesus claims them as His own works. Observe that Father and Son perform the same acts with the Son giving life to "whomever He wishes." His own will remains sovereign! How is this done? By the same THINKING (video-process) DOING arrangement described above. It is the Son

Who actually imparts life to men. It is the Son Who passes sentence or exonerates men in the judgment—yet in perfect harmony with the COMMON WILL between Father and Son. The Father thinks, the Son acts, with each exercising His own will.

 HONOR. From Jesus' mouth comes this claim to Deity. Monotheism, jealous for the honor of Jehovah, would never allow us to find two separate gods here. Yet that would clearly **appear** to be the case if we did not have the truth of God's omnipresence. Because the omnipresent God is present to the Incarnate Christ, we see only ONE GOD. The acts of the Father are revealed in the acts of the Son, the Father Himself is manifested in the BEING of the Son. Consequently Jesus MUST claim precisely the same honor as is due the Father. The unity of essence demands nothing less. Worship of the Father, therefore is impossible without worship of the Son. God Himself is an unreal abstraction without the Sonship of Christ. From our earthly point of view, Jesus is the only God we know! And Jesus, by virtue of His video-perception, is the only One Who knows the Father (John 1:18).

"Then when Jesus speaks, His words carry the same authority as those of the Father!"

24.   "Now believe this also, for again I speak in all truth. The man who gives heed to My Word, and puts his trust in the One Who sent Me, already has eternal life. That man will never face judgment for unbelief, having already passed out of the realm of death into life."

 HEED. This is passive. Man receives the Word, needing only to react in faith. Yet it is the **greatest work** of God, quickening men spiritually dead. The redemption scheme, based on the love of God and the sacrifice of Christ, is God's part. Man merely accepts Jesus' Word as the voice of God, reacts in faith, and the miracle happens. In that second a multitude of things happen to Him which he cannot see or feel. The most significant event is his change of attitude or disposition toward God. He changes his mind about God (repents) after coming in contact with the Word of Christ. Inasmuch as this is what is required for salvation, even children can hear the Word of the Lord and be saved.

WORD. Should someone say Jesus was all talk, this might be correct if we ignore His suffering and cross. Indeed His acts toward men were all talk. A word from Him and the blind saw, the lame walked and demons fled. He spoke, a storm subsided. He called Lazarus from the grave and once said, "Let there be light," and there was! Now He speaks and spiritually dead people come alive. But notice His claim to Deity. The Son speaks, but you believe the Father. So clearly is God's Word on Jesus' lips, one must exercise faith in the Father as Jesus speaks. Conversely, to disbelieve Jesus, is to ignore the voice of God! See the shift in grammar? After talking ABOUT Himself in the verses above, He now employs the first person, speaking directly to those around Him. This is unspeakably solemn, the Life-Giver is talking.

DEATH. Once a man accepts the Word of Christ **as the Voice of God** and responds in faith, he is instantly removed from the hordes awaiting judgment through unbelief. He joins those destined to spend eternity with God (Col. 1:13). Having changed his mind about God, he is no longer an enemy, but a child of God. The death spoken of here is that state of separation from God in which all unbelievers reside and remain hostile toward God (Eph. 2:1, 2). Man and God are enemies until this change (reconciliation) takes place. The fate of God's enemies is hell, the wrath of God awaiting all those disbelieving the Word of Christ (John 3:36). Inasmuch as there are degrees of hell, there is also a **judgment** to determine the **quality** of suffering. This is based on the works one does on earth.

"Does that mean there is life in the voice of Jesus, as well as in what He says—from the Father!"

25.   "Once more I tell you in all truth, an hour is coming, yea has already begun, when the dead shall hear the voice of the Son of God

and those who harken to it shall live. 26. For just as the Father contains within Himself the **source** of life, so also has He granted the Son to have the **gift** of life within Himself.''

LIFE-GIFT. Creation was made by a voice, "And God said . . . !" The source of life is in a voice. For if "all things were made by Him and for Him," (Col. 1:16) that life-giving voice belongs to Jesus! The text refers primarily to spiritual life here, for people are **responding** to that voice and receiving life. Those who do not respond, are thus eternally dead. The Greek indicates all hear, but **not all respond.** Thus, the **"new creation,"** is also accomplished by the same voice that gave substance to the old creation. "Granted the Son to," refers to the Incarnation, the temporal manifestation of God, which was a historical fact. In His humanity, Jesus was awarded the same power as resides in the Father.

"But didn't He say His was also the voice of judgment too!"

27. "What's more, He also gave Him authority to execute judgment because He is a Son of man! That shocks you, doesn't it? 28. Well the time is coming when all who are in the tombs will hear this same voice, 29. and come forth! The resurrection, as you know, will be either unto eternal life or eternal death, as indicated by whether people have done good or evil. 30. But I will make that decision. And My judgment will be just, for as I hear My Father's voice I will judge. Even in this, you see, I cannot, yea I will not act on my own initiative. I have only one desire and that is to do the will of Him that sent Me."

A MAN. The Greek article is missing because the point emphasized is that the Judge is a MAN. What grace! The Judge is One Who has "been tempted in all points like as we!" What wisdom! The Judge can sympathize with human temptation, yet burn with the divine passion for righteousness. The passage lumps the separate resurrections so as to speak to the FACT of the resurrections. Jesus' voice is the one which calls ALL from their graves, saved and unsaved alike. Human response is not the point here, Jesus' VOICE is. If above He claimed to SEE the Father's workings, here He claims to HEAR the Father's judgments. The closed circuit TV system has audio as well as video portions. "As I hear, I judge." See how He again refers to His divine origin as "sent" from the Father.

"Could the Jews be expected to believe such amazing claims from the lips of a Carpenter, even though He had miraculously healed the lame man!"

31. "Naturally you will say that My testimony is not valid, because I bear witness to Myself. 32. Well there is another Who bears witness of Me Whose testimony cannot be challenged. And I know that His witness is admissable as evidence. 33. But besides Him, there is John. You sent your messengers out to him and took his deposition to the truth. 34. Yet I mention him only for your sake and not because I require the testimony of any man. I speak of him because He did point the way to salvation. 35. He was a spectacular flare that burst forth, lighting up the darkness of this generation. For a while you found it entertaining to frolic in his light.

 FLARE. John was like a skyrocket that bursts suddenly against a dark sky and dies out. He was dazzling. He had all Israel tingling with Messianic excitement. As the last of the O.T. prophets, he arrived with the credentials needed to introduce the Messiah. From him, says Jesus, they received "the truth." The Greek calls John a "burning and shining torch," referring dually to his brilliance (zeal) and burning heat of conviction as he spoke of sin. Now John is dead and already a hollow memory. "Frolic in his light," is an image of people dancing to a party, their way lighted by torches. Jesus indicts their treatment of John's testimony. They were happy to tremble with Messianic excitement, but it quickly subsided when they learned what John asked of them. They were not interested in a "Lamb," they wanted a King.

"Then Jesus didn't use John's testimony to defend Himself?"

36. "The witness that I have is greater than that of John's, for the fact that I do the works of God indicates He **has given** them to Me to accomplish. The very works you **see** Me doing are themselves a certification that the Father has sent Me."

WORKS. "My works speak for themselves," says Jesus. And it is only necessary for people to observe HOW He did them . . . **by a Word.** More than the fact of the miracles is the way He performed them, by His will and Word of power! Thus, He offers them as the first proof of His Deity. What a witness they make! He gives hearing to the deaf, speech to the dumb, sight to the blind, cleansing to lepers, freedom to Satan's captives and life to the dead! Seas and winds are calmed, water is turned into wine, multitudes are fed with a few loaves and fishes and He walked on the waves . . . all in His own inherent power! His works were many, they were great, they were public, unrigged, unrehearsed, instantaneous . . . truly divine! Who but God or someone sent by Him could do such things?

37. Besides that, the Father has given His personal testimony to Me. Of course, it is an invisible witness, for you have never at any time heard His voice or beheld His form. 38. But alas, you have not embraced His witness, otherwise you would have believed on Him Whom He has sent.

FATHER. For His second witness, Jesus mentions the working of God inside every man. This is not the human conscience, neither is it the lamp of recognition. It is a distinct and separate witness of God's Spirit to the souls of men when they come in contact with the spoken or written Word of God. A different Greek word distinguishes the "witness" in verse 38 from the "Scriptures" (writings) in verse 39. It is by means of this INVISIBLE working of God that men are saved. Jesus mentions it again in the next chapter, i.e., "No man can come unto Me save the Father which sent Me draw him" (6:44). A good title for this inner working of God is PRE-SALVATION ILLUMINATION. For men, "dead in trespasses and sins," this working is absolutely necessary for salvation. But Jesus accuses the Jews of ignoring this internal, invisible witness of God and therefore they search the external (visible) O.T. Scriptures in vain.

39.   "You are constantly pouring over the Scriptures, imagining the very words somehow contain eternal life. Well, go on and search! And as you do, those words are bearing witness to Me.   40.   Yet you won't come to Me for that life."

SCRIPTURES. Here is the last witness the Lord cites in evidence of His Deity. His appeal to the Scriptures is the climax of His case. Beyond them there is no higher appeal. The Jews would agree. They loved the Word of God, so they said, bathing before they handled it, counting even the letters to avoid errors in copying it. The scribes even thought there was sacramental value in handling the sacred writings, but Jesus corrects that notion. Their value, He says, lies in their pointing to Him. The Greek for "search" is a command and Christians are rightly admonished to mine the Word for its wealth. But let none who reads think the Bible imparts life. It is a tool, a revelation, a book. It is a signpost to Jesus. Woe to any man, Jew or not, who knows the Book, but misses the Saviour revealed in that Book. For Jesus is a Person. All any book can do is tell ABOUT HIM!

"It sounds like the Master is beginning to turn the tables on His accusers."

41. "I do not say these things because I seek glory from men. Human approval or disapproval means nothing to Me."

APPROVAL. Jesus has made it clear He came to do the will of His Father, hence God's approval alone matters. But what an education to watch the Saviour handle Himself before these men! Imagine yourself on a TV show with the commentator poking fun at your faith, the audience mocking also. How would you respond? Watch Jesus. He has a three-step plan for such situations: (1) Testimony to His own works, i.e., the changes in our lives. We can speak with certainty about those. (2) Depend on the Father's witness to accompany our words as we speak the truth. Therefore make no DEFENSE of any kind, but instead, (3) refer always to the Word of God. That way the Bible is a buffer zone between us and the scoffers. The safest reply is . . . "The Bible says . . ." and let the Word do its work. But watch again, our Lord doesn't stop with that.

42. "But oh how different it is with you. Obviously you have no real love for God, 43. for here I am, fully attested to by My Father. I have come in His Name, yet you won't believe Me. But let someone else come along in his own name and him you will receive.

DIFFERENT. Different indeed. These Jews gloried in their worship of the one true God, but with their hunger for human glory, they were blind to the glory of God. Jesus' words bite deep with reproach. They are guilty of idolatry. The practice of seeking glory from man amounts to worship. By this glory giving and receiving process they made gods of one another in a disguised form of heathenism. Consequently they had many gods, for they exalted many men. What's worse they become vulnerable to the anti-christ. Jesus hints at this in speaking of someone who will "come in his own name," and in great human glory. In their passion for human glory, they will receive this man in place of God.

44.   How can you ever expect to exercise faith when the only glory you care about is that which you get from each other? Faith is impossible when you are not interested in the glory the true God bestows on a person."

 GLORY. Jesus says it is impossible to believe in God when people care more what others think than God, when human approval means more than divine approval. Thus glory-seeking is a barrier to faith. He cites Himself as proof of this. The glory of God is now standing in front of them and they can't recognize it. Why not? Their passion for human glory blinds them to God's glory. Were this not so, they would have recognized the glory of Jesus as that of the Father. Here is more incriminating evidence if they want it, for in saying this, Jesus claims to be equal to the Father in GLORY!

45.   "Don't think My mission is to gather evidence against you, planning to accuse you before the tribunal of God. I won't have to, someone else is going to do that. Moses will be your accuser. Yes, the same Moses on whom you have set all your hope. 46. For you see, if you had really believed Moses, you couldn't help but believe in Me. I am the One Moses wrote about.

MOSES. See the tables turn? They try Him before their human court. But He speaks of their coming trial, thereby projecting their vision to the final court of God. He says the one they claim to trust will be their accuser. What's wrong here? These people seemingly revered the writing of Moses. Did the Scriptures fail. No. They simply didn't believe them. Had they, they would have recognized at once the very One of Whom Moses wrote, particularly His words of Deut. 18:18. Had they believed the Law, they would have recognized the FULFILLMENT of it as HE stood there. Had they loved the Law, they would have sensed the VOICE which spoke to Moses was now speaking to them.

47. But of course, if you have no trust in Moses' writing, there is no way for you to believe My Words.

MY WORDS. Moses didn't invent the Law. God **spoke** to Moses in the mount, instructing him. Behind Moses' words was the One Who gave him the Law. The same Person now stands before this Jewish court accused of breaking the Law He gave to Moses. If they desire further evidence of blasphemy, they now have it. Here Jesus claims to be the AUTHOR of Moses' words. It follows then, if they don't really believe Moses, they can't believe Jesus. Moses' words and Jesus' have one source. Moses could rightly accuse them of ignoring his Law. Jesus now accuses them of not recognizing the Author of Moses' words. In effect Jesus is saying, "I am the One Who made the earth shake and the mount smoke that day when I called Moses up to Me and gave him the Word of the Law. Those Words you call the Law of Moses are Mine!" So disarmed are they by this authority, majesty and power, they discharge Him from their court.

"Apparently the rulers were bent on killing the Lord, but how did the masses feel about Him?"

6 1. Sometime after this, Jesus retired across the Sea of Galilee, embarking from Tiberias.

RETIRED. This could be one month or twelve after the events in Chapter Five. The disciples have been sent out on preaching missions, performing miracles and enjoying healing ministries of their own (Mark 6:7-13). Meantime the Lord also continued to perform many signs. At this time of the year, the west side of the lake is congested with people. Caravans are forming to go to the forthcoming Passover. Jesus will not go this time, the Jews at Jerusalem are seeking to kill Him (John 7:1). So he suggests to His disciples, "Come with Me to an isolated place and we'll rest awhile" (Mark 6:31). With boats for rent in the resort city of Tiberias, they anticipated a time of relaxation on the grassy knolls on the other side.

2.   And a huge crowd followed Him because they had seen the signs He was performing in healing the sick.   3.   But Jesus went up into the hillside and there sat down with His disciples.

CROWD. The lake area is now alive with news of Jesus' presence. The twelve have returned with exciting stories of their healing exploits. The Lord is mobbed. This prompted Him to suggest a boat trip across the lake. But the great crowd follows. Some take boats, but most go on foot, running around by the head of the lake. People swarm to healing meetings, and the dashing crowd reaches the other side before Jesus. When the Lord puts ashore He sees the crowd and is moved with compassion. Though tired, He spends most of the day healing their sick (Matt. 14:14). But as the day wears on, He becomes further exhausted. So He and His disciples ascend one of the green knolls to rest. It is now about 3 o'clock in the afternoon.

4.   The Passover, a feast of the Jews was at hand.

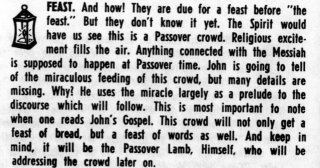

FEAST. And how! They are due for a feast before "the feast." But they don't know it yet. The Spirit would have us see this is a Passover crowd. Religious excitement fills the air. Anything connected with the Messiah is supposed to happen at Passover time. John is going to tell of the miraculous feeding of this crowd, but many details are missing. Why? He uses the miracle largely as a prelude to the discourse which will follow. This is most important to note when one reads John's Gospel. This crowd will not only get a feast of bread, but a feast of words as well. And keep in mind, it will be the Passover Lamb, Himself, who will be addressing the crowd later on.

5.   And Jesus, looking up and seeing this large crowd coming toward Him, said to Philip, "Where are we going to buy food enough to feed all these people?"

FOOD. Jesus and His disciples need time to themselves, but it appears impossible. The crowd is persistent, not about to be dispersed. The disciples, we learn from the other Gospels, sought to have the crowd dismissed in time to enter the villages and buy food. Evening is approaching. Possibly Philip made the suggestion to dismiss the crowd, but Jesus says, "They don't have to go. You feed them." This scene does not occur as abruptly as it appears here in John. Some discussion has preceded the Lord's question to Philip. The crowd is closing in as He speaks to Philip. So He will use it to teach them as He did in John Four, when the crowd was approaching them at the well.

"But why should the Lord ask Philip where food might be bought!"

6.   Inasmuch as the Lord already knew what He was going to do, His question amounted to a test for Philip.   7.   Whereupon Philip answered, "Why it would take at least twenty-five dollars worth of bread, and even that would provide only a tiny bit for each person."

PHILIP. Oh, Oh, Philip fails the test. What test? Would his eyes be on the Lord or the circumstances in meeting this dilemma? Jesus has every reason to test this man. He has just returned from a miraculous healing mission of his own. He should be full of faith. But what does he do? Studying the situation, he makes a hasty calculation, no doubt regarding the exact amount in their treasury, handled by Judas. Poor fellow, his eyes moved in the wrong direction. But before we judge, shouldn't we consider he was willing to spend all they had for the sake of the people? Would we do that?

8. Then Andrew, Simon Peter's brother, who was also one of His disciples, said to Him, 9. "There's a slave boy here who has five barley loaves and two sardines, but what are they when you have to feed a crowd such as this?"

ANDREW. He jumps in with an idea, maybe to rescue Philip. He was standing nearby. By some circumstance he has already made acquaintance with a baker's errand boy, a slave or apprentice who sold bread to the caravan. But alas, he has only a wee supply left. For a moment Andrew looks past the miserable loaves and two fish. With trembling heart he suspects maybe, just maybe the Master could do something with them. But then his eyes turn back to the hopelessness of the situation. For an instant it appeared the Master was to find faith in a disciple, but in vain does He search for such a thing. Oh that terrible unbelief which blinds our hearts.

"But you said Jesus already knew what He was going to do!"

10. "Have the people sit down," said Jesus. There was an abundance of grass in the place, so the men, numbering some five thousand, sat down.

GRASS. Around Passover time these hills are especially verdant. These are caravan people, meaning heads of families with women and children clustered about them. Entire households are found in such crowds. The command is to the men. They are to sit in a definite order, making food distribution easier and fairer. The Lord won't have people milling about while the disciples are trying to portion the food. Likely the women and children were served promiscuously, but the men SAT in ranks by hundreds and fifties (Mark 6:40). An arrangement, easiest to serve would be two semicircles with the outer rim in 30 hundreds and the inner circle, 40 fifties. The Lord is very systematic about this. It could take hours otherwise.

11. Then Jesus took the loaves, gave thanks, and distributed them to the companies of men seated there, as well as all the fish they wanted.

JOHN
6

———

101

DISTRIBUTED. The miracle occurs here in the hands of the Lord as all four evangelists report, though not one attempts to describe how it happened. Apparently what really occurred is indescribable, as with the water turned into wine. Likely it took place after the prayer and as the distribution went on. He "broke" the bread, says Mark (6:41), in a single act. But the Greek verb for "distributed" is one of continuous action. Somehow, as the bread comes from the hands of Jesus, there is that miracle, which reminds us of Elisha's oil which didn't cease until all the vessels were filled (2 Kings 4:6). The food flows until the **people** are filled. We learn from the other Gospels that Jesus' disciples took the bread from His hands, doing the actual work of distribution.

12. When everyone had enough, Jesus said to His disciples, "Gather up the broken pieces that are left over. Let nothing be wasted."
13. So they collected the excess pieces as He ordered, ending up with twelve baskets of leftovers. These were the unconsumed portions left by those who had eaten, with it all coming from the five barley loaves.

BASKETS. These were part of the traveling Jew's luggage and large enough for food and straw. This made them independent of Gentile provinder while enroute to the Passover. The likely reference is to the twelve disciples with each using his own basket to gather the surplus. If the disciples had wondered when they were to eat, they now had enough for days. The economy of seating the men further aids in gathering of the leftovers. These, incidentally, were handsome pieces, not crumbs. Mark says fish were left over too. Those who served the multitude were more blessed than the hungry crowd. A lesson for all who minister for Jesus. Yes, "a feast of the Jews was at hand," they just enjoyed a whopper!

"What did the people think when they found Jesus to be a miraculous Feeder as well as a Healer!"

14.   When the people beheld the mighty sign that Jesus had performed in power, they said: "How can there be any doubt? This has to be the Prophet that was to come into the world!"

PROPHET. Their stomachs filled, the people reflect on what has happened. The Passover season has them in a religious mood. Word begins to circulate, "This must be the Prophet Moses said would come" (Deut. 18:15), that is, the expected Messiah. A miracle restaurant would be great for those who must struggle to survive. Besides, He also healed the sick. What would a man scratch for if food and health were provided? Oh what a great King He'd make! The words, "that was to come into the world," show they consider Him to be the Messiah, as does the idea of making Him a King. How little does the crowd understand the Passover. A Messiah King is fine, but a Messiah Lamb—NO! As we shall see.

"Did Jesus like this sudden popularity and excitement that He could be the promised Messiah!"

15.   Realizing the people were about to seize Him and carry Him off to make a King of Him, Jesus withdrew once more into the hillside. This time to be quite alone.

ALONE. The festive pilgrims would like nothing better than a triumphal procession into Jerusalem at the Passover with King Messiah. Such a thing is in the plan of God, but not now. The timing is wrong, premature. John wants to show how pleased the people are with the Lord, in contrast with the rulers who sought to kill Him in the last chapter. But Jesus must escape the pressure of this crowd. He retires to the mountain again to be alone with the Father. His soul has been tempted and drained. Besides it is getting dark, and will soon be time to return to the other side.

16.   The sun was beginning to set so His disciples went down to the lake,   17.   and getting into the boat, started out across the water for Capernaum. Darkness had fallen and as yet Jesus had not come to them.

WENT. Jesus is not allowed much time to Himself, for His disciples come to Him (Luke 9:18). There's but a moment for a few questions. Darkness is descending. The crowd must be dispersed. So Jesus sends His disciples down to the boat with orders to head for Capernaum. He promises to join them later. This allows the boat to embark without interference from the multitude. As long as Jesus stays behind, the crowd will remain. But more is involved. Jesus is watching His disciples from the mountain. They are in for another test of faith before He rejoins them. It remains to be seen whether their faith has really grown after witnessing the miraculous feeding.

"His staying behind does seem to be a device for handling the crowd, but are you saying it was also a test for His disciples!"

18.   In time a heavy wind arose upon the lake and the water became turbulent.   19.   When they had rowed only 3 or 4 miles, after toiling for hours, they saw Jesus coming toward their boat, walking on the waves. They were terrified!   20.   But He called to them, "Don't be afraid. It is I!"

TERRIFIED. After hours of rowing they were but midlake, and fatigued. It's pitch dark. Fierce waves threaten to send them to the bottom. Yet they were safe, for Jesus was watching from the mountain (Mark 6:48). He was testing them. They had seen many miracles and now a huge crowd would make their Master a King. They too were becoming infected with "King-fever" (Mark 6:52). At the right moment He descends, meeting them not as they expected, but as a ghost gliding across the waves. Their terror compounds until His call identifies the assuring presence of the Great "I AM!" His voice stills the storm, but they fail the test.

21. They were so relieved, so very happy to receive Him and eagerly took Him on board. In that same instant the boat reached the land they were headed for.

INSTANT. The moment Jesus arrived, they arrived! Thus we have at least five miracles before us: (1) The healing of the sick within the crowd, (2) the feeding of the multitude, (3) Jesus coming upon the water, (4) the stilling of the storm, (5) the instant arrival of the ship at the destination. This series of miracles is recorded to prepare us for Jesus' Words which follow. Recall that John writes to set forth the Lord's claim to Deity. The miracles are preludes. The last, the instant arrival, finds the disciples so full of wonder and awe, they perhaps miss the motion of the ship. See how they go from terror to wonder in seconds? This flexing of their spirits and faith is calculated preparation for the astonishing Words which will fall from Jesus' lips in the city.

"It must have been a shock for a crowd bent on making Jesus King, to find Him suddenly gone!"

22. The next morning the multitude was still there, waiting on the shore. They had seen but one small boat there and observed that Jesus did not embark in this particular boat along with His disciples, but that they had left without Him. 23. Other small boats however, from Tiberias, had landed close to the place where the crowd had eaten the bread after the Lord had given thanks. 24. When the crowd finally realized that neither Jesus nor His disciples were still there, they got into these other boats and went to Capernaum looking for Jesus.

CROWD. John enters these details concerning the crowd left behind on the Eastern shore of the lake, so that the intensity of the scene will be in our minds. The people are panicky. There is no sign of Jesus, yet no one has seen Him depart. Picture a wall of people on the beach scouring the place for signs of Jesus. Now further up the shoreline there were some other boats tied. These had brought part of the crowd from Tiberias, the original point from which Jesus had embarked. Determining the Lord was no longer there, they piled into these boats and headed for Capernaum. This was now the place of His residence.

25.   When they found Him on the other side of the lake, they said to Him, "Rabbi, when did you come here?"

WHEN. The crowd finally locates Him at the synagogue. They talk at the door or else He is invited to speak a few words inside (vs. 59). In Greek the "when" implies the double idea of **when** and **how.** They are amazed to find Him here ahead of themselves. They don't see how, unless He traveled all night around the head of the lake, He could have arrived before they did. But having witnessed the miracles of healing and feeding they now expect a miraculous answer. Their real question is **how.** But He doesn't answer directly, preferring instead to unfold the symbolic meaning of the feeding of the multitude. This is John's style of presentation, you recall.

"Jesus must have known all along He would be going to use the feeding as basis for bringing a teaching to the people!"

26.   Jesus answered, "In solemn truth I say you seek Me now, not because you saw the signs, but because you ate the loaves and had your stomachs filled."

SIGNS. Had this crowd consisted of true believers waiting for God's Kingdom, they would have perceived the spiritual glory of Jesus' miracles. Here was supernatural evidence of God's presence, if they cared to see it. But alas, even their views of Messiah are carnal, sensuous, so they fasten their faith on the loaves. Their real god is their belly and so far, Jesus meets their expectations. Free food and miraculous healings match the tradition of their ancestors in the wilderness. Now if He would oust the Romans and establish His throne in Palestine, He would fulfill every ambition they held for Messiah. With a miracle worker on the scene, this crowd is not interested in such things as sin and righteousness and atonement.

27. "Labor not for that kind of food which perishes, but go to work for the eternal food, the kind which sustains one forever. The Son of Man can give you this food, since He is accredited and commissioned to appoint laborers for God."

FOOD. Observe the context, **working** for food. Food here symbolizes what people seek from life. See how two kinds are contrasted, temporary vs eternal, with people WORKING for one or the other. The idea of a "miracle restaurant" fascinates these Jews. To them it suggests a labor-free life. Hence Jesus uses the word WORK, cautioning them to invest in eternal, rather than passing things. Earthly food is not only perishable, says Jesus, but the man who seeks fulfillment for his life chasing it, is destroyed in the process. Only eternal food satisfies the soul forever. It is gained only by becoming a workman for God, both now and forever. Jesus declares Himself God's "Hiring Agent," with the miraculous feeding the sign of His commission. As God's Foreman, He pays off with this eternal food which brings everlasting satisfaction.

"Oh then He is picturing Himself as an employer securing workers for God."

28. This remark of His prompted them to ask, "What are we supposed to do then as workers in God's service?" 29. "This is the first work God expects of you, that you believe in the One Whom He has sent."

DO. Again, the context is work. See, they're willing to work for eternal food. But first they wish to know what specific tasks are involved. What will be required of them? Jesus answers, saying the first task God requires is unreserved faith in Himself as coming from heaven. Thus, any man desiring to earn this food must first hire on as a workman, and does so by submitting to Jesus. No one can do any work for God without first depositing his complete trust in Christ. Any reputed faith, without this first work, is also dead (James 2:17). Surrender to Jesus is the beginning point. The pay which comes after one has hired on, by this surrender, is eternal food. **But it must be earned.** Don't miss that. Our future wealth (satisfaction) in Christ is earned and should be thought of in terms of . . . "Lay up for yourselves treasure in heaven" (Matt. 6:20).

BELIEVE. Those seeing faith and works as different in KIND, perhaps divide too sharply. Salvation is indeed a gift, and the package (sonship, righteousness and authority) which comes with it is free. BUT accepting (receiving) it, is a **work.** The FIRST work of which Jesus speaks. True, it is simply a moral action (commitment-decision), nonetheless it is a WORK of faith. It is something a man must DO. Christ is God's gift to man, but receiving Him is a **work** of faith—moral work **done** by faith. When Christ is presented in soul-winning, people must DO something with Him or they are not saved. What they DO is the work spoken of here. There is no conflict between faith and works when faith is seen as man's first work in response to God's free offer.

"How did they react to the idea of complete trust in Him before they could become God's workers!"

30.   With that they challenged Him, "Well then, how about a sign, something we can see so as to believe you really are God's Agent? If you are yourself a Masterworker, what can you produce that would encourage us to serve you?"

AGENT. Jesus claimed to be God's Agent, avoiding the term Messiah. He refused their attempts to make Him king. Consequently they now demand further attestation that He is from God. They thrilled to the sample, but would like an extension of it so as to be sure He is the right Person. They are after **working** evidence that He is from heaven. They do not seek a sign from heaven, a perpetual supply of bread is closer to what they have in mind.

31. "Our forefathers ate manna in the desert like it says in the Scripture, 'He gave them bread from heaven to eat.' " 32. Jesus answered that, saying, "Believe Me, for in all truth I tell you, the bread which comes from heaven is not the kind Moses gave. The real bread, which comes directly from heaven itself, is given by My Father only. 33. The bread which God gives is that which not only comes out of heaven, but gives life to the whole world."

BREAD. Note how they sought a **continuance** of bread. If Moses, who was but a forerunner of Messiah, could feed a nation daily for 40 years, surely Messiah must do better. They would not accept His claim on the basis of one miraculous meal. He should be establishing His kingdom on the basis of a supply greater than Moses, and of superior manna. These Jews considered the desert manna the greatest of miracles and credited Moses for it. Moses' bread didn't come out of heaven, but was found on the ground. In effect, Jesus is saying, "I am speaking of a bread, which really does come directly from heaven. My Father is the Giver, and this bread is sufficient for the whole world, not just one nation!"

34. "Oh, that's the bread we want. Lord, give it to us continually."

LORD. See the increased respect after those words? They appear ready to assume He is God's Agent to administer this bread, of course they don't suspect He is speaking of Himself. This new bread sounds great. Their materialistic minds are about in the same place as the Samaritan woman when she said, "Give me this water." Her eyes were but half open as she pictured herself never having to draw water again. The Jews picture an everlasting supply of food which means no more work. Perpetual food from the hands of a Healer would solve all their problems, they think. At this point they regard bread as something separate from Jesus, with no thought that it might be spiritual.

35. Then Jesus said to them, "I Myself am the Bread of Life. He who comes to Me will never be hungry and he who believes in Me will never be thirsty."

MYSELF. Jesus makes a strong shift using the first person some 35 times throughout the discourse. Offering Himself as the Bread of Life He says, "The Heavenly Bread of which I spoke is standing in front of you. All you have to do to get it is **come** to Me, **believe** in Me." What a jolt for people thinking only of their stomachs, not their souls. At once the conversation shifts from the material realm to spiritual, for if a **Person** is the Bread of Life, then faith in Him is the ONLY way to get it. That raises a new problem. Do these Jews really wish to place their faith in Him?

COMES-BELIEVES. Things, of course, can never fill the soul whether things to eat, see, wear, do, or own. As one empty vessel cannot fill another, neither can one empty human fill another. Augustine put it: "Thou hast made us for Thyself and our hearts are restless until they rest in Thee." Only the infinitely full One can fill men. Inasmuch as Jesus says He is the fountain of human satisfaction, once more He is claiming to be God! But faith in Christ is like putting money in the bank. You not only must deposit it, you must leave it there to earn its benefits. So He says "come," the first act of depositing faith in Him. Then He says, "believe," the matter of **leaving** (maintaining) your faith there. As bread imparts nourishment to the body and sustains it, so Christ **imparts** life to the soul and **sustains** it with satisfaction.

36. "But as I said to you earlier, you have seen Me, and yet you do not believe."

 SEEN. In vs. 26, though using different words, He referred to their seeing the signs which indicate He came from God. But they were blinded, thinking only of their stomachs. They had witnessed the Messiah in action as Healer and Feeder and were but inches from salvation if they would but reach to Him by faith. They thought "seeing is believing," but after seeing they still didn't believe. Therefore it was not a matter of evidence, but the **will to believe.** For those who won't believe, it is never a matter of evidence, but of "an evil heart of unbelief" (Heb. 3:12). God supplies abundant evidence in nature, in history, in the practical effects where the Gospel has gone and in millions of changed lives—enough to satisfy any heart with the will to believe. Those who refuse to believe in Christ, plainly don't WANT to. And no amount of evidence will change their minds.

"Is Jesus hinting His ministry isn't worthwhile! Is He not to find satisfaction for His own Soul, also!"

37. "All that the Father gives Me will come to Me; and I will never turn away anyone who comes to Me."

ANYONE. Notice the **divine** side of salvation and the **human** side, like two sides of a coin. We have the **given** ones and the **coming** ones. The Greek is fascinating here, for the "all" given to Christ is a unit, a single package. Turn the coin over and you see each individual **in that package** coming to Jesus personally and processed individually. This is the same "all that the Father hath given Me," of John 17:24. We call this the "body of Christ," picturing all Christians as a unit. Jesus is saying that **package of people** is a gift from His Father. His ministry is therefore not futile, for a specific number (those written in the Lamb's Book of Life) will come to Him. This is comforting as He faces the unbelieving crowd. See how the only criterion is coming or not coming, nothing else.

38. "This is why I came down from heaven. I am not doing this independently on My own initiative, for I have come to execute the will of Him that sent Me. 39. And He Who sent Me has charged Me to preserve without a single loss all that He has given Me, even to the point of raising them all up on the last day. 40. I repeat, it is the will of My Father Who sent Me that all who believe in the Son after seeing Him rightly, should have eternal life. And I Myself will raise him up on the last day!"

SEEING. Earlier He accused them of beholding His miracles but not seeing Him for Who He is. Now He declares that "all" (the same gift package from the Father) who see Him properly so as to believe in Him, receive eternal life, plus guaranteed resurrection of the body. Why does He mention the last day? If He can keep people safe until then, all danger to the soul has passed. Beyond that point there is no danger. See how He has submitted Himself to the Father for the task of preserving all believers. From the divine side, Jesus is the Gift from God. From the human side, He is the object of our faith. To reinforce His claim of "safe-keeping" all believers, He says He, personally, will raise them on the last day.

"It must have shocked the Jews when He said He came from heaven to give life and guarantee spiritual safety to all who believe in Him!"

41. By now the Jews were beginning to grumble their disapproval of Him, because of His

saying, "I Myself am the bread which comes down from heaven." 42. "Is this not Jesus, the son of Joseph?" They reasoned, "We know His father and mother. How is it possible for Him to say, 'I have come down out of heaven?'"

 POSSIBLE! The Jews (Pharisee members of the synagogue perhaps) took offense at His Words. They considered they had knowledge of His parents, hence His claim, "came down from heaven," must be pretentious. They expected the Messiah to be a natural born Jew, not an angelic being. To their knowledge Jesus sprang from Nazareth, rose to be a Rabbi, but now claims to be from heaven, indicating divine Sonship. This is enough to turn their mood. They mumble complaints among themselves, neither whispering nor accusing Him openly. He hears what they are saying. John wants us to feel the rising offense so he has the Jews speaking from their own standpoint. The Lord, of course, does not correct their notions, for the truth of His supernatural character is revealed only to those convinced He is from God.

43. Jesus answered their antagonism by saying, "Stop murmuring among yourselves. 44. Nobody can come to Me without first being drawn to Me by the Father Who sent Me. And I will raise Him up on the last day."

DRAWN. The natural inability to come to Christ is neither physical nor intellectual, but spiritual. It is due to satanic blinding (2 Cor. 4:4), which results in **unwillingness.** Outside help is needed for ANYONE to see Jesus for Who He is and **come to Him.** A mysterious working of God, called PRE-SALVATION ILLUMINATION, makes it possible for ALL men to understand the truth of Christ **if they want to.** It is not compulsory, but an affectionate wooing which does not interfere with faith. It works like a magnet which attracts only iron. Some men respond to this illumination with hearts of WOOD, which cannot be drawn. Others respond with hearts of IRON.

They are powerfully drawn to Christ. See that the condition of each heart is an individual matter. Men are free to respond as they will. "Draw" in Greek expresses the drawing of a net, or dragging a culprit to jail. Hence it is strong, implying considerable resistance. Those blinding, satanic forces are mighty, amounting to real bondage.

45. "Even the prophets wrote of this, 'They shall all be taught of God.' Everyone who listens to the Father and learns of Me, comes to Me."

PROPHETS. Jesus expands on the Father's drawing, quoting Isaiah 54:13. Throughout the prophets, universal illumination was promised during the time of Messiah. In O.T. times, illumination was isolated, but during the N.T. era it is to be general. Not everyone listens to the Father. Therefore some will not learn of Christ so as to come to Him. **"If you were of those who listen to the Father to let Him teach you,"** Jesus says to the Jews, **"you would know Who I am and come to Me. But you resist His working, grumbling against His Spirit with your murmuring."** Even as He spoke, there was a witness to their hearts. But they would not heed it. Today, as the Word is read, the same witness attends the truth. The Holy Spirit makes it possible for souls to be saved as they encounter the Word of God. For those who will not heed it, there is nothing else (Heb. 6:4-6).

46. "I am not suggesting that anyone has ever seen the Father. No one has done that except the One Who comes from God—He has seen the Father."

SEEN. Moses stood before the burning bush. He ascended the mount to talk with God. But He did not see Him, only His Name (Glory) was declared to Him (Ex. 33:22; 34:5-7). It is not to deny Moses that Jesus says this, but to assert His own essential nature. Only One Who is Himself of the absolute nature of God could view the fullness of divine essence. Neither did He wish them to think that He Himself was speaking to them as one simply taught by God, merely reciting what He had "learned" of the Father. He would have them understand that what He was saying was the result of His immediate access to the fullness of God. Thus Jesus declares Himself not only the absolute Prophet of God with perfect vision of Him, but completely different in that the naked essence of Deity was open before Him.

47. "That is why I can say in very truth that the believer has eternal life."

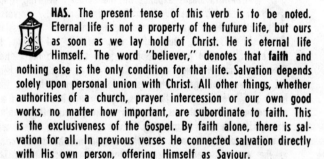 **HAS.** The present tense of this verb is to be noted. Eternal life is not a property of the future life, but ours as soon as we lay hold of Christ. He is eternal life Himself. The word "believer," denotes that faith and nothing else is the only condition for that life. Salvation depends solely upon personal union with Christ. All other things, whether authorities of a church, prayer intercession or our own good works, no matter how important, are subordinate to faith. This is the exclusiveness of the Gospel. By faith alone, there is salvation for all. In previous verses He connected salvation directly with His own person, offering Himself as Saviour.

"After countering the murmurings of the Jews, will He go on to explain what He means by His being the Bread of Life!"

48. "I am the Bread of Life. 49. Your fathers, who ate manna in the desert, nonetheless died. 50. But the bread which comes down from heaven is such that a man may eat of it and never die. 51. I Myself am the living bread which has come down from heaven. If anyone eats of this bread, he shall live forever. And what precisely is this bread? It is My own flesh which I give for the life of the world."

MYSELF. He is, of course, speaking of His PERSON. Jesus is HIMSELF the life-communicating bread. That they may understand He means that His person is to be appropriated by faith, He uses the figure of eating His flesh. Taken literally, this is an abomination. He has already insisted that **faith alone** is the condition for eternal life, therefore this statement has to be consistent with faith. Thus it is but a stronger idea of the appropriation of His Person. When He speaks of GIVING His flesh, it obviously means death. But since it is a death designed to bring life to others, it has to be a **sacrifice.** Thus He is saying, "You must partake of My sacrifice." The eating of His flesh was only a figure, yet familiar to Jews under the sacrificial system. The idea of a **dying** Messiah, was the last thing this king-hungry crowd wanted to hear.

"How did the bread seekers react to such a remark!"

52.   The Jews then fell to a fierce disputing among themselves, with some saying, "How can this man give us His body to eat?"

HOW! The Lord's mention of His divine origin upset the Jews. When He says He is a sacrifice for the world, they are shocked. But now when He suggests they "eat" the sacrifice, they are so mad they fight with each other over His Words. Since they want to believe He is Messiah, they don't fight with Him. Who fights a miracle worker? They appear repulsed at the thought of eating His flesh, yet this crowd is headed for Jerusalem to "eat" the paschal lamb. In saying, "this man," they start to show contempt for Him. Notice how Jesus moves next to intensify His Words, rather than placate this crowd.

53.   Jesus therefore replied, "Believe Me for in all truth I tell you that unless you eat the body of the Son of Man and drink His blood, you have no life in you."

BLOOD. Now it is clear that He means His death as a sacrifice. The Jews killed the sacrificial lamb by stunning it and then cutting the throat so as to separate the blood from the body. It was the separation of the blood from the flesh that brought the death. And Jesus indicates this when He says they must "drink His blood." It would be almost impossible for them to take Him literally now. But their minds are so against the idea of a dead Messiah, they prefer to think He is teaching cannibalism. They ignore the spiritual meaning of His Words. The literal drinking of blood, of course, is an abomination. See how Jesus answers their dissent by pressing further still.

**"But the Jews were forbidden to drink the blood
of any animal, weren't they!"**

54. "He who eats My flesh and drinks My blood possesses eternal life and I will raise him up on the last day."

 ETERNAL LIFE. See again how eternal life is a **present** possession. It is something a Christian has right now, but the resurrection of the body is clearly a **future event** —hence a separate matter. Jesus makes a sharp distinction between the life we now have from Him and the future body when He says, "I will raise him up." The present body, has a life of its own and apparently holds the man inside a prisoner. Eternal life, then, belongs to the soul, with the quickening of the body a separate and detached event.

 EAT-DRINK. What does it mean to eat the flesh and drink the blood of the Son? Is Jesus teaching the Last Supper? Indeed not. When the Lord instituted the ordinance He did say, "This is My body . . . My blood," but neither there, nor in His reference here, is He referring to the actual eating or drinking of anything. Physical things cannot give spiritual life to the soul, yet that is what He says happens in this verse. These are but mystical expressions for spiritual reality. They are metaphors which speak to the act of receiving Christ. How do we know? Jesus said so, back in verse 35.

"He who COMES to Me shall never hunger; he who BELIEVES in Me, shall never thirst." If coming and believing take care of hunger and thirst, then **coming is the eating, believing the drinking.** This is the Lord's own interpretation of His Words.

55. "For My flesh is real food, and My blood is real drink."

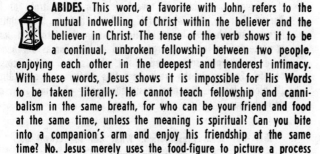

REAL. Eat poisonous food, death results. Eat nutritious food, health follows. It is not the eating which produces such results, but **what is eaten.** Thus our Lord notes that it is the eating **Himself** that makes the difference. Faith by itself does not save, but faith in HIM. Hell will be full of believers in the **fact of God,** but whose faith did not digest Christ. He teaches an actual appropriation of Himself is needed. As one takes food into his mouth for the body's sake, Christ must be received into one's heart for the soul's sake. The experience of receiving Him must be as real as that of eating food. Natural food is a temporary necessity, but Christ is the eternal necessity—thus the real food.

56. "He who eats My flesh and drinks My blood abides in Me and I in Him."

ABIDES. This word, a favorite with John, refers to the mutual indwelling of Christ within the believer and the believer in Christ. The tense of the verb shows it to be a continual, unbroken fellowship between two people, enjoying each other in the deepest and tenderest intimacy. With these words, Jesus shows it is impossible for His **Words** to be taken literally. He cannot teach fellowship and cannibalism in the same breath, for who can be your friend and food at the same time, unless the meaning is spiritual? Can you bite into a companion's arm and enjoy his friendship at the same time? No. Jesus merely uses the food-figure to picture a process which occurs in the spirit. As food is taken to become part of our bodies, so Christ is received to live in our souls. This is what happens when Jesus is invited into one's heart.

57. "As the Living Father has sent Me and I am alive because of Him; so the man who eats Me shall live because of Me."

ALIVE. Jesus declares His own life is that of the Father, "My life and His being one." He pictures the Father as the Fountain of Life, ("Living Father"), with Himself alive in the same flow. He lives because the Father lives. Yet, He calls Himself a Mediator ("sent") between God and man. As the "sent" One, men can EAT Him and share the same life. Just as any food which is eaten gives its life to a man's body, so Christ Jesus gives His life to the soul. "Every man," of course, is every man who has EATEN Christ. That is how the life is obtained. Thus ceremonies (communion included) and rituals cannot produce such a thing. Receiving Christ, a definite experience, is the only way.

58. "This then, is the bread which has descended out of heaven; and it is not at all like the bread your ancestors ate—and died. The man who eats this bread shall live forever."

THIS BREAD. Jesus returns to the bread symbol, using it to close His discourse to the crowd. He finishes as He began, letting His opening remark serve as a summary of what He has said. One might wish He would strip away the symbol to reveal a more naked truth of His Person. But no, He wants this truth clothed in this sublime form of speech—the bread of life. It is in this form that Jesus is presented as the most urgent need of life. For as our bodies need bread, our souls need Christ. He is the real necessity of life. To remove the truth from this metaphor, would dilute its glory. Jesus is the most basic commodity of living . . . our daily bread!

"That was some presentation. What did the crowd do when He finished speaking!"

59. Now these things were spoken in a syna-

gogue in which Jesus was teaching in Capernaum.

SYNAGOGUE. By this historical note the Holy Spirit reveals the nature of the crowd. Many of Jesus' followers, who lived in Capernaum, were here as well as those who had followed from the other side of the lake—the "miracle-bread" seekers. All seem to have a judaistic spirit, quick to place a sensuous, physical construction on His Words. Not hungry for God's True Bread, they want to be offended by His Words. They prefer to think He is teaching a cannibalistic eating of Himself, rather than see Him appropriated by faith. A variant form of this is found in those who view the Sacrament of the Supper as fulfilling His Words. We should note that while Jesus' Words do not teach the Last Supper, the Last Supper does teach what He is saying.

60.   Upon hearing these things, many of His disciples said, "This is more than we can take! Who could possibly accept such hard words as these?"

HARD. Someone has noted, "It was not in His Words that the hardness lay, but in their hearts." True, but we must also understand these Jews wanted, in the worst way, to accept Jesus as Messiah. Yet they wanted a live Messiah, not a dead one. Consequently when He spoke of giving "His life for the world," they closed their ears. The concept of a suffering Messiah was repugnant to them. So they chose to regard the letter of what He was saying, rather than the meaning. And it became a scandulous suggestion of man-eating. By giving His Words a materialistic hearing, they crossed with the laws of Jewish purity (drinking blood) and became the abomination of human sacrifice. Thus they choked on His Word complaining no Jew should listen to such things.

"Does Jesus bother to explain what He really means!"

61.   But Jesus, intuitively aware of the grumbling of His disciples, asked them, "Does this

shock you? Is it really too much for you? 62. What would you do then, if you were to see the Son of Man ascending back to the place where He was before!"

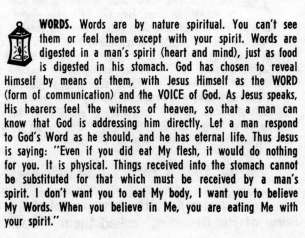

ASCENDING. The idea contained here is that of His exaltation in glory and not simply His visible ascent out of sight as in Acts 1:9. To expose the condition of their hearts, He is asking: "If you saw Me in My glory would it make any difference? Would you still be offended with My Words if I addressed you as the God of Israel?" Whether Jesus speaks as a Rabbi walking among them, or as the sound which thundered at Sinai, the words would be the same, the voice the same. But is it a question of His exalted state versus His humble state? No. It is a matter of the hardness of their hearts. The truth is changeless no matter how it reaches one's ears. It is a question of responding to the truth, not the status of the speaker.

63. "Only the Spirit can give life; flesh (physical things) can do nothing for you spiritually. The Words that I have spoken to you are spirit and they bring life."

WORDS. Words are by nature spiritual. You can't see them or feel them except with your spirit. Words are digested in a man's spirit (heart and mind), just as food is digested in his stomach. God has chosen to reveal Himself by means of them, with Jesus Himself as the WORD (form of communication) and the VOICE of God. As Jesus speaks, His hearers feel the witness of heaven, so that a man can know that God is addressing him directly. Let a man respond to God's Word as he should, and he has eternal life. Thus Jesus is saying: "Even if you did eat My flesh, it would do nothing for you. It is physical. Things received into the stomach cannot be substituted for that which must be received by a man's spirit. I don't want you to eat My body, I want you to believe My Words. When you believe in Me, you are eating Me with your spirit."

64. "But there are some among you who do not believe." Jesus was aware from the first which of His followers were without faith, right down to the man who was to betray Him, 65. adding, "This is why I said, 'No man can come to Me unless the Father does a work in His heart.'"

AWARE. Unbelief registered sharply upon the Lord's spirit. He could feel it. Thus His discourse began with, "You seek Me not, etc. . . ." He was aware of the unbelief surrounding Him, not only in the outer crowd, but also within the circle of His followers. Surely, many **professed** to believe in Him, but His sensitive spirit responded to **true faith,** intuitively, even metaphysically. Consequently He reacts also to the secret germs of unbelief in Judas, which His Words trigger. Judas is barely coming into the realization now, but Jesus knew him as the betrayer even when He chose him. Before He comments on Judas, He tells the unbelieving crowd they are strangers to the working of God in their hearts, and that is why they do not recognize Him. This is the last straw, they won't listen to Him anymore.

"Did this settle it for most of them!"

66. As a result of this, many of His followers returned to their old ways, keeping company with Him no longer. 67. Jesus then turned to The Twelve and asked, "How about you, would you also like to leave Me?"

LEAVE. When He said it required a supernatural work of God for people to believe in Him, it was too much. The crowd turns away. Besides, His talk of self-sacrifice didn't square with their estimate of Messiah. His miracles indeed attracted them, but His Words repelled them, becoming a disgusting offense. This discourse completely shatters their hopes that He might be a miraculous king. Surely these Words were equally startling to His intimates, The Twelve. As the crowd moves out, He turns asking if they too wish to leave. The Greek shows He expects a negative answer. Judas stays. He will not betray himself by withdrawing with the offended disciples.

68. "Lord," answered Simon Peter, "to whom would we go? Yours are the Words of eternal life. 69. And we have believed and have come to know that You are the Holy One of God!"

KNOW. Peter acts as the mouthpiece for The Twelve assuming a priority he enjoys down to the days of Paul. With no second Messiah scheduled to appear, they'd have to keep searching and seeking. If Jesus is not the One, He is saying, there is no other. Notice the order here: faith preceding knowledge. In the past 8 hours they have seen staggering things—masses healed, multitudes fed, Jesus walking on the water, with their spirits flexed from terror to wonder. Normally "faith cometh by hearing" (Rom. 10:17), but in their case, faith has come by experience, producing a solid conviction. The Greek indicates a completed action within them, a permanent result. Jesus' disciples respond to His **Words,** whereas the crowd was attracted to His **miracles.** Instead of being offended, they acknowledge them to contain eternal life.

HOLY ONE. Observe the unique testimony of Peter. He declares Jesus to be anointed (Holy One) by God. What a remarkable coincidence with the testimony of the demons, who with clear perception of the spirit-world, instantly recognized the real character of Jesus (Matt. 8:29). Peter makes this statement on the basis of the working within his own heart. Such anointed words can come only from the "Anointed One." This same working is true in all who harken to the Spirit's witness. While Peter was the spokesman for the group, he was mistaken about the "we." At least one disciple (Judas) did not share this conviction, though he didn't mind hiding under Peter's words.

"Then Judas, who didn't believe in the Lord, chose to stay with Him as a phony disciple!"

JOHN
6

123

70. Jesus answered, "Did I not choose you twelve? Yet one of you is a devil." 71. Now He meant Judas, son of Simon Iscariot. He it was of The Twelve who was going to betray Him.

DEVIL. This is strong, transcending the idea of sons or children of the devil. It indicates a willing and deliberate tool of Satan, i.e., the devil's own man. By this word, Jesus informs Judas that He is aware of the unbelief in his heart, also perhaps, the treachery to surface later. To Peter He is saying, "Well spoken, but the simplicity of your heart doesn't apply to all, for one in our group is an enemy agent." If Judas' eyes met Jesus', surely his first disaffection crystallized that same second. No doubt he felt deceived in his glowing expectations. It is not to be supposed the disciples had any idea whom the Lord meant.

WHY JUDAS! The Lord constantly employed visual aids as teaching devices, vis., communion, baptism, healings, feeding the crowd, etc. His selection of Judas was an ingenious one. Satan's methods are unfolded in his man: 1. **Closeness:** Judas was intimate with Jesus, convinced of His public and private innocence, yet betrayed Him. 2. **Hideous:** In betraying innocence for money, we see the exaltation of "mammon" as the real god of unbelievers. 3. **Disguised:** Satan's agents are found among the servants of the Lord. 4. **Immune to truth:** Judas was a participator in Jesus' miracles, a sharer of His Words of life, yet never saved, i.e., like some raised in Christian homes. 5. **Treacherous:** Posing as a friend, Judas schemed to betray Him. Satan uses a man's family and friends for hate and hurt. In Judas we see how sin works. Demonstrating evil in action, he is a visual-aid, hand picked by Jesus in accord with the prophetic Word (Psa. 41:9).

7 1. Even after this occurred, Jesus continued to minister in Galilee. He avoided traveling in Judea inasmuch as the Jews were scheming to kill Him.

AFTER THIS. The Galilean crowds turned their backs on Jesus, ignoring His remarkable signs and words. One might expect Him to move to greener pastures, but heavenly wisdom guards His steps. He remains in the vicinity, not merely to extend His grace to the thankless Galileans, **but as a precaution.** They sought to kill Him in Judea, but the Jews lacked authority here. Until the very hour when He is to sacrifice His life, He guards it with divine precaution. He would avoid a premature death. It required heavenly wisdom for Jesus to survive as long He did. He was not about to risk Himself with needless boldness. God's saints may have to exercise similar wisdom to survive in the last days.

"Yes, but He couldn't stay in the North indefinitely. Jerusalem is the faith-center of Judaism."

2. And now one of the Jewish feasts, the Feast of Tabernacles, was drawing near.

TABERNACLES. By law all males were required to attend this feast at Jerusalem, one of the three great feasts of the Jewish year. Occurring at harvest time (October), this was one of the happiest and most joyful of all the festivals. It was something of a national Mardi Gras. For seven days, the men left their homes and lived in rudely constructed booths (tents) of branches, on the streets and rooftops. This was God's way of reminding them of their homeless wanderings in the wilderness and not to forget Him in the midst of plenty. Hence at harvest time, Jesus would like to go, having been away from Jerusalem for approximately 19 months.

3. So His brothers said to Him, "This is no place for you to be carrying on your ministry;

go to Judea so that your disciples there can see the kind of things you are doing. 4. No one who really thinks to claim a public ministry ever keeps his credentials a secret. If you really are what you claim, you should be exposing yourself to the whole world." 5. For not even His brothers had any faith in Him.

 BROTHERS. These would be James, Joseph, Simon and Judas (Matt. 13:55). All four were distinct from the Apostles since none of the brothers was converted until after the resurrection. Yet they are found in the "upper room" awaiting Pentecost. As to whether these are OLDER brothers from a former marriage of Joseph, or YOUNGER children of Joseph and Mary, is not settled. See their patronizing tone, acting as His advisers? Indeed, His residence in Galilee had been half-concealed. But now they propose He should declare Himself in Jerusalem. The "feast" would provide a perfect time for some of His heavenly fireworks. They didn't see that His claim to Messiahship meant anything in Galilee, those peasants couldn't do anything for Him. To their minds, He needed the approval of the rulers at Jerusalem, for that's where Messiah was to appear and reign.

"Sooner or later He does have to go to Jerusalem, doesn't He!"

6. Whereupon Jesus said to them, "It is not yet the right time for Me to go, but as for you, any time is the right time. 7. It is impossible, you see, for the world to hate you. But it already hates Me, because I denounce its evils and show how bad it is. 8. So you go on to the feast by yourselves. For the present I am not going up. It isn't time for Me to go to the feast yet." 9. Having told them that, He stayed behind in Galilee.

HATE. Jesus knows the world hates Him, thus His care with His life. He will not risk Himself in foolish displays for publicity. Actually, He seeks the opposite, forbidding His disciples to reveal His true identity. His way is not the world's way. One campaigning for office would not do as He did. But Jesus operates in the safety of The Father's will, by His timetable, not the world's. His brothers, with no timetable, were free to live blindly from day to day. See how He refers to the unbelief of His brothers, calling them men of the world. Since the world cannot hate itself, it cannot hate them. But inasmuch as He is "not of this world," it does hate Him. His presence is an indictment of evil. Note the contrast between Jesus' discernment of "His hour," and the arbitrary, whimsical way men use their hours.

"Then He knew there was a precise time when He should go up to the feast!"

10. Later, when His brothers had already gone up to the festival, He too went up, but not as a member of a caravan. He went by Himself, traveling secretly.

SECRETLY. Jesus no doubt saw His brothers off on the convoy for Jerusalem, staying behind so as to time His arrival at the feast. When He set out, it was not as a pilgrim with a happy caravan. That would be a mistake. The happy people would have betrayed His presence. Instead He made the trip alone, stopping over perhaps, at Bethany. "Secret," does not mean He disguised Himself, only that He did not travel as a pilgrim planning to participate in the ceremonies. He traveled as a Prophet, keeping out of sight until the **right moment** for His appearance at the feast. His brothers, arriving well before Him, surely alerted the city to His coming.

11. Therefore the Jews were looking for Him to be at this feast. They went about asking, "Where is that man?" 12. Within the crowds there was constant whispering about Him. Some

were saying, "He is a good man;" others vigorously disagreed, maintaining He was not a good man at all, but was merely fooling the people. 13. However, of those who favored Him, none dared to speak openly for Him out of fear of the Jews.

 LOOKING. Advised of His coming, the Jews (rulers/Sanhedrin) had their spies seeking after, "that man." That same "Man" Who had baffled them after healing the cripple at the pool (Ch. 5). But the inquiries merely start the crowd murmuring. Inadvertently, these spies spark city-wide discussions, filling the pilgrims with expectancy over Jesus and His possible appearance at the feast. See how the hostility of the rulers pervaded the people? The sentiment of the city was against the Lord. Those who were in favor of Him, dared say only, "He is a good man." Oh, the fear of man! How often is a faithful witness of Jesus silenced by it!

"Just when did Jesus appear at this festival?"

14. It was not until the feast was half over that Jesus went into the temple and began to teach.

 TEACH. As soon as the commotion about Him settled down, the Lord suddenly appeared in the temple and began to teach. His actions show masterful insight to human nature. So startling was His appearance, everyone was caught off guard. An aura of mystery was about Him. A halo of psychological shock accompanied His presence. Nobody knew what to do. Before the priests could get into motion to break the spell, He delivered a lengthy discourse. John doesn't tell us exactly what He taught. But knowing the Lord's methods and pattern, we can be fairly sure it was a remarkable exposition of the feast itself, displaying unusual knowledge and insight to the O.T. passages relating to it. Obviously, He showed how it pictured man's wanderings in this world, with the promised land (heaven) a place of soul satisfaction. His listeners were spellbound. Heaven truth would be new to them.

15. "How," asked the Jews, "did this untrained man ever acquire such learning?"

UNTRAINED. Like some today, these Jewish leaders worshipped at the altar of education. Their minds burned with curiosity. Their hearts should have burned with conviction. It is clear the leaders were themselves entranced with Jesus' teaching, even to the point of asking where He learned such things. But that was as far as it went. They sensed His authority, yet they were at a loss to account for His learning. They are reluctant to credit Him with a heavenly anointing, choosing rather to regard Him as a self-made, self-appointed upstart. In any age, where there is a religious hierarchy, there is also a strong prejudice against the unauthorized, unlicensed minister, who serves God without denominational approval. Yet a man who listens to the Spirit of God, whose heart is fired by that Spirit, is more learned and approved than the best seminarian who lacks God's counsel within his spirit.

16. Jesus answered, "This teaching I am bringing is not Mine, but that of the One Who sent Me. **17.** Anyone determined to do God's will, will recognize at once whether My teaching is from God or I am bringing a message on My own."

RECOGNIZE. The Jews are baffled by Jesus' learning, asking how He came by such knowledge (vs. 15). Jesus disclaims any authorship of the message, declaring Himself to be only a spokesman for The Father. He then says that anyone who desires to do the will of God, will recognize the true Source of His teaching at once. Many who are curious about God's Word have no thought of obeying it. Hence much of it remains closed to them. The WILL is the inlet for spiritual light. Wherever a servant of God speaks His Word, there is an accompanying witness of the Spirit. Yet this witness is not overpowering. It is merely sufficient to satisfy any heart that WILLS to do God's will. The Jews were not willing, thus the truth was closed to them.

**JOHN
7**

129

"With none eager to do God's will, shouldn't the Lord use
more practical language!"

18. "Anyone who brings forth a teaching on his own initiative, is concerned for his own reputation. He seeks to enhance his stature by means of his message. But He Who is concerned only for the glory of the One Who sent Him, is detached from self-interest, and free from the desire for self-aggrandizement. Consequently, there is no unrighteousness in Him."

REPUTATION. The mark of a man who speaks for himself is **ambition.** But one who glorifies ONLY God, is free from evil motive. Jesus here displays a certain disinterest, as if to say, "If I hadn't been sent with a message, I wouldn't even be here. A person who comes seeking God's glory alone, is no imposter." He asks His hearers to weigh His exaltation of God against any exaltation of Himself, in judging whether or not He speaks truly. Beyond that, His entire ministry has not been for Himself, but others. He hasn't asked anything for Himself, He doesn't own anything. He is purely a Messenger, a Servant, Who has come to give them the Words of the Father. This righteousness in His life should evidence His truthfulness. See also how this condemns the spirit of self-exaltation wherever found in any servant of the Lord.

19. "Take Moses for example. Did he not give you the Law? Yet not a one of you seeks to obey it as evidenced by your plot to kill Me. Why is that?" 20. The multitude answered, "You must be insane! Who is trying to kill you?"

KILL. They've charged Jesus with having no authority. Now He turns the tables, charging them with refusing to obey Moses even when they did accept his authority. Therefore it is not a matter of authority at all, but of submitting to the will of God. He cites the murder plot of the hierarchy as evidence of their disobedience, which is as yet unknown to the mass of pilgrims jamming the city. With wisdom, He exposes the secret design of His enemies to publicity. The people know the leaders seek Jesus, but they see nothing in His actions or Words to warrant arrest. That they would kill Him is a shock to the crowd. The leaders now are speechless before His Words, considering it dangerous to have their secret plot aired before the people. The charge of insanity (demon) is likely proverbial. We say, "You must be crazy, man!" But we don't mean insanity.

21. Jesus' reply to that was, "I do just one work on the Sabbath and it shocks everybody. 22. Well, consider this: Moses gave you the Law of circumcision (actually it originated with the Patriarchs, not Moses) and you are willing to circumcise on the Sabbath. 23. If therefore a child is cut on the Sabbath to avoid breaking the Law of Moses, why are you angry with Me for making a man's body completely whole on the Sabbath? 24. Therefore quit judging Me on the basis of appearance only, and honestly weigh the facts before making a judgment."

CIRCUMCISION. Jesus doesn't react to their sarcasm, but presses His argument for healing on the Sabbath. If Jews, out of respect for Moses' authority cut a child (symbolical healing), why should they indict Him for making a man completely well? Jesus is saying, "Moses had the same thing in mind, when he ordered circumcision. The fact is, My work is more **Sabbatical** than his, and you would see this if you judged on the basis of truth rather than appearances." Anyone considering the Sabbath honestly could see that healing the man at the pool two years prior and helping souls is

even more humane than man's need for rest. This is but another way of saying the Sabbath was made for man, not man for
the Sabbath. Exalting ceremonial requirements over human
requirements is pure legalism.

"That must have jolted the people. Surely everyone felt the weight of what He said."

25. At this, some of those who resided in the city of Jerusalem began to voice them- selves, "Say! Isn't this the man they are trying to kill? 26. And here He is, speaking in public with nobody challenging Him. You don't suppose the rulers have found out He really is the Messiah, do you? 27. And yet, that can't be. We know the origin of this man. When Messiah comes, no one is to know where He comes from."

RESIDED. This is a different class of people, distinct from the pilgrims which flock to Jerusalem three times a year. These are the permanent residents of the city. See, they know of the rulers' plot to kill Jesus. They've been silent until now. But with Jesus speaking openly, it appears the plot has been relaxed—the leaders perhaps chang- ing their minds. But note how they regard themselves better instructed than their leaders . . . "We know the origin of this man." They show no eagerness to discover the truth of Christ for themselves, hence are no better than their leaders. See how the crowds don't want Jesus, nor yet the inhabitants of the city, and certainly not the rulers. Human nature is the same regardless of class—class makes no difference when it comes to Christ.

28. Whereupon Jesus, continuing His teach- ing in the temple, emphatically replied to them, "All right, so you do know Me and even my origin. But I have not come on My own. The

Person Who sent Me truly exists. He is alive and real, but you do not know Him. 29. But I know Him, because I am from Him and He has sent Me."

REAL. An imposter would be shaken by an attack on his origin, but not Jesus. He emphatically agrees that they do know of His earthly parents and residence (wisely side-stepping debate), but they do not know the One Who sent Him. And that's what counts. This class of Jews (city residents), were used to playing religion. They had a symbolical God, camouflaged sins, phony forgiveness and a tradition of heroes regarded as the noble line of Israel. Everything about Judaism was fake. How could they know the real, the true, the living God? Here was Jesus, a real live Person coming from a real live Father. Jesus' claim was staggering. He was either the most amazing pretender the world had ever seen, or He was actually from God. His Word means, "To ignore Me is to spurn the true, living God of Israel!"

"That must have stirred things up!"

30. Consequently, they were of a mind to seize Him, yet none laid a hand on Him for His time had not yet come. 31. For many in the crowd had come to believe in Him, saying, "Can Messiah, when He comes, be expected to do more miracles than this man has done?"

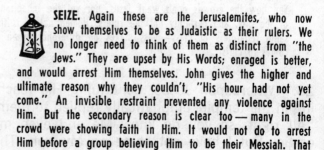

SEIZE. Again these are the Jerusalemites, who now show themselves to be as Judaistic as their rulers. We no longer need to think of them as distinct from "the Jews." They are upset by His Words; enraged is better, and would arrest Him themselves. John gives the higher and ultimate reason why they couldn't, "His hour had not yet come." An invisible restraint prevented any violence against Him. But the secondary reason is clear too — many in the crowd were showing faith in Him. It would not do to arrest Him before a group believing Him to be their Messiah. That would cause a riot. The faith of these people cannot be saving faith, but parallel to that of John 2:23, where "many came to believe in His Name after seeing all the miracles which He did." Again it is faith based on seeing miracles, not a commitment to Jesus. Another restraint of violence is found in the fact that the Roman governor was under orders to keep down all violence in Jerusalem which was a hard to defend city at the perimeter of the Empire. During these feasts, the Governor took up residence in the city and soldiers were alerted to watch for trouble.

"Surely the leaders wouldn't allow Jesus to continue like this."

32. When the Pharisees heard that the crowd was whispering such things about Him, both they and the chief priests dispatched temple police to arrest Him. **33.** Upon seeing them, Jesus said, "For a little while longer I shall be with you, and then I will go back to Him Who sent Me.

A LITTLE WHILE. The "hour" of Jesus' departure is fixed, but still six months away. Things move quickly now. Word of the popular mood reaches the Pharisees who consort at once with the chief priests. They have the power to issue hierarchical warrants, so temple police are hastily sent to the assembly. The officers enter, mixing with the crowd to await the right moment to seize Him. He spies them, hence His tantalizing words . . . "For a little while longer I SHALL be with you." No human or satanic power can shorten that "while" one iota. Those words mean to the police, "You can't arrest Me now"; to the crowd, "My work among you draws to a close, then I return to Him that sent Me!" Where's that? To us, it means heaven. To them, Abraham's Bosom. Heaven is unknown to them as yet.

34. "You shall seek Me, and shall not find Me; and where I am, you cannot come."

SEEK. "Seek and ye shall find," is the invitation of Revelation. Is Jesus contradicting that truth here? No. The answer lies in the KIND of seeking. The Jews had their own ideas about Messiah and if they continue seeking Him on those terms, they'll never find Him. It refers to the same false-seeking Israel has continued through the centuries since. It does NOT refer to the unavailability of Christ, nor to the hostile officers. In six months they do find Him and crucify Him. To the mass of Jews it means, "as long as you are looking only for a political Messiah, a miracle worker, an anti-Roman king, you will never find Me." But let an individual in any crowd behold Jesus with simple faith and the Lord is already found. But such people are not in view here. Jesus' words are meant to communicate the impossibility of going where He is going.

AM. Here is fascination. "Where I AM you cannot come." He does **not** say, "Where I will **be**," or yet, "Where I **then** am." He is still on earth making this statement. How it marks His Deity. Before, He had said, "I GO to Him . . ." but here, "Where I AM." See the two natures of our Lord? In terms of His humanity He was going to the Father. With respect to His divinity, He **ALREADY** was in the bosom of the Father (1:18). The Jews caught something of His meaning. They gathered He was referring to some dark, mysterious region as yet unknown to them. In the back of their minds they believe He means paradise in Sheol. But they can't allow themselves to think that, for then His words indicate they couldn't go to Abraham's bosom. They seek to come up with some other explanation for His words.

35.   Whereupon the Jews began inquiring among themselves, "Where is this He is about to go so that we cannot find Him? Do you suppose He means to go among the Jews scattered about the Gentile world? Maybe He even means to teach Gentiles?"   36.   But what can it possibly mean when He says, "You shall seek Me, and shall not find Me; and where I am, you cannot come?"

INQUIRING. The Jerusalemites are baffled. They are stirred to inquire among themselves: (1) "Where is He going that we cannot follow? To paradise! No, that's out. We expect to go to Abraham's Bosom." (2) "Does He think to find acceptance among the Jews scattered among the nations, because they are less orthodox than we? They might be dumb enough to believe Him." (3) "Chances are He will go to the Gentiles. His teaching seems to fit them better than us, anyway." Indeed, God's invitation has sounded better to Gentiles. Note how they cannot shake the penetrating mystery of His Words. They are haunted by . . . "you cannot come." Truth bothers people even when they don't receive it. The Holy Spirit sees to that.

"The Lord has not as yet brought His message to the holiday crowd, has He!"

37.   On the last and most important day of the feast, Jesus stood up and cried out to the people, "Let anyone who thirsts, come to Me! And whoever believes in Me, drink!   38.   And then, as the Scripture says, 'Rivers of living water shall surge forth from deep within his being.' "

DAY. The 8th day was most solemn, marking the close of the feast. For each of seven days before, the priests, in ceremonial procession, carried golden vessels of water from the pool of Siloam into the temple courts and poured them out upon the altar. This pictured the carrying of water in the Wilderness. On the 8th day this was NOT done, celebrating the entrance of Israel into the promised land where the people drank from live springs. The pool of Siloam was fed from a spring beneath the altar. When Jesus speaks of Himself as a fountain, He employs the imagery of the living spring under the altar which fed the pool. On this day, the people took boughs from their dismantled booths and beat on the side of the altar, picturing the rock smitten by Moses. Hence Jesus is also offering Himself as the Smitten Rock.

THIRST. In Chapter six the Lord used the figures of hunger and bread. Now He uses water and thirst for bringing His message to the crowd. The fathers ate bread in the wilderness and died. They also drank of Moses' water (smitten rock) and died. But now He offers "living water," (as to the woman at the well) of which a man may drink and never thirst. Water means life in that part of the world, so the meaning is clear. There is a thirst deep within man which nothing physical can quench. Jesus says He is the answer to that great thirst deep inside man, which nothing in this world can satisfy.

 RIVERS. Scripture prophesied a great fountain should one day open in Jerusalem to send water gushing into the desert causing it to burst into life (Ezek. 47:1). Jesus uses this familiar prophecy which will one day be literally fulfilled, to teach the result of drinking Him (His Words) by faith. The man who drinks of Christ in turn becomes a fountain. From deep within his once thirsty being, rises a torrent of words. They pour from his mouth. They are "spirit and they are life." Christians are vessels from which life-giving words pour forth to others. Christ is thus pictured as the spring, deep beneath the temple, while the Christian is the temple from which (as per the prophecy) gushes forth the water of life. The teaching is clearly that of Christ indwelling the believer, the hidden source of the life-giving flow from his mouth.

39.   Now here He was speaking of the Spirit, which those who believed in Him where to receive later. As yet the Spirit (Holy Ghost) was not yet given to men, inasmuch as Jesus was not yet glorified.

 SPIRIT. The reference is to the Holy Spirit, though neither the word "holy" or "the" appear in most Greek texts. Literally it reads, "Spirit was not yet." Therefore "given to men" is supplied to avoid any thought that God's Spirit did not exist until later. Since God is eternal, His Spirit is eternal. John is here referring to an unusual working of the Spirit yet to occur **after** Jesus' death. The King James translators repeatedly added the term "ghost" to picture this working, though the word in Greek is "spirit." It is a working

truth, not simply middle age superstition. What Ghost? Jesus'
Ghost. He told His disciples He would not leave them orphaned,
but would return to them (John 14:18). He does, as a
Ghost. Or by another Name, the "Spirit of Christ." It is as a
"Ghost" that He indwells the believer. The term "ghost" al-
ways refers to the spirit-return of someone who has died.

 LATER. Jesus' work in humiliation ends with His cross
and ascension. Then at another feast (Pentecost) fifty
days later, His Holy Ghost comes to indwell. Jesus'
arrival as the Spirit of Christ was attended with great
fanfare (fire-sound-tongues) and the church was born that day
as He took up His residence with individual believers. He
really is the fountain flowing deep inside the Christian, satisfying and overflowing. Until recent times this working remained a mystery, but now we behold a modern illustration
every time we watch a TV program. A man speaking in a
studio can appear simultaneously on millions of sets. By means
of the carrier waves (Spirit), the Ghost/image (Christ) is
received by the set (Christian). In a body Jesus was limited
to one place at a time, but in the studio (heaven), He can
appear in any heart tuning in J-E-S-U-S!

 GLORIFIED. For Jesus to return as a ghost to indwell
His disciples, requires that His work in the body be
finished and the resumption of His **former glory** in the
Spirit. Notice that He is "led" of the Spirit while in
the body, but that He, as the King of heaven, "sends" His
Replacement (Jn 16:7). His glorification means His taking on once
again all that He laid aside in His humiliation (Phil. 2:6-8)
while He participated in humanity as a "bondslave." By virtue
of His omnipresence, He can indwell each Christian once He is
out of the body (Col. 1:27). This is a critical verse in the
King James translation where the term "Spirit" appears twice
in the same sentence. The King James translators, eager to
show the ghost-ministry of our Lord, deliberately substituted
the words "Holy Ghost" for Spirit.

**"Did the drama of the feast and the familiar prophecies help the
people to understand His message!"**

40. On hearing these words, part of the multitude began to say, "How can there be any

doubt about it, this has to be the Prophet!"
41. Some went so far as to claim, "This is
the Messiah!" But others, a little confused
said, "Surely the Christ is not to come from
Galilee, is He? 42. Don't the Scriptures say
clearly that Christ is of the line of David and
to be born in David's village, in Bethlehem?"
43. Consequently the opinion of the multitude was divided on Him. 44. Some even
wanted to arrest Him, but no one laid hands
on Him.

DIVIDED. The Lord's Words burn deep into the hearts
of the people. All He has spoken so far at this feast
convinces most He is the Prophet Moses said would
come (Deut. 18:15), if not the Messiah Himself. Some
hesitate to go that far, having difficulty with His Galilean origin. As yet Christ's birth in Bethlehem is unknown. Verse 44
shows the effect of His Words in other hearts. One group becomes downright hostile, perhaps seeking to rally the police
(mixed in the crowd) to make an arrest. The Greek for "wanted," indicates desire but no power. Not only are they divinely
restrained, but apparently the police cautiously stay out of
sight, no doubt ordered by the Sanhedrin to do nothing **openly.**
See how the counsel of God binds all hands until "His hour?"
Both the majesty of Jesus' Words and fear of His followers serve
this purpose.

"His Words must have been amazing when even the police were
afraid to lay hands on Him!"

45. The temple police returned to the
Pharisees and chief priests who inquired of
them, "Why didn't you bring Him with you?"
46. The guards explained, "Nobody has ever
spoken the way this man spoke!" 47. "Ah,
so you've been deceived too," retorted the
Pharisees. 48. "Can you find a single ruler

who believes in Him, or any of the Pharisees? 49. But as for that stupid rabble which seems to believe in Him, they are ignorant of the Law and cursed by God!''

DECEIVED. The guards, struck by the power of Jesus' Words, return empty-handed. The rulers are enraged, for they were set to try Him secretly. The entire Sanhedrin has been gathered for the occasion, thinking thereby to avoid any future challenge of their decision. In anger they rail against their servants, accusing them of denying the example of Jewish aristocracy and falling in with the people, whom they call scum and vermin. With their hearts bent on killing Jesus, they seek to coerce the police to emulate their haughtiness above the people and share their determination to slay the Lord. It was the power of Jesus' **Words** which benumbed the officers, not His miracles. Is He not THE **WORD**? But a man in their midst squirms as they speak of Jesus. He has felt the power of those Words himself.

"Was that really true! Did not a single ruler believe Jesus could be the Messiah!"

50. At this point, Nicodemus, who was one of them (the same man who had previously visited Jesus), interrupted. 51. "Does our Law," he asked, "condemn a man before he has had a hearing and we have had a chance to determine the facts in his case?"

NICODEMUS. Good boy! After a long silence he speaks out amidst this Christ-hating body. He knows the feelings of his colleagues, but he can stand it no longer. The words of the guards shake him. With courage he rises, calling attention to the Law. All knew what he said was true. But they had gathered to kill, not reason. Speaking as he did **at this moment,** reveals not all the rulers oppose the Lord. This one could easily be a disciple. "We may condemn the people for ignorance of the Law," he says, "but we condemn ourselves for despising its precepts." He accuses them of prejudice so strong as to make them act in defiance of the Law. The police know at least one ruler is probably a believer in Jesus, thereby deflating the rulers' claim. With Jesus not present, plus the amazing words of the guards plus Nicodemus' statement, the council cannot take any action. The secret trial method for killing Him won't work.

"Were the other rulers upset with Nicodemus for his stand!"

52. They reacted to that saying, "Oh, so you would be a Galilean too, would you! Look in the Scriptures. Where does it say any prophet should arise out of Galilee?" 53. And so the council adjourned, each member going to his own home.

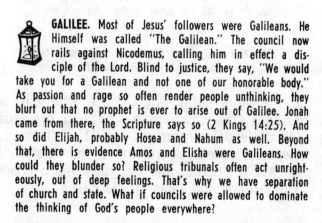

GALILEE. Most of Jesus' followers were Galileans. He Himself was called "The Galilean." The council now rails against Nicodemus, calling him in effect a disciple of the Lord. Blind to justice, they say, "We would take you for a Galilean and not one of our honorable body." As passion and rage so often render people unthinking, they blurt out that no prophet is ever to arise out of Galilee. Jonah came from there, the Scripture says so (2 Kings 14:25). And so did Elijah, probably Hosea and Nahum as well. Beyond that, there is evidence Amos and Elisha were Galileans. How could they blunder so? Religious tribunals often act unrighteously, out of deep feelings. That's why we have separation of church and state. What if councils were allowed to dominate the thinking of God's people everywhere?

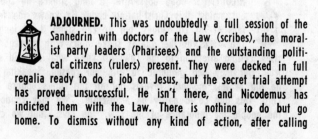

ADJOURNED. This was undoubtedly a full session of the Sanhedrin with doctors of the Law (scribes), the moralist party leaders (Pharisees) and the outstanding political citizens (rulers) present. They were decked in full regalia ready to do a job on Jesus, but the secret trial attempt has proved unsuccessful. He isn't there, and Nicodemus has indicted them with the Law. There is nothing to do but go home. To dismiss without any kind of action, after calling such an extraordinary session must have been mortifying. It gives a clue to the exalted position Nicodemus held and **risked** for Christ. Verse 53, usually connected with the next chapter, is significant for it shows the effect of Nicodemus' words to frustrate council action against the Lord. Some method other than the "secret trial" will have to be found now. Their plot has failed, their evil has been exposed.

8 1.   But Jesus, meanwhile, went to the Mount of Olives.

MOUNT. The feast is over. But few pilgrims leave for their villages. Too much excitement—Messiah is at hand. Jesus makes His way to the Mount. This became His custom during His last stay in Jerusalem. The rulers unable to try Jesus privately, need a new scheme for their attempts against His life. Next they will try to discredit Him before the public or catch Him on the horns of a dilemma, hoping to create grounds for charges against Him. From now on they will seek to trap Him openly with words, that is, get Him to disqualify Himself no matter how He defends against their questions. They will use this device continually during the last days of His ministry. He is six months away from the cross.

❖   ❖   ❖   ❖   ❖   ❖

AN INCIDENT occurs in the following verses which is not in the style of John. It is missing from some of the earliest and most valuable manuscripts, where the accounts not only vary but are found in different places. Scholars generally pronounce Verses 7:53-8:11 inclusive as NOT belonging to John's Gospel. Nearly all agree, however, that the story is true on the basis of internal evidence. Otherwise it would be hard to account for its presence in the N.T. The question is: **where does it belong!** If it is left where it is, the events are shifted up one day. If it is moved to the end of the chapter, the discourse of Jesus continues uninterrupted. He was not arrested, only the guards returned to the council. Yet it is not inconceivable that Jesus also withdrew to the Mount of Olives for reasons of security. If so, He would be in just the right place for the event of Chapter 8 verse 1.

JOHN
8

TWO DISTINCT MESSAGES are given by the Lord in these chapters. In Chapter 7 He offers Himself as the source of "Living Water." This took place near the altar of the temple the DAY AFTER the water ceased. But His message in Chapter 8, offering Him as the "Light of the World," occurs in the Treasury (Court of Women) where stood the golden candelabra. Lighted during the feast and seen all over Jerusalem, they are now out. It is the sight of these **extinguished** candelabra which no doubt occasions the Lord's invitation. In Chapter 7 He offers Himself after the **water** has ceased. In Chapter 8, He offers Himself after the **light** has ceased. It seems satisfactory to leave the account where it is. The shifting of events one day accommodates the two different messages delivered in two different places. The truth is unaffected regardless of the shift.

✻ ✻ ✻ ✻ ✻ ✻

2.   Just as day was breaking, He again appeared in the temple and all the common people flocked to Him. So He sat down and began to teach them.   3.   Then some professors of the Law and Pharisees brought to Him a woman arrested in the act of adultery. They made her stand in front of Him, in full view of everyone.

PHARISEES. John gives us a picture of the mass of remaining pilgrims rushing upon Jesus as He reappears in the temple. He was a sensation the day before. Now He is back on the job at dawn. Then some Pharisees and legal doctors attempt a subtlety. They produce a woman caught in adultery and display her before Him. Her guilt is unquestioned. Since the death penalty is involved here, the Sanhedrin has to be in on the conspiracy (Lev. 20:10). Perhaps the case has already been before a local Jewish court, when they are inspired (by Satan) to use her in a scheme to trap the Lord publicly. With diabolical concession they will say, "Since you are the Messiah, you decide her fate." They think they have Him trapped.

4.   "Master," they said to Him, "this woman has been caught in the very act of adultery.

5.   Now in the Law, Moses commanded that such a person should be stoned to death. But what do you say? What would be your judgment in this matter?"

JUDGMENT. The trap is set. The Lord repeatedly announced that He had come to SAVE, not condemn. They would impale Him on His own words. Will He minister mercy or justice? If He says, "Release her," He breaks Moses' Law. If He says, "Stone her;" He condemns her, violating His stated purpose in coming. Further, they could then tell the Romans He was prescribing death for persons on His own initiative. This was illegal. So, would He defy Moses and contradict God's Law, or would He affirm Moses and prove Himself false before the people? "Master," is spoken tongue in cheek, ironically, a device for luring Him into the trap.

"What a trap! He has to decide one way or the other, doesn't He!"

6.   Of course they said this to trap Him, hoping His answer would provide grounds for a charge against Him. But Jesus bent over and began writing on the ground with His finger.

FINGER. This is the finger of God, the same that etched Moses' tablets and Belshazzar's walls. What did He write? The Holy Spirit didn't regard it important enough to be in the text. It seems almost idle to raise the question. Some say He wrote nothing, but was merely doodling in the dust. This was an oriental custom, one used to show contempt or indifference to people around him. Others say He wrote out the sins of the elders, or drew a saying from one of the prophets designed to convict the conscience. If His action is one of contemptuous indifference to their plot, then it has the meaning of "Why tempt Me you hypocrites!" (Matt. 22:18).

7.   But when they persisted in pressing their question, He straightened up and said to them,

"All right, let the one among you who is without sin, be the first to throw a stone at her."
8. And then He bent down again and continued writing on the ground.

 PERSISTED. Whatever His silence meant to them, they failed to interpret it, and continued pressing for an answer. See Him rise. He turns to face them. He speaks. Remember, Words from Jesus are "spirit and life," and have power—power sufficient to paralyze the police. What He says has convicting force as well as the weight of wisdom and truth. "Never spake a man like this man!" said the guards as they returned impotent to the Sanhedrin. The Pharisees are about to taste it for themselves. Recall too, that John is revealing the Lord Jesus to us as the WORD of God. God speaks directly to these proud men who mercilessly used this woman to trap Him.

 WITHOUT. Jesus' Words for "without sin," are used only here in the N.T. and mean **sinless perfection.** He is saying, "Let the one who is flawless before the Law, heave away." Yet it is more penetrating than that. He is affirming that the Law of Moses is perfect, requiring a PERFECT EXECUTIONER to administer it. With that, He throws the responsibility back to them, NOT as a group, but as INDIVIDUALS. Usually the first stone brought death. He makes no judgment of the woman, but turns the tables by saying, "The one who would find this woman guilty, must first find himself innocent." With such wisdom He upholds the Law, but lays the matter on individual consciences. "Who qualifies," He asks, "as a perfect executioner of the PERFECT Law?" If we were to guess about His writing, it might have to do with Moses' Law so as to advance its convicting power to their evil hearts. Notice the "heard" of the next verse.

9. And when they heard what He said, they began to go out, one by one, beginning with the eldest until Jesus was left alone. The woman was still standing there where they had placed her.

ALONE. The Light of God had flashed upon their black hearts. They saw and felt the filth of their uncleanness. Jesus' Word stabbed deep. The older ones feel it first. They had the most accumulated sin, the most reputation to preserve. The evangelist wants us to see their orderly retreat, one at a time, so as to avoid suspicion of a plot. They came with the long robes and haughty looks, but they leave not so proud. Court is out, but no decision has been rendered. The accusers have all gone without casting a vote. The disciples are there. The crowd of pilgrims looks on. What an impression this must have made on them.

"Is the woman just standing there now, saying nothing!"

10. So Jesus stood up. Facing the woman He asked, "Where are all your accusers? Didn't any of them condemn you?" 11. "No one, Lord," she said. To which Jesus replied, "I am not going to condemn you either. You are free to go, but don't sin like that any more."

FREE TO GO. Without an **accuser** she was free under Jewish Law. Yet she remains, because Jesus hasn't given His verdict. Then He says, "I won't condemn you either." See what happened? He neither condemns her, nor defies the Law of Moses. Still He doesn't approve her sinful act, but announces the verdict of the court convened before Him. She is legally free. She was tried in a court, she is freed by the court. The Judge turns her loose without any statement on His part. He is aware of her guilt of course, and therefore exhorts her to break with her sin once and for all. That's the way to handle a bad habit. His Holy Light shines in her heart too!

"After the incident of the woman, does the Lord continue applying the truths of the feast to Himself!"

12.   Once again Jesus addressed the people saying, "I am the Light of the world. The man who follows Me will never walk in darkness, but shall have the light of life."

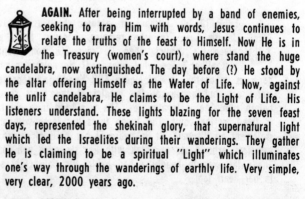

AGAIN. After being interrupted by a band of enemies, seeking to trap Him with words, Jesus continues to relate the truths of the feast to Himself. Now He is in the Treasury (women's court), where stand the huge candelabra, now extinguished. The day before (?) He stood by the altar offering Himself as the Water of Life. Now, against the unlit candelabra, He claims to be the Light of Life. His listeners understand. These lights blazing for the seven feast days, represented the shekinah glory, that supernatural light which led the Israelites during their wanderings. They gather He is claiming to be a spiritual "Light" which illuminates one's way through the wanderings of earthly life. Very simple, very clear, 2000 years ago.

LIGHT. Light is for seeing. Physical light (sun/fire/electrical) provides **external** illumination. Spiritual light, **internal**. With physical light a man moves and works; in darkness he cannot see where he is, what he is doing or where he is going. In spiritual darkness the same is true. A man does not know WHO or WHY or WHAT he is, where he is from or where he is going. But with spiritual light, he does. Spiritual light is **insight,** or awareness, and comes by way of WORDS. Since Jesus is the WORD, He is also LIGHT. By Him, a man can see what life is all about, what God is like and what man is. To go through life without reason, purpose or explanation is to be in the dark. Apart from Jesus, life makes no sense. A man might as well be a bug, knowing only that he is here today and gone tomorrow.

13.   Whereupon the Pharisees challenged Him, "You are testifying on your own behalf, that's not legal. Your personal testimony isn't valid as evidence."

PHARISEES. Some in His crowd were Pharisees, doubtless miffed by what He did to their fellows. They throw back to Him words which He uttered when He healed the lame man, i.e., "If I bear witness of Myself, My witness is not true" (5:31). They want to prove Him inconsistent, quoting Him against Himself. Yet it is only a testimony to their blindness. Light is always its own testimony. Does a street light need a sign on it before people walk in its rays? Does the sun need to be certificated before people get up and go to work? The only time people cannot behold a light is when they are BLIND! Only the spiritually blind cannot respond to spiritual light (insight).

"If Jesus is the Light, then should He not speak like a man full of light!"

14.   "My testimony is valid," replied Jesus, "even though I am bearing witness to Myself. I know where I have come from and where I am going. But you yourselves have no idea where I am from or where I am going.   15.   You are incapable of evaluating Me. Your judgments are based on outward appearances, on carnal reasonings. As for Myself, I haven't come to

judge any man, that's not why I am here. 16. Yet, if I were to pass judgment on someone it could only be just, for I am not acting alone in what I do—the Father Who sent Me is with Me."

TESTIMONY. Spiritual light tells a man who he is, where he is going and why he is here. Without such light (insight), no man can explain himself except to say he is like a bug, here today and gone tomorrow. But Jesus knew Who He was etc., and adds, "This is proof that I am the Light." Of course, the blind Pharisees were incapable of recognizing Him, neither would they take His Word for it. "You judge Me," says Jesus, "only by what you see, a man like yourselves. Because you behold a Carpenter-Rabbi, you think I cannot be the Light of the world. Though you judge Me by your physical standards, I do not judge you. I've come to save, not judge. Yet if I did judge, it would be just, for My judgment is the judgment of God."

"But He did say in Chapter Five that His testimony by itself was invalid, didn't He! Shouldn't He have witnesses to confirm His claim!"

17. "Besides, is it not written in your own law that the testimony of two witnesses is valid as evidence? 18. Well, one of those witnesses is Myself, testifying on My own behalf. The other is the Father Who sent Me. He testifies on My behalf too." 19. "And just where is your Father?" they ask. To which Jesus replied, "You do not know My Father any more than you know Me. For if you really knew Me, you'd know My Father as well."

WHERE! The Pharisees are not hinting an insult concerning His birth, but trying to trap Him into saying, "God is My Father." They want to provoke Him to stronger language suitable for a charge of blasphemy. They know

God is invisible. So they are asking, "Just HOW does He witness to your statement?" They ask for **tangible evidence** that God is with Him. He answers them much as He later did Philip, **"If you knew Me you'd know My Father also."** For God to reveal Himself **as a man** requires He operate in a body. The stumbling block is that His body also belonged to a Carpenter of Galilee. Just how that Carpenter is the invisible God of glory is a matter for faith, _not merely human measurement.

20.   These words He spoke in the temple Treasury where He was teaching the people. Still, no one arrested Him, for His hour had not yet come.

 TREASURY. Not the treasure chamber of the temple, but the treasury hall (court of women) where offerings were received. Women did not go beyond this point. Men stopped here to deposit gifts before proceeding to the altar area. This was the most public part of the temple, covering several hundred square feet or more. The Lord could have easily been seized, yet no one attempted it in spite of His astonishing claim. They are enraged, but Jesus is secure from hostility until God's restraint is removed. This location is in keeping with the account of the woman taken in adultery. To this court (women's court) only could she have been brought.

"If some are enraged enough to try seizing Him, did He continue teaching! By now many were surely mocking Him!"

21.   Therefore He spoke to them again, "I am going away. You will try to find Me, but you will die in your sins. Where I am going you cannot come."

 THEREFORE. Jesus' attitude changes. No longer is He offering Himself, but warning those who would seize Him. It is futile to look for a political Messiah when one needs a Savior from sin. Their unbelief, evidenced by their murderous spirit toward Him as God's Messenger, seals their fate. By refusing the Lord, they consign themselves to Satan's bitter end — that place of eternal punishment. An impassible gulf exists between heaven and hell, hence they "cannot come," yea never come where He is going. This mocking, ranting group reminds Him His hour is approaching. He thinks once more of His return to glory. Of course the Jews don't understand He is speaking of heaven.

22. At this the Jews began to inquire among themselves, "Do you suppose He means to kill Himself? That would explain why He says, 'Where I am going you cannot come.'"

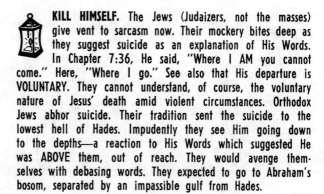

KILL HIMSELF. The Jews (Judaizers, not the masses) give vent to sarcasm now. Their mockery bites deep as they suggest suicide as an explanation of His Words. In Chapter 7:36, He said, "Where I AM you cannot come." Here, "Where I go." See also that His departure is VOLUNTARY. They cannot understand, of course, the voluntary nature of Jesus' death amid violent circumstances. Orthodox Jews abhor suicide. Their tradition sent the suicide to the lowest hell of Hades. Impudently they see Him going down to the depths—a reaction to His Words which suggested He was ABOVE them, out of reach. They would avenge themselves with debasing words. They expected to go to Abraham's bosom, separated by an impassible gulf from Hades.

"What ridicule! They put Him in a different class from themselves, don't they!"

23. "There is a difference between us," continued Jesus, "you are from below, while I am from above; you belong to this world, but I belong to another."

BELOW. Jesus agrees not only are their destinations different, but their **origins** also. They are from BELOW refers not to the earth, but their diabolical natures. They spring from Satan's headquarters, that is their spiritual home. Jesus is from above. Heaven is His home. That fact is obscure to them, so He explains with a second sentence. "This world," to the Jews meant the heathen world headed for condemnation. Thus He declares Himself from another world, therefore separated from them by origin and nature. He meets their suicide mockery by saying Hades is their spiritual home. It was for this reason He told Nicodemus he had to be born **"from above"** (John 3:3).

24.   "This is why I told you that you will die in your sins. For unless you believe that I AM, you will die in your sins."

 I AM. Most authorities connect this with "I AM THAT I AM" (Ex. 3:14). Supplying the pronoun "HE" it means "I am the Messiah." Without it, it is a strange expression of His being. They know He is claiming to be Messiah, but He avoids an outright declaration. He won't give them grounds for a charge against Him. So He says, "I am Who I am," which they instantly associate with "I AM THAT I AM." To understand Who He is, they must sum His declarations so far to see how they reveal a Person Who is from above, sent by the Father, Who is the Light of the world and the quickener of men. He is saying, "If you do not acknowledge ME as a **divine being,** you will die in your sins." This is still necessary today, even though entire religious movements deny His Deity.

DIE. To die in sin means the continuation of evil. Without Christ, a man's sins follow him, so that he continues to be evil forever. In hell, where grace is removed, evil surges unrestrained toward an unapproachable climax. Haters, for example, hate as never on earth. Jealousy compounds into a sickness not known among men. Unquenchable lust thirsts for satisfaction, fear has limitless objects, viciousness feeds on itself. Well do men picture hell as fire, but it is **fire of soul.** It is not the place that burns, but **the people.** Their natures are on fire—forever! God does not have to create hell, only provide a place for its occupants. Hell already smolders in the hearts of men. It bursts into flame when men reach a place where God's grace is removed. God need only supply the place, hellions make it hell.

"They must have smarted under the wisdom of His Words!"

25. "Who then are you?" they asked. "Just exactly what I have been telling you from the beginning," said Jesus.

BEGINNING. See how He avoids the trap? They want Him to voice a claim which might be used to frame a charge against Him. But He disappoints them, "If you'll sum up My statements from the beginning, you'll know exactly Who I am." Without stating so directly, He is telling them He is the Messiah, that He is from God and their only hope of deliverance from sin. The force of His Words mean, "I AM WHO I AM," and they sense a subtle connection with the ancient Name of Jehovah. But His Words also mean, "I am exactly Who I say I am," making it impossible to fix a definite charge. They get the message. He is free of any charge. What wisdom!

26. "There is so much I could tell you about Myself, but unfortunately there are too many things which I could judge in you. So I speak to the world only that which I have heard from Him Who sent Me—the True One." 27. In all this, they never once realized He was speaking to them about the Father.

FATHER. What blindness! All that He has said of Himself adds up to the fact that He brings a message from God to His people. Blinded by passion for a political Messiah, instead of a Redeemer, their hard hearts make it impossible for Jesus to reveal Himself to them as He did to the Samaritan woman. "There's too much wrong with you," He says, "for Me to tell you precisely Who I am." He must deal with them as wicked schemers, using Words with double meaning to which the heart of faith could respond, but the unbelieving mind could not comprehend. This is why He often taught in parables (Matt. 13:10-13).

28.   Then Jesus said to them, "When you have lifted up the Son of Man, you will realize that I AM and that I have not acted on My own initiative, but have spoken exactly as the Father has counseled Me to speak."

 LIFTED. The Lord uses an expression capable of double meaning. By lifted up, He refers to His cross and subsequent glorification. The Jews take it to mean the day when He is exalted as the Messiah and political ruler. To them His Words hint He is acting under secret orders not to reveal Himself, but later they will perceive Who He is. This suggests He may yet be the One they want. "Lifted up," you see, also means to elevate one to a throne. So they put their own construction on His Words, thinking it means the Messianic people will elevate their Messiah to power. "YOU have lifted up . . ." implies this. He is speaking of being "lifted" on a cross, they see Him "lifted" to a throne. This twist of meaning now presents a ray of hope to many of the listeners.

29.   "And He Who sent Me is with Me right now. He has never once left Me alone; for I always do what pleases Him.   30.   While He was saying these things, many began to exhibit some faith in Him."

 WITH ME. The double meaning continues. The Jews interpret His Words as an expression of confidence in the success of His mission with the help of God. They picture a secret meeting between Jesus and God where a strategy is worked out for overthrowing the Romans to establish the crown of Israel. But of course, the Lord is not referring to God's help at all. Such would be contrary to the essential unity of Father and Son. In His unconditional **obedience,** He enjoys the seal of unconditional **confidence.** But they see a plan being worked out which will shortly find this Rabbi revealed as the King of Israel. Consequently many began to believe in Him on this basis. This is faith in His Word (not miracles), but their false interpretation of it. The sequel shows what kind of faith this is. The Lord is aware their faith is based only on their Messianic expectations.

31. Turning then to those who appeared to believe in Him, Jesus said, "If you allow your lives to be regulated by My teaching, you will become real disciples of Mine. 32. In that way you will come to know the truth, and the truth will set you free!"

THEN. Mark the continuity. The Lord addresses the group which put the wrong construction on His words to become half-converts. He admonishes them to go on to real discipleship by submitting to His Word, rather than admiring Him as their potential king. By centering their lives in His teaching, they could escape the bondage of sin and error. The "IF" shows He knows theirs is an emotional attraction and not a commitment of themselves. He exposes their superficial discipleship shortly. See how He associates liberty with truth? Truth is light (insight), but it comes by **submission** to His Word, not just hearing it. It is not truth resting in one's mind, but operative in his life. Submission to Christ's Word means He becomes one's Master. Jesus wants disciples, not fans. It is slavery to Jesus that frees men from the slavery of sin and the fate of this world (Rom. 6:16, 22).

"Did this group of would-be disciples appreciate His Words of promised freedom!"

33. "But we are Abraham's descendants," they protested, "and nobody has ever yet enslaved us. What do you mean by saying, 'You will be set free?' "

DESCENDANTS. See how fast they turn? Some faith that. They now discover their mistake. His Words, they see, were not political, but **spiritual**. Truth frees from error and ignorance, not the Romans. So twisting His Words again, they claim never once to have yielded their spirits to a foreign power. They had been outwardly oppressed by the Egyptians, Babylonians, Syrians and now the Romans. Yet never once had they surrendered their right to be free or fight for freedom. Only rarely had they been politically free. They are speaking here of their unbroken Jewish spirit which survives even today. Jesus doesn't argue. He knows Jews have always considered themselves free, though dominated by outside powers. But He is speaking of moral freedom, spiritual freedom.

"How does the Lord get them to see that He is speaking of moral bondage rather than any political enslavement of men's souls?"

34. "In all truth I tell you," replied Jesus, "that every man who participates in the life of sin, is a slave to sin. 35. And a slave has no permanent bond to any household. A son, on the other hand, is an essential and organic part of the family and belongs to it forever. 36. Therefore, if the Son shall set you free, you will have true freedom."

SLAVE. The definite article in Greek points to the sin-life, rather than any specific sin. When Jesus mentions SIN, He expels any political meaning to His Words. The bondage He means is moral enslavement. Every sinner is a servant of sin—**including Abraham.** And if a servant, certainly in no position to free anyone. The Jews were staggered to have Jesus make this application of custom to Abraham, much as Catholics are rocked to have Mary called a sinner. With Abraham a sinner and therefore a servant, he needed to look to another for his own freedom. The Son (Jesus) in concert with the Father (the Lord of the royal house) is the only One Who can release souls from spiritual bondage. Thus Jesus is greater than Abraham, even as a Master is over a servant.

37. "I know you are descended from Abraham, yet you seek to kill Me because you can't stand My words. 38. I am merely putting into words what I have seen in the presence of My Father. But you, on the other hand, are doing what the presence of your father causes you to do."

 ABRAHAM. Jesus acknowledges their human descent from Abraham. But as such, they are bent on MURDER. Why? The revelation of God turns them to wrath. Abraham's seed they are, God's children they are not. Their enmity to His Word is proof. Jesus says this is due to their difference in parentage, leading up to their **spiritual** ancestor—Satan. With these Words He explains the infinite gulf between them as one of parentage, they come from different households. Now they begin to catch what He meant when He said He was from ABOVE, while they were from BELOW. They may have Abraham's blood in their veins, but their spirits originate with a different father. Abraham's godly spirit is foreign to them.

"Did they understand the terrible implication of Jesus' Words!"

39. "Abraham is our father," they retorted. "If you really were Abraham's children," said Jesus, "you would act like it. 40. But here you are trying to kill Me, a man telling you the truth, even as I hear it from God. Surely Abraham would never do that! 41. You do the works of your father, all right, but it is not Abraham." They snapped back, "We are not spiritual bastards! We have only one father— God, and God alone!"

A MAN. Jesus is NOT accusing them of killing the Christ, but a man from God. Abraham would not do that, it was contrary to his spirit. He gladly received God's messengers. They knew Abraham had welcomed the

"Angel of the Lord," and Melchizedek. Therefore they must be copying some terrible father as yet un-named. This was a real blow. They regarded themselves the "offspring" of God inasmuch as Abraham was chosen to sire the holy race. When Jesus says Abraham is NOT their father, He puts them **outside** the holy family, with another god for their father. This was precisely how they regarded the Samaritans, as spiritual bastards. Jesus' Words sting with fire. They finally mention God. The conversation is spiritual now.

42. "If God were your father," replied Jesus, "you would love Me, for I have come directly from His presence to stand before you. I am not here on My own initiative, He sent Me. 43. So why is it that you do not understand what I am saying? It is because you don't want to hear a message from God! 44. You are just like your father the devil! And you are just as determined to satisfy your desires. He was a murderer from the beginning, it is his nature to kill. There is nothing truthful about him, because there is no truth in him. Consequently when he speaks, he gives voice to his lying nature. Only lies can come from him. He is the father of both the lie and all liars."

DEVIL. What a striking testimony! Jesus reveals Satan. He is alive. He motivates and prompts these Jews. He is their father . . . clearly so because of their opposition to the truth. There are but two households, God's and Satan's. At one time the devil rejoiced in the truth (Ezek. 28:14, 15). Therefore evil began with him. He is the first liar, with his first twist of truth recorded . . . "You shall surely not die" (Gen. 3:4). He hates life, authoring Abel's murder. With no light in himself, darkness is his center of gravity: meaning he deceives even himself. Thus he is the father of all deception. He rules the world of spiritual darkness which opposes God's truth. The hostility facing Jesus clearly has its source in Satan. Christians denying the existence and activity of Satan today, also resist Jesus' testimony to the devil's presence and power.

45. "It is because it is I, Myself, Who is speaking the truth to you that you do not believe Me."

MYSELF. The Greek emphasizes the EGO of Jesus here. The Jews are not merely resisting truth, but a PERSON from God. It is the Person Who offends them, for He offers HIMSELF. His Words kindle their diabolic natures. Were He to lie, they'd love Him. And were He to tell them what they wanted to hear, it would be a lie. He can only speak the truth, since He is the Truth. Since these Jews are by nature, children of the LIAR, they hate His SELF-REVELATION of the Truth. One day anti-christ will come saying things they want to hear and they will receive him, thus identifying their true parentage. The cults today honor Jesus, but not as God. As God, they want no part of Him. It is **God in Person** they hate, as did the Jews.

46. "Can any of you convict Me of sin? If I speak the truth, why do you not believe Me? **47.** I'll tell you why. The one who has God for his Father, harkens to the Words of God. That's why you will not listen to Me. You are not the children of God."

CONVICT. Jesus challenges them to find a flaw in His life. Sin here means not only error in speech, but sinlessness of life. If He is from God, He must stand out in sharp contrast to the evil of the world. If His life is pure, then so is His doctrine. If He is without sin, He is also without error. Since none of the Jews can find Him guilty of anything, the only reason they refuse His Word is because they HATE GOD. His bearing and character are truth-compelling, but since He disappoints the popular view of the expected Messiah, they turn a deaf ear to Him. That these Jews reject the Word of God is proof they are not of God. Jesus' claim to sinlessness is a vital verse in the Word. He must be the Great Exception men can behold and believe. As God in Person He can be no less than sinless.

"What an indictment! Surely such Words could only kindle their rage against Him!"

48. That prompted the Jews to snap back, "We were right when we said you were a Samaritan and a demon-possessed one at that!" 49. "I am not possessed," answered Jesus calmly, "the truth is, you want to dishonor Me because I honor My Father. 50. And as for My reputation, that isn't My concern. Someone else takes care of that, the One Who judges between us."

SAMARITAN. When they referred to Him as being demon-possessed in John 7:20, it was a figure of speech. But now they say it fits Him beautifully. To them a Samaritan was the exact opposite of a Jew. Calmly He answers as a self-possessed person, "I am not possessed." But He says nothing about the Samaritan charge. Those Samaritans welcomed Him and He refers to Himself as the "Good Samaritan" in another place (Luke 10:33). He accuses them of hating God and taking it out on Him, because He is from God. See how He says nothing in self-glory, content to leave His personal glory in the hands of His Father. A lesson for all of us.

"But He does defend His Word doesn't He, even if He refuses to defend His reputation!"

51. "In all truth I tell you, the one who submits himself to My teaching shall never see death!"

DEATH. Above Jesus said He had NO CONCERN for His reputation, now He says His disciples need have NO CONCERN about death. Those who let His Word regulate their lives can forget about it. The Greek: "SEE death," expresses the thought a man won't have to give death a serious look. He is NOT saying a man won't die, but that he can ignore death since it no longer holds any terror for him. This is the opposite of natural man who lives in fear of death. But note that such fearlessness comes only to those whose lives are lived in actual submission to the Word, not those who merely believe it and embrace it as being true. Discipleship is a step beyond that faith which merely approves the Word of God. It has to do with obedience.

"Could they understand such Words! That is a rather deep spiritual truth, isn't it!"

52. "Now we know you are demon-possessed. Only a demented man would say that 'The one who submits to my teaching will never experience death.' Abraham died, so did the prophets. 53. Are you now saying that you are greater than our father Abraham who died, and the prophets who died also? What are you making yourself out to be? Who do you think you are, anyway?"

GREATER. He offers Words of mercy, they reply with bitter enmity. Now they take His Word to SEE death to mean His disciples won't TASTE death. But He isn't referring to the death-experience, only to its harm and terror. They feel He is claiming the power to immunize His followers against physical death, and thereby doing something Abraham couldn't do. Which of the prophets or patriarchs escaped death? He must be claiming a greatness beyond theirs. But this is because they take His Words SEE DEATH to mean EXPERIENCE death. To their minds only a madman would talk like this.

54. "It would be pointless for Me to defend

Myself to you," answered Jesus, "self-glory is worthless. It is My Father Who exalts Me, the very One you claim as your God, 55. although you are unable to recognize Him. But I know Him intimately and were I to say I didn't, I would be as much a liar as you! The truth is, I have direct, personal acquaintance with Him, and am even this minute carrying out His Word. 56. As for your father Abraham, the delight of his life was to see My day, and to his great joy he did see it!"

 MY DAY. Leaving His reputation in HIS Father's hands, Jesus now refers to THEIR father, Abraham, declaring he beheld the DAY OF CHRIST. What is that? We take it to mean the total advent of Jesus as God incarnate, from birth to His final exaltation. Or, stated another way, the entire story of redemption and revelation as found in Jesus. Just HOW Abraham saw this we are not told. Whether by prophetic vision (which is most likely) or by conversations with the Angel of the Lord (a theophany), we don't know. But we do know how the Jews understand Him. They regard His Words to mean a face to face contact with the patriarch. Their reply to Him reveals this clearly.

57. "You are not yet fifty," replied the Jews, "and you mean to say that you have actually seen Abraham?"

SEEN. Notice how they reverse the situation. It was Abraham who had the privilege of seeing Jesus, not the other way around. But they refuse to give a pretender such honor. It would appear their reverence for Abraham transcends their reverence for God. Jesus' claim to intimacy with the One they call GOD, doesn't inflame them nearly as much as claiming contact with Abraham. Their minds are so bound to earthly estimates, they weigh Jesus' human maturity against Abraham's day 1900 years before. The reference to "fifty" is a Jewish expression for maturity.

"Will Jesus explain further how it was possible for Abraham to behold Him!"

58. "In all truth," said Jesus, "I tell you that before Abraham became, I AM." 59. Upon hearing that, they picked up stones to throw at Him, but Jesus slipped out of sight and made His way from the temple.

I AM. No one can mistake this claim to Deity. No trick of grammar or theology can confuse this sublime truth. There is only one meaning: before Abraham came into being, Jesus already existed. The truth lies in contrasting two Greek verbs. The one referring to Abraham means "became." The verb referring to Jesus means "exist," which is not the same as became. Whereas Abraham was created, Jesus always was! This statement declares His eternal pre-existence, therefore His supremacy of Being. Either these are the words of an amazing blasphemer or of God incarnate!

STONES. The Jews are enraged. They understand Him perfectly. They are so furious they are ready to be judge, jury and executioners. No waiting for councils, no regard for Roman warnings, they are bent on killing Him on the spot. Gathered about the Lord are His adherents. So He disappears into the friendly group. It is not necessary to think of Him as being made invisible to effect this escape. The Greek indicates He "withdrew Himself," whereas another word would have been used if the Spirit meant for us to understand that He "vanished." Jesus then conceals Himself in the temple until the timetable of His Father moves Him on. He has an appointment with a blind beggar. He will emerge from the temple to keep it.

"Does Jesus remain in the vicinity and continue His presentation in spite of the hostility!"

9 1. And as He was passing by, He saw a man who had been blind from birth.
2. "Master," inquired His disciples, "whose sin caused this man to be born blind, his own or his parents?"

SAW. The feast-action of Chapter 8 continues. Some time has passed. Jesus is leaving the temple. The crowd has dispersed, tempers have cooled. We are probably to picture the beggar seated at the entrance. Jesus pauses, His eyes rest on the beggar. The disciples watch Him. They may have seen this man often. They think it is a good time to have Him answer a baffling question, i.e., how close is the connection between sickness and sin? Israel's teachers had no satisfactory answer. They were correct in relating sickness to sin, but Jesus will have no part of their question. He has more urgent business than discussions of theology. He has come to Jerusalem to reveal Himself.

3. "It is not a question of whether this man or his parents sinned," answered Jesus, "but of beholding the working of God in him. 4. We must perform the works of Him Who sent Me while the daylight lasts. Night is coming when no man can work. 5. As long as I am in the world, I am the Light of the world."

DAYLIGHT. Time is running out. The cross is six months away. He is going to heal this man and He doesn't want His disciples fussing with theology when He is about to dramatize the truth of Himself. He would shift their focus to the **urgency** of God's work, rather than explanations of Satan's work. He uses the SUN as a figure of Himself. He has little time left in the world and is eager to press home the truth that He is the LIGHT of the world. He first declared this symbolically as He stood by the candelabra in the women's court. Now He is going to prove He can give LIGHT to people with a dramatic visual aid. He is going to bring **daylight** and **spiritual light** to a blind man. How that man became blind in the first place is aside from the lesson. A discussion of sickness and sin is theological trivia compared to what He is about to demonstrate.

"You mean He is going to prove He is the Light of the world!"

6. With that He spat upon the ground and made some clay with the saliva. Then He applied the muddy clay to the eyes of the blind man, 7. and told him, "Go wash in the pool of Siloam." (The word Siloam means 'sent.') And so the man went away and when he returned he could see.

 CLAY. The clay-making is incidental to the miracle, but it is vital to the story. The clay was unnecessary, He could heal with a Word. This is akin to the quilt-carrying of Chapter 5, where the cripple was used to gain the attention of the Sanhedrin. Once again Jesus does something to bring news of His work before the ruling Jews. And again there will be **walking evidence** of His claim. The healing of a man of congenital blindness is proof that He is from God. Note the pool is the same from which the priests drew the "water of life," for the seven days of the feast.

"Then the making of the mud was more for the sake of the Pharisees than the blind man!"

8. His neighbors and all who were used to seeing him as a beggar, began to remark, "Isn't this the man who used to sit here and beg?" 9. Some were certain about it. "Yes this is the man," they said. But others thought differently, "No, it is merely someone who looks like him." However the man himself kept insisting, "I am the one."

NEIGHBORS. Notice the precise detail of this account. So minute and true to life we can only suppose John was on the scene to receive them from the blind man himself. Recall that Jesus did this work as He was "passing by" out of the temple. The man, therefore did not return to the Lord, but to his family. He wouldn't have known where the Lord was. The Master deliberately sent the man away from Himself. He wanted no crowd about Him now. He prefers that the Pharisees come seeking Him after they get word of His "clay-making" on the Sabbath. This was specifically forbidden by Law. The man is a city-wide sensation as he goes about seeing his friends for the first time.

10. Satisfied it was he, they began to ask, "How then were your eyes opened?" 11. "The man called Jesus," he replied, "made some clay and pasted it over my eyes. Then He told me to go to the pool of Siloam and wash. I did. I went there and washed and that's how I received my sight." 12. "Where is He now," they asked. "I don't know," he replied.

 WHERE. Notice his straightforward answers. He told only what he knew, offering no theories for the miracle. Many commentators have traced the rise of this man's faith. He moves from "The man called Jesus," to the place where he worships Him as God (Vs. 38). It can be fascinating to see how the inquisition of the Pharisees forces him to reach the right conclusion about Jesus. Yet John writes to record Jesus' claim to Deity. Thus the miracle and the man's faith are secondary to the message Jesus will deliver to the Pharisees. This healing occasions His "Good Shepherd" message which ends at Chapter 10:21. The attention should be fixed on Jesus. The miracle is but evidence that He is the "Light of the world."

"Surely the matter didn't stop there!"

13. So they escorted the man who had been born blind into the presence of the Pharisees. 14. Bear in mind the day on which Jesus had made the clay and opened the man's eyes. was a Sabbath.

ESCORTED. Right on schedule the blind man's neighbors take him before a theocratic court, feeling no doubt, it was their duty to appraise the rulers of this great miracle. This is as Jesus planned, knowing full well the question of Sabbath-breaking would be raised. This matter persists as the crux of His controversy with the Jews. Israel has stumbled over tiny points of Law, blind to the massive revelation of their own Messiah. Their Maker was close enough to touch, but legal specks blinded their eyes. The major speck was Sabbath-keeping. Jesus deliberately makes this the target of His work so as to show the awful spiritual condition of the nation. Thus the healing of this BLIND man is related to the BLINDNESS of Israel as led by her blind rulers.

"How will the Pharisees react to the report of this amazing healing!"

15. The Pharisees asked him to repeat his story and explain to them how it was he had received his sight. The man told them simply, "He put some clay on my eyes. I washed it off. And now I can see." 16. Some of the Pharisees said, "This man can't be from God, He doesn't keep the Sabbath." But others of them disagreed, "How can a sinner perform such great signs as these?" This resulted in a division among them. 17. So they decide to question the man further, "This man who opened your eyes, what can you tell us about him?" He replied, "He is a prophet."

PHARISEES. This may not be the great Sanhedrin itself, but one of the minor sanhedrins. There were two in Jerusalem. They were synagogue-courts consisting of 23 assessors, with the right to levy the lower grades of excommunication. The power to isolate a person from the privileges of religion and business and society forever, was in the hands of the great Sanhedrin only. The man before this group is unquestioned evidence of God's working in their midst, but the Pharisees divide on how a sinner could perform such a feat. So they begin an inquisition of the man. He states his honest feelings. To him the Healer can be nothing less than a prophet.

18.   The Jews then began to question whether or not the man had in fact been born blind. They just couldn't believe he had actually received his sight, so they summoned his parents,   19.   and questioned them: "Is this your son? And do you say he was born blind? And if so, will you explain to us how it is that he is now able to see."

PARENTS. These poor people are scared to death. It had already been agreed by the rulers that anyone claiming Jesus was the Messiah should be excommunicated from the synagogue and cut off from the religion of Israel. A lower court could levy 30 days excommunication, which meant they would be treated as lepers. No one was allowed to eat or drink with them or conduct any kind of business. People had to keep their distance. Under such threat the poor parents are easily intimidated. They guard their words. They face the prospect of 30 days excommunication.

"Even though his parents are scared, will they deny what they know to be the truth!"

20.   The parents replied, "We know that he is our son and that he was born blind.   21.   But as to how he can now see or who it was that

opened his eyes, we have no way of knowing. Why don't you ask him? He is of age as a legal witness. He can speak for himself." 22. It was their fear of the Jews which made his parents talk like this; for the Jewish authorities had already agreed that anyone acknowledging Jesus as Messiah should be barred from the synagogue. 23. It was because of this that his parents said, "He is old enough to speak for himself."

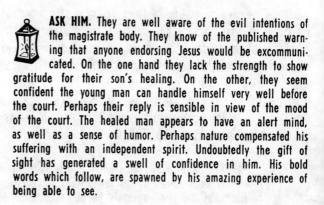

ASK HIM. They are well aware of the evil intentions of the magistrate body. They know of the published warning that anyone endorsing Jesus would be excommunicated. On the one hand they lack the strength to show gratitude for their son's healing. On the other, they seem confident the young man can handle himself very well before the court. Perhaps their reply is sensible in view of the mood of the court. The healed man appears to have an alert mind, as well as a sense of humor. Perhaps nature compensated his suffering with an independent spirit. Undoubtedly the gift of sight has generated a swell of confidence in him. His bold words which follow, are spawned by his amazing experience of being able to see.

24. So for the second time they called back the man who had been born blind and admonished him, "You should give God the credit for what has happened to you. We know this man is a sinner." 25. "Whether or not He is a sinner," replied the man, "I wouldn't be able to say. But one thing I do know is that once I was blind, but now I can see!"

CREDIT. The man was no doubt asked to step from the examination room while his parents were interrogated. Now he is called back. The court tries a different technique. This time they seek to influence his testimony by first saying, "We know," hoping he will think twice before going against them. He understands they wish him to lie and go along with the hierarchy in discrediting Jesus. Of course it is only by insinuation, but he knows what they want. Yet, how can he ignore something as precious as the gift of sight or denounce Someone as remarkable as his Healer? He is not about to please the court, excommunication or not. He refuses to contradict his own experience of, "I know."

"Surely the court won't let it go at that."

26. So they pressed him again, "Tell us, what exactly did he do to you? That is, just how did he open your eyes?" 27. "I told you already," he answered, "but apparently you weren't listening. Why is it that you want to hear it all again? Would you too become His disciples?"

DISCIPLES. What boldness in this man! What a daring sense of humor. He detects their bafflement. Instead of denying his benefactor, he now considers himself a disciple, asking if they aren't interested in joining too. See how he leaves the dogma of the court unanswered. He doesn't care what they think. His experience is real, making their accusations false in his eyes. They return to the HOW of the Sabbath-breaking, but he knows it is only to find a charge against his Healer. He is filled with scorn. Irony mingles with his words. He senses they are going to brand him a disciple of the Lord anyway if he doesn't go along with them. So he beats them to the punch. Their reaction is no surprise to him.

28. With that they became abusive. Furiously they turned on him, "You're the one who is his disciple, we're the disciples of Moses. 29. We know for certain that God spoke to Moses, but as for this man, we don't even know where he came from." 30. The man

reacted as though flabbergasted, "I can't believe it! A man comes along and gives me sight
and you don't know where He is from? This is
incredible!"

INCREDIBLE! See how he takes their words, turning them
around to indict the court. They say they don't know
where this Man is from. He says he's shocked to hear
such a confession from the leaders of Israel. A Man
appears, obviously from God and a Prophet, and they find His
origin a mystery. The healed man now seems well convinced.
His spiritual eyes are opening. Every Jew knew that Messiah
would arrive as a Healer, with the giving of sight to the blind
as a specific credential. So he begins to present a case for
the Lord, basing his argument on a common creed.

31. "Everybody knows that God does not give
heed to sinners, but harkens only to the God-
fearing and those who do His will. 32. And
where, since the beginning of the world, has it
ever been heard that a man should open the
eyes of one born blind? 33. No, if this Man
were not of God, He wouldn't have the power
to do such a thing!"

HARKENS. The miracle of sight to one born blind appears
unique in history. So the healed man uses it, along
with a common creed, for leverage against the court.
With all miracles of God regarded as answers to prayer
—and since God does not bend to the will of sinners—it
could only mean that Jesus was a devout Man in the will of
God. Feel the exultation of this man's soul as he testifies to
the innocence and piety of the Lord. He knows the court
embraces this creed. He is also aware of the truth of what
he is saying, "If He were not of God, He couldn't do such
a thing!" The force of his argument was compelling. The
conclusion should have brought this court to its knees.

34. "How dare you teach us!" they roared back at him, "You who were not only born in sin, but raised in it!" And with that they threw him bodily from the courtroom.

 BODILY. With those words they finally admit he was born blind. They explain his blindness as **born in sin.** People who hate truth don't care about inconsistencies. In rage they throw him out, following it no doubt with judicial excommunication. If they lacked the authority, they could get the great Sanhedrin to do it. He had defied the decree before witnesses, earning the excommunication. But he expected it. As he picks himself up from the dust, the real truth is he has excommunicated them. If the organized religion of his day was too blind to recognize a Man from God, he'd as soon be done with it. True, he wouldn't like being barred from his own people for life, but a strange new excitement now surges within his soul.

"What will Jesus do for the man now?"

35. When Jesus heard that they had expelled him, He sought the man out. Finding him He asked, "Do you believe in the Son of Man?"

SON OF MAN. This was Jesus' reference for Himself as He linked Himself with humanity. Some Mss. read, "Son of God." The reference is open for debate. Either would be the same for the man. Divorced from the religion of his day, he now needs a precise target for his faith. Jesus is going to provide it. The man has moved from "a man called Jesus" to "a Prophet" to "from God." He already has the faith for salvation, now he needs the proper object. So Jesus asks him, "Do you really believe in the Son of Man now that you have borne such testimony to Him?" The Greek shows Jesus expects an affirmative answer.

36. Eagerly the man replied, "Tell me Sir, Who is He that I may believe in Him." 37. "You have already perceived Who it is," said Jesus, "and now you have seen Him. It is He Who is speaking to you." 38. "Lord, I do believe," he said, and bowed down to worship Him.

172

WORSHIP. This word is rare, used only three times in John. It speaks of the attitude of the soul in the presence of God. The Greek text is animated, indicating the eagerness of both Jesus and the man, who has now found the target for his faith. When Jesus says "perceived," it shows His awareness of the man's growing insight and desire for his Healer. He had never seen the Lord with physical eyes. In haste, Jesus reveals Himself to him, much as He did the woman of Samaria. See how a man is put out of the synagogue to be received into the fellowship of Jesus? A blind beggar was able to "perceive,"—"then behold"—"then believe"— "then worship" Him! But Israel couldn't recognize her own God! Were Jesus not God, it would have been blasphemous for Him to accept this worship. What proof of His Deity!

"Wouldn't the sight of an excommunicated man kneeling before Jesus attract quite a crowd!"

JOHN
9

173

39. "My coming into the world," said Jesus, "is in itself a judgment. My very presence separates the sightless from the seeing. Those who do not see, receive sight. Those who claim to see, become blind."

 JUDGMENT. What a sight! The healing sensation of the city kneeling before the mysterious Rabbi! The feast crowd gathers. An amazing visual aid is before them. A man, kicked out of the synagogue, now SEES and bows before his God. He represents the believing remnant within Israel. Those preferring to cling to the Jewish system remain blind to their own God. With Words loud enough for all to hear, Jesus says He is the Separator of men on the basis of **seeing.** The spiritually humble, asking for sight, receive it. The spiritually proud, refusing the "Light of the world," remain in darkness. Blindness is darkness. The Pharisees catch what He means.

40. Some Pharisees in the company with Him overheard these Words and said to Him, "Surely you don't mean to include us among the blind, do you?"

 US! These are the very ones He does mean. They are in His party for the express purpose of catching Him in the act of clay-making. Learned in the Scriptures and intellectually proud, they wouldn't dream of asking for spiritual sight. They insist their spiritual eyes are already open. Thus their blindness is self-imposed. Their passion for Sabbath-keeping blinds them to any recognition of the truth. An amazing wonder of God has taken place before their eyes, but they see it only as a trespass of their legal system and not as a sign of the Messiah. It is similar to that parental blindness which refuses to see the faults of their own children.

41. "If you were truly blind," explained Jesus, "so that there was no way at all for you to apprehend what I have been saying, you wouldn't be guilty. But since you claim to be able to see, what then is your excuse for not recognizing Me? You are blind because you want to be blind, therefore you remain guilty."

GUILTY. Earlier, Jesus had said, "If you believe NOT that I AM, you will die in your sins." Had the Pharisees permitted themselves to see Him for Who He was, or Who He might be, they could have arrived at the same conclusion as did the blind beggar. But they refused to see Him as anything other than a Sabbath-breaking sinner. Their refusal was willful. Therefore their blindness was a matter of choice, not incapacity. Were it impossible for them to recognize Him, it would have been different. Then they would have an excuse. But now their guilt must remain. In selecting a blind, uneducated beggar, Jesus shows how easily people can SEE their Messiah if they want to. For coming to Him, as He is about to teach, is as easy as a sheep recognizing the VOICE of its own shepherd.

"Now that the healing of the blind man has attracted the desired audience, will Jesus bring His teaching!"

10 **1.** "Believe Me when I tell you this: the man who enters the sheepfold by climbing in some way other than by entering the door, is a thief and has come to plunder. **2.** But the one who enters by the door is the shepherd who owns the flock."

SHEEP. The Lord has healed a man and led him OUT of spiritually blind Judaism. The stage is now set for His teaching. The sheep reference is familiar to Jews. They are a shepherd people, their Scriptures full of prophecies of the Shepherd Who was to come. Israel is the sheepfold. This man is one of God's sheep who recognized the voice of the True Shepherd. Jesus has come to the fold, bearing God's credentials, the Spirit's witness. The rulers, therefore, are NOT true shepherds. They lack heaven's approval and their motives are evil. Jesus says they exploit the sheep rather than guide them, calling them thieves who seek only to plunder the sheep.

3. "The doorkeeper opens the way for him as he approaches, and his sheep perk up at the sound of his voice. Then he calls by name those sheep which are his and leads them out of the fold. 4. When he is sure all of his own are out, he walks ahead of them. They follow him because they recognize the sound of his voice. 5. Should a stranger come along, they'll run from him. His unfamiliar voice frightens them."

FOLD. A number of flocks were kept within a low-walled enclosure at night, a keeper guarding the entrance. When a shepherd arrived in the morning, he'd call out his own by name. A sheep is a simple animal which follows only the voice of its shepherd, no one else. Oriental sheep were named much as we name dogs and horses. Once certain his sheep were out of the fold, the shepherd walked before them, chanting often, so that his voice assured them of his presence, even when he is temporarily out of sight. Sheep are alarmed by a strange voice, they flee a stranger. Jesus now portrays Himself as the True Shepherd of God's sheep. He has arrived on the scene, calling His own from the fold of Israel. Only His own come to Him, the rest belong to the false shepherds, the rulers of Israel. Only His own recognize His voice.

6. Though Jesus' illustration was familiar to them, they still did not understand what He meant by it.

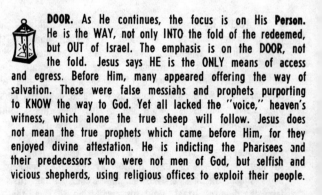

MEANT. A sheep was now kneeling in front of Jesus, called out of blind Israel. This is why He used a blind man for the visual aid—the man recognized the **voice** of the True Shepherd, his Messiah. The Holy Spirit (the Doorkeeper?) opened the gate. The man is now in the fold of the redeemed. The truth is quite simple. The ruling Jews, also shepherds, had sheep which followed them. Yet, within the one fold of Israel, were those who also belonged to Christ. Upon hearing His voice, they would detach themselves from Israel and follow Him. While the Pharisees were familiar with shepherd operations, they didn't understand the parable meant the calling out of God's people from within apostate Israel. They thought all in Israel were God's sheep. The Lord will have to explain further.

7. So Jesus spoke to them again, "Most assuredly I tell you I, Myself, am the Door of the sheep. 8. All who came before Me, claiming to be sheep-doors, are thieves and robbers. But My sheep paid no attention to them."

DOOR. As He continues, the focus is on His **Person.** He is the WAY, not only INTO the fold of the redeemed, but OUT of Israel. The emphasis is on the DOOR, not the fold. Jesus says HE is the ONLY means of access and egress. Before Him, many appeared offering the way of salvation. These were false messiahs and prophets purporting to KNOW the way to God. Yet all lacked the "voice," heaven's witness, which alone the true sheep will follow. Jesus does not mean the true prophets which came before Him, for they enjoyed divine attestation. He is indicting the Pharisees and their predecessors who were not men of God, but selfish and vicious shepherds, using religious offices to exploit their people.

9. "I alone am the Door. It is through Me a man can enter in and be saved. Not only can he come in to find safety, but he can go out to find pasture as he pleases. 10. I alone have come to give life to the sheep, that true life which allows one to live his life in the

fullest of exuberance and satisfaction. A thief, on the other hand, comes only to steal, lay waste or destroy."

ALONE. Note the narrowness of Jesus' claim. The way to heaven, despite the liberal tendencies of modern times, is no wider than the **Person** of Christ. There is no other way to God. But the life He gives is the opposite —unlimited expression and satisfaction. All other claimants have to be false for none can give life, they can only take from people or use them, finally destroying them. The "come in— go out" speaks of Christian freedom. Heaven and earth are spread before us and we can safely range in both places. The "pasture" refers to the richness of life in Christ on which we feed. Nothing else can satisfy the infinite appetite of man. The "exuberance" is the abundant living which a man can enjoy as he presses toward intimacy with the Godhead (John 14:20; Col. 2:9, 10). Only Jesus can give people the life God intended for man when He made him.

11. "I am the Good Shepherd, a genuine shepherd, willing to lay down His life for the sheep, 12. and not like a hired herder who runs at the first sight of a wolf. He doesn't care about the sheep, they aren't his. Concerned most for his own safety, he quickly abandons the sheep to the wolf, permitting him to snatch them and scatter the flock. 13. Because he is a hired man and interested in his salary rather than the sheep, he flees upon the threat of danger."

SHEPHERD. Jesus shifts from the "Door" figure to that of the "Shepherd." It is deliberate. The metaphors should not be mixed when handling these verses. The Greek reads, "the Shepherd, the Good," distinguishing Jesus as a **True** Shepherd from the commercial herders. Since the true shepherd is the flock's owner, the scene is a heroic risking of the shepherd's life as he combats the wolf. The Pharisees, the commercial herders, have not this concern for God's people. Caring more for their skin than the safety of their people (which they called "rabble"), they easily abandon them to the wolf. The Greek hints their flight long before the wolf reaches the flock. The wolf represents all spiritual danger, with Satan as the instigator.

14. "I am the Good Shepherd. I know My own and My own know Me, 15. just as the Father knows Me and I know the Father. And I am laying down My life for the sheep."

KNOW. Jesus is speaking of acquaintance and recognition among kindred personalities. Here is the interpretation of the parable: His sheep are His people, as closely connected to Him as He is to the Father. The "just as," denotes a similarity of manner, also kind. Thus He is saying, "The relationship between the sheep and Me is no different than the relationship between the Father and Me." There is therefore some marvelous communion in the Godhead we are yet to enjoy. The Lord entered humanity, that we might be partakers of the divine nature (2 Peter 1:4). He is therefore a **supernatural** shepherd. His contest with the wolf (Satan) a supernatural struggle. His sacrificial death will make it possible for His sheep to enter into intimacy with Deity.

'What about His sheep who are outside of the fold of Israel—those eager Samaritans, for example!"

16. "But I have other sheep which do not belong to this fold. These I must bring in as well, for they too will listen to My voice. Then there will be but one flock with one shepherd."

ONE FLOCK. Notice Jesus says, "Other sheep," not "other folds," for these are people scattered throughout the world. Yet there is only one kingdom into which all will ultimately be gathered. He does not mean Jewish residents outside of Palestine, for that fold included all Jews no matter where they lived. It is the heathen to whom He refers. Among them, as in the case of the Samaritans, are those who will respond to His voice. While He did come to the lost sheep of Israel, He sees this restriction abolished by His death. All of His sheep become one flock because there is ONLY ONE Shepherd.

17. "And here is why the Father loves Me: I lay down My life for the sheep, with the confident expectation of taking it up again. 18. No one forcibly takes My life from Me. I am laying it down of My own free will. I have the power to do this and I also have the right to take it back again, because My Father has commanded that I do this very thing."

LOVES. Two things about Jesus' death please His Father: His **voluntary** sacrifice for His sheep, His **confident** expectation of resurrection. Yes, He has been commanded to do this, but He also WANTS to. When it is remembered that He faced death as **a human,** this confidence is striking. He was willing to die for His people, but He had a fear of death (Heb. 5:7), which makes His sacrifice more marvelous. His agony in the garden reveals He had no appetite for death by crucifixion (Luke 22:39-46). The Father's command is His confidence. His love for us makes Him willing. The fact that He is aware of His power of resurrection does not diminish the extent of His fear of what He faced—for us! His Deity did not cancel what He felt as a man!

"This message must have staggered His listeners. Surely they never heard such teaching from any man before this!"

19. And so once again, His words divided the Jews. 20. Many of them said, "He is demon-possessed, He is raving mad! Why do you listen to Him?" 21. But others disagreed, "No demon-possessed man could talk like this.

Besides, who ever heard of a demon opening the eyes of the blind?''

DIVIDED. The Master has performed His sign (healing the man) and made His claim (the True Shepherd). Once more His words divide His listeners. The Pharisees who challenged Him at the close of Chapter 9 are now divided. His teaching has hardened the bitter majority which now regards Him as a madman and will pay no more attention to Him. The friendly minority is intimidated. The strongest defense they can make for Jesus is that His work seems too great to be accomplished by demonic agency. With His work now finished for a time in the city of Jerusalem (coinciding with the Feast of the Tabernacles), He will move out into the Judean countryside for about two months. He will re-appear in the city on December 25th for the Feast of Dedication.

"Does Jesus stay away for the two months to let His words soak in!"

22.   Then came the Feast of Dedication which was held in Jerusalem.   23.   And since it was winter, Jesus walked about inside a sheltered arcade of the temple, known as Solomon's porch.

FEAST. This feast has to do with the temple itself. And now Jesus appears within the enclosure, walking between the walls of the outer court. The weather is inclement. He has not yet broken with the temple, so it is proper for Him to be here. This feast, a happy one, commemorates the restoration of the temple by Judas Maccabeus (B.C. 165) and commonly called the "Feast of Lights." The people longed for another Maccabeus to appear and deliver them from their oppressors. So again, a unique occasion will bring Jesus and the rulers together. They find Him walking alone, the raw weather perhaps depriving Him of His customary circle of faithful followers. Word reaches the rulers, "Jesus is back!" This time they don't mean to let Him get away without a specific answer to their question.

24.   So the Jews encircled Him and said,
"How long do you intend to keep us in sus-
pense? If you really are the Christ why don't
you come out with it and say so?"

SAY SO! Bear in mind the ardent longing of these
people. They yearn for a Messiah who matches their
dreams. For centuries they have waited. His appearance at this feast kindles their hope in Him once
again. If there is the slightest chance Jesus is the One, they
will listen to Him. His works attract them, but His words
infuriate them to the point of stoning Him. They cool off each
time hoping against hope He is the promised One. They want
concise statements of Messiahship. He never gives them, but
offers words revealing Himself as something **greater.** For that
they hate Him, but since He hasn't denied He is the Messiah,
they listen again and hope. These rulers have had two months
to ponder His last words, now they close in on Him purposing
to extract an explicit answer.

25.   "I have told you," said Jesus, "but you
refuse to believe Me. All the works which I
have done in My Father's Name, bear ample
testimony to Me,   26.   but you will not believe because you are not My sheep!"

SHEEP. He picks up where He left off two months ago.
They have encircled Him as if to bar His escape, they
mean to find out once and for all. He takes them back
to the WORKS which are sufficient enough for faith,
but they will not believe, therefore they are not His sheep.
Not once does He tell them He is Messiah. But He does say
who are NOT His sheep. That's plain enough. To the Samaritan
woman He said, "I am He!" To the blind man, "I am He that
speaketh with thee!" But to the Pharisees only, "I am the
Door . . . the Shepherd." They must put together the truth
of the Shepherd King and the sheepfold of God. But that's
fair since they claimed to know so much about divine truth.
It should be easy for them, after all they said, "We're not
blind, are we!"

"The Pharisees still don't get it, do they!"

27. "My own sheep recognize My voice and respond. I know them and they follow Me. 28. I give them eternal life and they shall never perish. No one can tear them out of my hand. 29. My Father, Who has given them to Me, is greater than all and certainly no one can tear them out of the Father's hand. 30. I and the Father are One."

LIFE. Note the human side of salvation: to know (recognize) Jesus and follow Him. See the divine side as He cites a 3-fold proposition: (1) He knows each sheep personally (by name), (2) He gives them eternal life, guaranteeing they will never perish, (3) Inasmuch as no one can tear anything from the Father's hand—and since Jesus and the Father are One—no one can tear anything from Jesus' hand. The wolf imagery is continued. This last statement, a syllogism, is the strongest possible word on the keeping power of Christ, the safety of the saints. He has avoided any reference to His Messiahship, offering instead, an even larger claim to supernatural power and Deity. The Pharisees can't miss it. John writes to set forth Jesus' claim to Deity.

ONE! The Greek "One" is neuter. Rendered literally it means, "We are the same Thing!" But that's awkward. Yet it cannot be rendered, "We are the same Person." That requires the masculine gender. The context provides the key. Notice the WORKS claimed by Jesus—"life-giving" and "safe-keeping." He claims He can do this because, "I and the Father are One!" In effect He is saying, "This is possible because We are one in nature and substance, therefore also in POWER. It takes power to do this, so it is not referring only to purpose and will as some claim. Note the "I." To the Jews this meant the One speaking to them. Then see "THE Father," which means the God of Israel. He doesn't say, "MY Father," but identifies Himself with the Almighty by the common plural verb, "are." He says, God and I are one in kind, thereby claiming equality in essence and nature. The Jews pick up stones because His meaning is clear—equality with God!

"Wouldn't that provoke the Jews to hostility once again!"

31. Once more the Jews picked up stones to stone Him.

> **STONES.** They understand Him perfectly. And they react just as they did when He said, "Before Abraham became, I am!" Such a claim, to them, is worthy of instant death. They pick up rocks, but see how they are powerless to throw them? They may hem in the Lord for questions, but do Him violence—no. They will be impotent until "His hour" arrives. They have demanded He be explicit. He has. Precise about His Deity and His sheep, but not about His Messiahship. They are furious over His claim to be one in substance with God, but this time He remains on the scene. He is going to ask them a question, one which betrays a touch of playful irony.

32. "Right before your eyes," said Jesus, "I have performed many merciful works in My Father's power. For which of these good deeds would you stone Me?" **33.** "We are not going to stone you for doing a good deed," answered the Jews, "but for extreme blasphemy because you pretend to be God when you are just a man!"

> **WORKS.** It is for WORDS they mean to stone Him. But He subtly speaks of the WORKS which prove He is from God. They are sufficient to convince any informed Jew that His claim is valid. They are so set on a **political deliverer,** they won't accept any other kind—even One Who delivers from sin. So blinded are they by this single passion they are not able to recognize the Lord's credentials. It means nothing to them that a man of 38 years blind dereliction is restored, even though it proves Jesus' unity with God. Blinded by rage and disappointment, they see Him as an astonishing blasphemer deserving death on the spot. Their hands are stayed as He continues to talk with them.

"Does the Lord mean to debate their charge!"

34. "Is it not written in your Law," replied Jesus, "'I said: you are gods?' 35. Well then, if those men to whom the Word of God came, received the title of gods—and there is no way to annul the Scriptures— 36. why would you call blasphemous Someone Who has actually been sanctified and sent into the world directly from the Father—because He says, 'I am the Son of God!' "

 GODS. This title was given to every judge in the time of the Judges, to David and Solomon and every priestly individual anointed to minister the Word of God. (Psa. 82:6). Even though they were anointed by other men, they bore the title, "gods." Jesus argues that if the indissoluble Scriptures called these Word-handlers "gods," why are the Jews upset with Him for calling Himself the "Son of God," when He has been anointed by God Himself. Inasmuch as He is directly from the Father, as His works testify, He is not guilty of blasphemy. John has already noted that Jesus IS the "Word become flesh," whereas the "gods" of the O.T. merely received the Word.

SON. In the past, Jesus elected to call Himself the "Son of Man." He has never once said to the Pharisees, "I am the Son of God." But now see HOW He makes use of this title. He has just told them that He gives eternal life to His sheep, sheep which are strangely in His hand and the Father's at the same time—the non-destructible property of both. In effect He says to them, "Put those words together and they mean, 'I am the Son of God.' " He is saying that all that He has told them really means that He is One with God in nature, yea, somehow mysteriously God Himself. That is why they picked up the rocks, actually paving stones from the floor of the temple court.

37. "If I am not acting like the Son of My Father, then don't believe Me. 38. But if My works are those of God in action, then let those works convince you where My words cannot. Even if you don't believe in Me, accept the evidence of My works. Then you will recognize and gradually come to believe that the Father is in Me, and I am in the Father."

CONVINCE. Jesus is very patient with these vicious people, making a last effort to reach them with the truth of Himself. He is saying, in effect, "If My words upset you so much, forget about them for a moment and take an honest look at My works. Let them speak to you." It is as though they owe it to themselves to take a good look, since they reveal God in action. If they can comprehend what they see, it could lead them to faith in Him. Therefore Jesus is appealing to them to let His works do for them what His words seem unable to do. If they will accept the testimony of His works, it could lead them to an understanding of mutual indwelling of the Father and Son, which would then explain how Jesus can be God and yet the Son of His Father at the same time.

39. Again they were of a mind to seize Him but He escaped from their hands, 40. and returned once more to the other side of the Jordan, to the place where John was baptizing at the first. And there He stayed.

ESCAPED. True to their original understanding of His words, they act to arrest Him. His softer words have softened their attitude some, so that now they would arrest Him rather than stone Him. But they have no doubt as to what His WORDS and His WORKS mean: a clear and unmistakable claim to be God. Nothing He can do or say will win this crowd. So He withdraws for a time to an area of greater susceptibility. He will return to Jerusalem when the whole nation will be assembled for the paschal feast. On that occasion, the "Lamb of God," will be slain for the sin of the world. Jesus will remain in this area until it is time for Him to go to Bethany, in about 3½ months. A message from the home of Lazarus will signal His return to Judea.

41.   A great many people came to Him while He waited there. "John," they said, "never did any miracles, but all that John told us about this Man certainly proved to be true." 42.   And in that place many found faith in Him.

JOHN. There were many people in this area on whom John the Baptist's words made a permanent impression. They believed John to be a prophet and now they saw how Jesus fulfilled his account of the Messiah. Here there is no intimidation from the rulers, the people are free to think for themselves. This is likely the same place where Jesus said to John and Andrew . . . "Come and see." What the people now saw and heard confirmed the words of John. His work pays off as "many believed on Him there." John the Baptist worked only with words. He did no miracles lest there be confusion between himself and Messiah. Yet he himself was a miracle (Luke 1:7). There were lots of sheep on the other side of the Jordan who "heard" Jesus' voice and "followed."

"With the mood of the city so hostile, will Jesus now stay away from Jerusalem until time for His final entry at the Passover?"

11 1.   Now there was a man called Lazarus who became gravely ill. He lived with his sisters Mary and Martha in their village, Bethany. 2.   This Mary, whose brother had fallen sick, was the same who had anointed the Lord with perfume and wiped His feet with her hair. 3.   The sisters sent word to Jesus, "Lord, You should know that Your friend, of whom You are so fond, is very sick."

FOND. Jesus has been across the Jordan with His disciples for about 3 months. Then a messenger arrives from Bethany, a suburb of Jerusalem, lying about 2 miles to the S.E. This village is the home of a family Jesus loves. He learns that the younger brother is dying. The Greek indicates Jesus is "fond" of Lazarus. The sisters make no request, leaving it with the Lord what He should do. See how John identifies Mary? Writing long after the event, which is recorded in the next chapter, he refers to her as the one who anointed the Lord. He assumes his readers are familiar with the story. She was famous for her act. The Greek hints she is the prominent member of the family.

"Wouldn't it be dangerous for Jesus to rush to the aid of Lazarus, with Bethany so close to Jerusalem!"

4.   But when Jesus received the message, He said, "The purpose of this sickness is not the death of Lazarus. It has occurred to bring glory to God and reveal the glory of the Son of God."

PURPOSE. Lazarus is dead when Jesus gets the message. He knows it. Everything He now says is based on that. He knows exactly what He will do. A wonderful teaching situation has arrived, both for His disciples and the sisters. His words are for the messenger to take back, even though Lazarus is dead. What a test they will be for the sisters. He speaks loud enough for His disciples to hear. Recall how similar words were given on the occasion of the blind man and how that event was used so mightily to reveal the glory of the Son. We enter now upon another remarkable incident, calculated to reveal the Deity of the Lord in spectacular fashion.

5.   Now Jesus loved Martha and her sister and Lazarus,   6.   and for that reason deliberately stayed where He was for two more days.

JOHN 11

188

DELIBERATELY. Upon a death we grab phones, send messages and make hasty trips. Jesus continued with what He was doing, operating on God's timetable. He deliberately let the situation degenerate to the worst so as to display His glory at its best. Four days will pass so that there can be no doubt about the miracle He will perform. Bethany is 15 miles away, requiring one day for the trip. When He arrives, the sisters will have all but despaired of hope. From the days of Moses God has been dealing with His people in this fashion, so that someone has noted, "Man's extremity is God's opportunity." That is the case here. He allows the situation to become an extremity.

MARTHA. See how she is here named first, though Mary is the prominent member? She is to profit most from this event. This touch of death is largely for her, except that it occasions a great sign of the Lord's Deity. Luke identifies her as a fussy person, a neurotic worrier. She is busy when she should be listening (Luke 10:41). Out of love for this family, Jesus lets the heartache compound. The Greek verb shows it to be divine love, the kind which allows suffering in order to bring blessing. Because of Jesus' divine love for Martha in particular, He delays His departure for Bethany.

"You mean He stayed away just so He could bring a spiritual blessing to this family?"

7. Then, after the two day interval, He said to His disciples, "Let us return to Judea."
8. "Rabbi," protested His disciples, "It wasn't long ago that the Jews were trying to kill You! Do You really want to go back there again?"

RETURN. His disciples fear for His safety, knowing the mood of the city is dangerous. To them it is like going back into the lion's den. Human reasoning says stay away, explaining why, perhaps, the sister's message didn't ask Him to come. But the Lord is operating within the Father's will, the safest place regardless of any danger. His calm majesty is revealed by His answer to their protest.

It amounts to a lesson for His disciples. They are occupied with the threat of danger, when they should be occupied with the Father's will.

9. "Are there not but twelve hours of daylight," answered Jesus. "A man can walk in the daytime without stumbling, because he has this world's light to see by. 10. It is only when a man walks after dark that he stumbles, for then he has no light by which to see."

DAYLIGHT. In Palestine the days are of nearly equal duration, thus they are divided into twelve hour periods throughout the whole year. As God has appointed daylight hours for the laborer, so does the Son have His appointed hours to minister. Nothing can shorten them, anymore than the days can be shortened. Jesus is therefore saying, "I can make the trip without danger, My twelve hours are not yet ended." As the daylight worker sees where he can go and what to avoid, so Jesus knows exactly what He can and cannot do. For the man who is out of God's will (in darkness) the way is filled with peril. Jesus also knows His twelve hours will be ending soon, so His words carry the effect of "I must finish the work given Me while it is still light." The disciples understand this kind of teaching.

11. After giving these words a little time to soak in, Jesus added, "Our friend Lazarus has fallen asleep. But I am going to awaken him." 12. "But Lord," replied His disciples, "if he is sleeping, that is good for him. It can save his life. He will then recover." 13. All along they supposed that He had been referring to natural sleep, when actually He was speaking of Lazarus' death. 14. Therefore Jesus told them plainly, "Lazarus is dead."

SLEEP. Jesus uses Christian language here, such as Paul later employs, "We shall not all sleep." But it is strange talk, human talk. It has the idea of a man taking temporary rest. The disciples, of course, don't understand this language. They conclude Lazarus is snoozing and that is the best thing for someone who is ill. Therefore Jesus is forced to use the language of men and says plainly, "Lazarus is dead." But Jesus has come to remove the sting of death. He has twice raised people before, people who were not dead, but whose bodies were dead while the people themselves were somewhere else. It would appear then, that Jesus speaks only of the **body** when He uses the term sleep, for souls never sleep. Even today we say that bodies are—"laid to rest"—anticipating they will one day awaken.

**"Will His disciples remember that He referred to death in this way!
It could be a shocking lesson!"**

15. "For your sakes I'm glad I wasn't there at the time. Now you will be able to believe. So come, let us go to him."

GLAD. Jesus doesn't mean He is happy He didn't have to see Lazarus die. He is glad that now a greater miracle can be performed for their faith. Had the Lord been present, He would have no doubt healed Lazarus. As it is, the raising of the "dead" can occur instead of healing the sick. The absence of the Lord was needed to bring this sign. Had He been there and NOT healed Lazarus (which is unthinkable), it would have troubled the minds of His disciples and shaken the faith of the sisters. They would never be able to understand His **apparent** helplessness to save His friend from death when He had been healing crowds of people for over three years.

HIM. See how Jesus speaks of Lazarus as being ALIVE. He is. Only his body is dead. Death does not affect one's person, for the life of the soul is independent of the body. The Lord will make that abundantly clear as He teaches, finally demonstrating the truth with His own body. Until Jesus arrived in history, it was not known that only a man's body dies and that the man himself is unaffected by the experience. Thus Paul teaches that Jesus "brought life and immortality to light . . ." (2 Tim. 1:10). He uses Lazarus as a visual aid for this very teaching. He will pass through death unscathed. It will have no more effect on him than taking a nap. Jesus was right to give death a new name—"sleep." It is not the "King of Terrors," but a harmless event.

16. Then Thomas, sometimes called "The Twin," said to his fellow-disciples, "Let us go too and be killed along with Him."

 THOMAS. A strange gloomy person, Thomas. He sees always the dismal side of things. Lazarus is dead, death awaits his Master in Judea. Melancholy keeps him from seeing the promise in Jesus' words. It is his nature to be negative and critical and skeptical. But he has his good points too. He cares not to live if his Master is to be sacrificed. Hence he is strong in love, but weak in faith. It is to his credit that he despairs of living without Jesus. So great is his affection for Christ (not faith), that he would rather die than be without Him. What a disciple he'd be if his faith matched his affection! Like most pessimistic Christians, Thomas yields only after he has been convinced the hard way. Tradition says he suffered martyrdom in India.

"Did Jesus and His disciples then leave the Jordan to go back into Judea!"

17. When Jesus arrived He found that Lazarus had already been in the tomb four days. 18. And with Bethany less than two miles from Jerusalem, 19. many people came from the city to console Martha and Mary in the loss of their brother.

 ARRIVED. Jewish custom required Lazarus to be buried the day he died. Jesus had remained in Perea two days, another was needed for the trip to Bethany and the messenger took one day. Therefore Lazarus was dead when Jesus got the message. Gathered about the sisters are numerous mourners. Some were family friends, but many Jews from the city came also. Hoping, perhaps, to regain the friendship of the family since Jesus was away. These are surely Pharisees, though not necessarily members of the Sanhedrin (vs. 46). Greater lamentations were carried on in those times, with professional mourners hired for wailing.

20.   As soon as Martha learned that Jesus was approaching, she went out to meet Him. Mary remained in the house.   21.   "Lord, if only You had been here," said Martha, "my brother would not have died.   22.   Yet I know full well that whatever You ask of God, God will give it to You."

ASK. Martha's attitude is one of slight protest, not humility. And this in spite of Jesus' reply-message . . . "This sickness is not unto death." Had she believed it, she would have relaxed. She knows of the raising of Jairus' daughter and the youth at Nain. She has reason for confidence in Christ. It shows as she makes an excursion in faith . . . "whatever you ask, God will give it to you!" She is like Andrew who momentarily flared in faith over five loaves and two fishes. However her choice of words reveals she doesn't comprehend the dignity of Jesus. She speaks of Him as an **inferior** seeking a favor of His Superior. Her knowledge of Him is far from perfect.

"Will Jesus now test what she has just said!"

23.   "Your brother will rise again," said Jesus. 24.   "I know he will rise again in the resurrection," said Martha, "but that doesn't take place until the very last day!"

RESURRECTION. Jesus' words can be taken two ways. Either He means Lazarus will rise NOW, or in the future resurrection. Depending on the sincerity of her statement above, she will interpret His reply. She flunks the test, presuming He means the future resurrection, rather than an immediate raising of Lazarus. Had she honestly trusted the Lord, her response would have been one of joyful thanks. Jesus must now work with Martha so as to help her faith in Him match His true identity. He is not only her Messiah, He is her God. This is why He deliberately stayed away from Bethany. He purposed to deal with Martha so that she might believe in Him as the One Who gives life to men, a work only God can do.

> **"Then Martha's faith wasn't sufficient to grasp the meaning of Jesus' words!"**

25.   Jesus said, "I am the Resurrection and the Life. He who believes in Me shall continue to live, even though his body dies.   26.   And everyone who is alive and believes in Me shall never die. Do you believe this?"

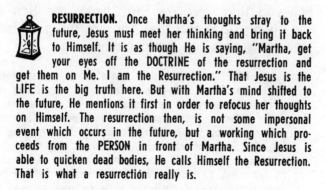

RESURRECTION. Once Martha's thoughts stray to the future, Jesus must meet her thinking and bring it back to Himself. It is as though He is saying, "Martha, get your eyes off the DOCTRINE of the resurrection and get them on Me. I am the Resurrection." That Jesus is the LIFE is the big truth here. But with Martha's mind shifted to the future, He mentions it first in order to refocus her thoughts on Himself. The resurrection then, is not some impersonal event which occurs in the future, but a working which proceeds from the PERSON in front of Martha. Since Jesus is able to quicken dead bodies, He calls Himself the Resurrection. That is what a resurrection really is.

I AM. John brings us to the last public "I AM" of Jesus, and to the central idea of this chapter. The miracle which follows is but supporting evidence of His claim to Deity. He declares Himself the source of life for men's souls AND their bodies. Notice He does NOT say, "I raise the dead," or "I perform the resurrection," but, "I AM the Resurrection!" The Resurrection was standing on two legs, face to face with Martha. Inasmuch as He gives life to men's souls, though their bodies be dead, He opens the truth of the separate existence of the soul from the body. A fact which is illustrated by a watch whose works, when separated from the case, keep ticking. A man in Christ lives regardless what happens to his body.

 BELIEVE THIS! What? That Lazarus is still alive! That is what Jesus' words add up to, for Lazarus was a believer. His body may be dead, **but he isn't!** Jesus challenges Martha's faith to rise to meet His statement. Will her faith ascend to such a height? No. Not for the moment anyway. Shortly He will back His claim with the certifying miracle. Then she will be able to believe it. This entire discourse and miracle which follows appear to be for Martha's sake. It shows how far the Lord will go in order to change a life.

"Surely Martha isn't able to believe her brother is still alive, is she!"

27.   "Yes Lord," replied Martha, "I have long believed that You are the Christ, the Son of the Living God, and that You are the promised One for Whom the world has waited."

 YES. Poor Martha—she's sincere enough, but she hasn't the faintest idea of what He has just said. If she did, her soul would have shouted for joy. Lazarus was a believer. Jesus' words mean that He is ALIVE! Her testimony shows she doesn't understand WHO is speaking to her. The Greek indicates she is restating a long held belief in Jesus as Messiah, NOT an affirmative answer to the question He just asked. It is beyond her for the moment. To state that Jesus is the expected Messiah is a far cry from believing He has given life to Lazarus and is the Resurrection in Person. She is probably a little sad, hoping He might have come up with something more practical than mere words about life and resurrection.

28.   Having said this she went away and called her sister aside. She whispered to her, "The

Master is here. He wants to see you." 29. The moment she heard that she got up quickly to go to Him. 30. As yet Jesus had not come into the village, but remained in the place where Martha had met Him. 31. When the Jews who were in the house comforting Mary saw how quickly she arose and went out, they followed her. They assumed she was going to the grave to weep.

MARY. The explosive Martha rushed from the house to meet the Lord, eager to express her disappointment that He wasn't there when Lazarus died. Then she returns. She beckons Mary aside and whispers this interesting detail not found in the narrative. Jesus wanted the girls to come to Him privately. He would deal with their faith away from the influence of the Jews. This is of greater concern to the Lord than the raising of Lazarus. It was for this purpose He deliberately stayed away from Bethany. Mary, the trusting one, rises to go to the Lord ahead of the crowd of mourners. Notice how differently she handles herself before the Master.

32. So when Mary came to the place where Jesus was and saw Him, she fell at His feet. "Lord," she said, "if You had only been here, my brother would not have died." 33. When Jesus beheld her weeping and saw the Jews who were following her, also weeping, it stirred within Him feelings of such magnitude that His emotions became outwardly visible to all.

EMOTIONS. The Lord has feelings which glow in the text. The Greek is violent, using "deeply agitated"— "troubled Himself"—"vehemently stirred" to express His internal conflict. There is a collision of emotion within Him. (1) He is pained to see the agony of this family which

He loves. (2) He is reminded of His own death and burial coming up soon. (3) He is incensed over the desolation sin brings, (4) furious with the pagan lamentations. (5) He feels rage at the terror death holds for man. (6) Yet He is excited about what He is going to do. (7) There is exultation as He pictures the family's joy restored with the raising of Lazarus. (8) He thrills to the prospect of displaying the Father's power. These feelings collide within Him to produce an emotional volcano which erupts outwardly.

34. "Where have you laid him?" Jesus asked. "Come and see, Lord." 35. Then Jesus burst into tears, weeping silently.

TEARS. God cries. He is not merely a spectator to human heartache, but a participator. "Jesus wept," reads the A.V., but the Greek indicates gentle weeping as the tender expression of **controlled** grief. His furnace erupts in tears, yet He is restrained. A different Greek word describes the weeping of the sisters. Their wailing exhibits numerous **external** agonies of grief. His is the disciplined ventilation of human sorrow. Observe that knowing what He was about to do did not cancel His ability to share their grief. Tears then are not a defect, but perfectly in order for God and man. Our Savior is far more attractive as a weeping, loving Lord, than as an unfeeling, unconcerned stoic! He felt Mary's pain—even as He feels ours!

"What did the people think when they saw the Master crying!"

36. "See," said some of the Jews, "how much He loved him!" 37. But others noted, "If He could open the eyes of the blind, why then didn't He save this man from death?"

WHY! Jesus' tears divide the people. John reveals some were kindly disposed toward the Lord, others hostile. Jesus could have prevented Lazarus' death, but here it is a question of **purpose,** not power. God is limited in

JOHN 11

196

many things by His own purposes. Many of these Jews had come from the city with the hope of winning the sisters back to Judaism. Most of them are untouched by sympathy. They interpret Jesus' tears as sadness over His powerlessness to prevent Lazarus' death. They would even cast doubt on His healing of the blind man in Jerusalem. Their hypocrisy and unbelief register bitterly on the Lord's spirit.

"Did the presence of these Jews actually bother the Lord?"

38. With these words bringing fresh agitation to His spirit, the Lord arrived at the tomb. Actually it was a cave with a stone covering the entrance.

AGITATION. The Lord winces from the vicious stabs and hostile presence of these Jewish "mourners." Added to it, may have been a reluctance to return Lazarus to this world of evil hostility and hate. This is what Lazarus was coming back to. Usually Jesus went about healing the sick, raising but three from the dead. It might not be such a kindness to take a man from the freedom of the spirit-world and return him to a new series of trials and encounters. Enemies such as the Sadducees, who deny the resurrection, would be especially vicious. Though Lazarus' death proved to be a harmless experience, he had to face it twice. Surely this is on the Lord's mind as well.

CAVE. Wealthy families had private tombs excavated in rock or fashioned from natural cavities in the terrain. The entrances were closed with large stones rolled or slid into place. Rarely were the chambers lower than the doors. Sometimes niches in the walls provided resting places for the bodies. A teaching of the Talmud says that corruption sets in the 3rd day after death, and until that time the spirit hovers over the corpse in case there is a resuscitation. This cave, the costly ointment of Mary, and the big crowd from Jerusalem indicate this family is well to do. Jesus is about to give a command to the servants of the family.

39. "Remove the stone," said Jesus. But Martha, the dead man's sister, protested, "Lord, by now the stench will be terrible. He's a fourth day man!"

PROTESTED. Martha's faith is insufficient to accept Jesus' promise of life for Lazarus. Instead of marvelling at His command to move the stone, she protests His first move to fulfill His word to her. She pictures her brother's putrefying form. She fears the scandal of corruption odor before the big crowd assembled. Her word choice, "fourth day man," a peculiar Greek idiom, shows she is more inclined to believe the Talmud tradition than Jesus. Believing the situation beyond Him, she hesitates to let the servants remove the stone. She still doesn't know Who Jesus really is. He asked her, "Do you believe this?" Though she said, "Yes," we now see she didn't.

"Then Jesus is doing all this to deal with her lack of faith!"

40. Jesus said, "Didn't I tell you that if you would believe, you would see the glory of God!" 41. And so they removed the stone. Then Jesus, looking upward, spoke aloud, "Father I thank You for hearing Me! 42. I know that You always hear Me, but for the sake of this crowd here, I am talking to You like this so that they can believe that You sent Me!"

REMOVED. Jesus' words are stern, almost a reprimand for Martha's failure to believe His word. He had clearly told her Lazarus' sickness was not to end in death (vs. 4). But she is so blinded by circumstances her faith has been overpowered. She needs this sharp word from the Lord. It does the job. Shaking off the stupor of unbelief, she signals the servants to move the stone. Martha's faith is restored BEFORE Lazarus is called back. She responds to the WORD of the Lord as Lazarus will shortly.

THANK YOU. Jesus, via His uninterrupted prayer-life with the Father had already worked out the resurrection details. But this restoration of Martha's faith is a mightier work of the Spirit than restoring Lazarus, as God views things. Jesus looks heavenward to **dramatize** His communion with the Father. The people see it. He speaks aloud permitting them to eavesdrop. These words and the miracle which follows are His credentials that He is from God. He has just demonstrated His **direct communication** with God and is ready to back it up with an amazing sign.

43.   With that He gave out a loud cry, "Come here Lazarus! Out!"   44.   And the dead man came out, his hands and feet securely bound with grave wrappings. His face was also bound with a cloth around it. "Untie him," said Jesus, "and let him go free!"

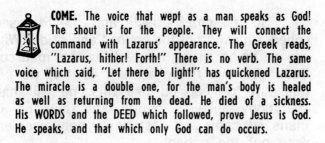

COME. The voice that wept as a man speaks as God! The shout is for the people. They will connect the command with Lazarus' appearance. The Greek reads, "Lazarus, hither! Forth!" There is no verb. The same voice which said, "Let there be light!" has quickened Lazarus. The miracle is a double one, for the man's body is healed as well as returning from the dead. He died of a sickness. His WORDS and the DEED which followed, prove Jesus is God. He speaks, and that which only God can do occurs.

UNTIE. We don't know whether Egyptian style windings (arms and legs separately) were used, or if the sisters wrapped him snugly the night he died. The latter idea has led some commentators to think Lazarus' walking is also a miracle. But Jesus will no more untie him than He would roll away the stone by Himself. That which man can do, God lets him do. And so Lazarus is liberated by human hands that he might return home without help. John leaves it to our imaginations to picture the happy group returning to Bethany. He prefers to pass on to the consequences of the miracle as it affects the ministry of the Lord.

"Surely this miracle had a startling effect on the crowd!"

45. After this, many of the Jews which came out to be with Mary and Martha and saw what Jesus did, believed in Him. 46. But certain ones among them hastened to report to the Pharisees what Jesus had done.

REPORT. Large crowds had come from the city to comfort the sisters during the mourning, hoping to win them back to Judaism. But Jesus' words and miracle turn most of them to Christ. This dramatic shift in events is a shock to those remaining hostile to Jesus. They rush to inform the Sanhedrin. With the Lord now convincing large numbers of Jews, splitting the Pharisee party, He is a dangerous threat. These are not the common people (the so called "rabble"), but important wealthy upper class residents of the city. The tide has turned in Jesus' favor. A public acclamation appears likely.

"That ought to spur the rulers to open action against the Lord!"

47. So the chief priests and the Pharisees called a meeting of the council and said, "What are we doing sitting here letting this man continue with his many signs? 48. If we permit him to keep on like this, he will have everybody believing in him. And then the Romans will come and destroy our holy place and wipe out the nation!"

COUNCIL. Panic occurs within the Sanhedrin. An emergency session convenes to meet the danger of Jesus' rising popularity. With the raising of Lazarus at the city gates, it now appears Jesus could sweep the population before Him in their enthusiasm over His miracles. It is no longer a question of legalities now, the safety of the nation is at stake. They had asked the Lord for a sign and now they have a whopper convulsing the crowds. They fear a revolt against their authority and Rome, which could bring legions from Damascus to destroy the city. They must now take action on some basis other than Jesus' defiance of the Sabbath Law.

49. But one of them, Caiaphas, who was High Priest that memorable year, addressed the council. "You don't seem to understand at all what is happening here. 50. Hasn't it occurred to you that it is better to have one man die in order to save the people than to have the whole nation destroyed?"

 CAIAPHAS. He is a Sadducee. The Sadducees deny the resurrection of the dead. With the raising of Lazarus (a "fourth day" man) they are very much a part of this meeting. Caiaphas is ready to give aggressive leadership. He was High Priest for 18 years and in office "that year" when Jesus died. His scheming mind offers a quick solution—get rid of the disturber—but not on religious grounds. Do it in the national interest. Make it a government act and thus change it from a supercrime to a good deed done for the sake of the people. It has long been the council's purpose to kill Jesus out of hate, only now does it occur to them to cover the crime by performing it in the national interest. A Sadducee conceives the idea—**with the Spirit's help.**

"Caiaphas spoke more truly than he realized, didn't he!"

51. Actually he didn't say this entirely on his own impulse. Since he was in the High Priest's office that year, he was also prophesying that Jesus was to die for the nation, 52. and it wasn't for that nation only that He died, but to bring together into one people all the children of God scattered throughout the world.

 PROPHESYING. Caiaphas, of course, didn't realize he was being used to make a heavenly announcement. His intention was purely wicked. But the Spirit used his office as head of God's visible people for the prediction. It pleased God to have the official announcement come via these evil lips. John adds a comment to insure the benefits of Christ's death are not limited to the Jewish nation. Jesus died, says John, "for the sins of the whole world" (1st John 2:2). Writing years after the city had been destroyed, John refers to the Jews as a "nation," not a people. He uses a different Greek word to speak of them as a **nation among nations.** Israel is a "nation" today, no longer the people of God. Christians are the people of God, gathered on the basis of Jesus' death (1 Peter 2:9).

"Did Caiaphas' suggestion appeal to both the Pharisees and Sadducees!"

53. From that day on they cooperated with each other planning just how they might kill Jesus. 54. Therefore Jesus made no more public appearances among the Jews. He withdrew with His disciples to the edge of the Judean desert, staying at a place called Ephraim.

EPHRAIM. It is no longer safe for Jesus to appear openly without prematurely sacrificing Himself. Panic has united the council in the task of killing. All that remains is HOW it should be done. With His presence also endangering Lazarus' family, Jesus withdraws to a village about 15 miles N.E. of Jerusalem, overlooking the Jordan valley. From here He can see the Passover caravan as it comes down from the North. He and His disciples will join it near Jericho to begin the last trip into Jerusalem. The countryside is notified by the council to give information on Jesus' whereabouts on pain of excommunication. The cross is now about 30 or 40 days away.

"After the raising of Lazarus, isn't everyone eager to see Jesus!"

55. The Jewish Passover was now approaching and many people journeyed from the countryside to go up to Jerusalem and receive ceremonial cleansing before the Passover feast

began. 56. They expected to see Jesus there. As they gathered in the temple, they began to inquire of one another, "What do you think, will He come to the feast or won't He?" 57. It was widely known that the chief priests and Pharisees had issued a mandate that anyone who knew the whereabouts of Jesus should report it, so they could arrest Him.

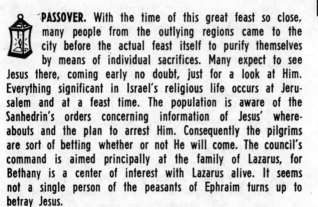

PASSOVER. With the time of this great feast so close, many people from the outlying regions came to the city before the actual feast itself to purify themselves by means of individual sacrifices. Many expect to see Jesus there, coming early no doubt, just for a look at Him. Everything significant in Israel's religious life occurs at Jerusalem and at a feast time. The population is aware of the Sanhedrin's orders concerning information of Jesus' whereabouts and the plan to arrest Him. Consequently the pilgrims are sort of betting whether or not He will come. The council's command is aimed principally at the family of Lazarus, for Bethany is a center of interest with Lazarus alive. It seems not a single person of the peasants of Ephraim turns up to betray Jesus.

"When did Jesus leave the countryside to return to Jerusalem for the last time!"

12 1. Six days before the Passover, Jesus came to Bethany, the village of Lazarus whom He had raised from the dead. 2. Here they prepared a banquet in His honor. While Martha served, Lazarus joined Jesus at the table.

PASSOVER. This year Jesus will be offered as God's Lamb in accord with the High Priest's announcement. He left Ephraim to join the paschal caravan on Friday, meeting it no doubt at Jericho. The happy throng journeyed to the Mt. of Olives where they would rest, for the next day was the Sabbath. Bethany is in the neighborhood of the Mt. of Olives. After the legal Sabbath time passes, Jesus and His disciples go to the home of Simon the leper. Here a dinner is held in His honor. The trophies of His power are with Him at the table, Lazarus (resurrected) on one side, Simon (healed) on the other. It is a happy time of praise and thanksgiving.

3.   And then Mary brought out a whole pound of very expensive perfume and poured it over Jesus' feet and wiped them with her hair. The fragrance of the perfume was such that it saturated the entire house.

MARY. Mary enters the room, bearing a sealed flask. She breaks it open. The fragrance is fantastic, fit for an emperor. As per the custom of refreshing travelers, Mary anointed Jesus' head. But then John reports a detail Mark and Matthew omit, she also anoints His feet. Using her hair (her glory), she wipes His feet. This was an amazing act of devotion, amounting to great honor conferred upon Jesus. God was pleased to have this precious event occur just prior to Judas' treachery. The odor of royalty saturated the house and perhaps even to the countryside. It is hard for us to conceive the value of this act, for we do not count oriental perfumes among our family treasures. To use a full pound in such fashion was unheard of, no matter how wealthy a person might be. Water, which was scarce, was always considered sufficient for washing feet.

4.   At this, Judas Iscariot, one of His disciples —the one who was going to betray Jesus— when he saw this, burst out,   5.   "Why wasn't this perfume sold? It could have brought three hundred pieces of silver which could have been given to the poor!"   6.   Now he said this not out of any concern for the poor, but because he was a thief. As treasurer of the Twelve, he

was used to helping himself to the funds in the money box!

 JUDAS. Judas' first recorded words are a hypocritical protest against squandering this rare perfume on Jesus. He has no love for the Lord, his disaffection already beginning at another feast. Like Satan, his real master, he cloaks his evil intent behind a noble suggestion. The Holy Spirit tells us he cared not for the poor—he loved money (mammon). A shrewd businessman, he instantly calculates the perfume's worth—a year's wages for a working man. Nobody challenged his estimate, the exotic fragrance had already created the atmosphere of a royal courtroom. Mary lavished 300 pieces of silver on Jesus' feet, Judas sold Him for thirty. It is to the praise of Jesus that He said and did nothing to give away the true identity of this evil man among the Twelve.

7. "Let her alone!" replied Jesus to this outburst. "Isn't it enough that she has sacrificed to keep this for the day of preparation in advance of my burial! 8. You will always have the poor with you, but you will not always have Me!"

DAY OF PREPARATION. Mary does this act of devotion in silence, but Jesus explains it for us. Sensing His approaching death as a sacrifice, she anoints His body for burial. Others will anoint Him after death, she 6 days before. That's what makes it an act of faith. To the Lord her act means, "I know, I understand what lies ahead of You!" The cost meant nothing to her when it came to honoring Him. She lavished the family treasure on Him while she could. He wouldn't be there in the morning. Others will be treating Him like a King on the morrow. Jesus therefore rebukes Judas, though indirectly. He uses a plural pronoun and addresses the Twelve, for Judas' words had caused them to grumble also (Mark 14:4). Jesus acknowledges Mary's sacrifice by declaring a perpetual memorial in her honor.

"**What happened when word of Jesus' presence got around!**"

9. When the masses who resided in Jerusalem heard that Jesus was back in the vicinity, they came out to Bethany, not only to see Jesus, but to get a glimpse of Lazarus whom He had raised from the dead. 10. This caused the chief priests to plot against the life of Lazarus as well, 11. for on account of him, many of the Jews were going over to Jesus and putting their faith in Him.

PLOT. Word of Lazarus' resurrection swept through Judea. It was the sensation of the hour. When news reached the city that Jesus had returned to Bethany, the residents streamed forth for a look. With the Passover at hand, Jesus' return triggered overwhelming excitement and expectation in the people. It could only mean one thing to the masses—the hour of deliverance had come. With Lazarus a living memorial to the miraculous power of Jesus, the "counsel of blood" must find a way to get rid of him too. The Sadducees would especially be interested in killing Lazarus for he cancelled their doctrine. With this great upsurge of the people, Judaism is now in great danger.

"**Isn't it just about time for Jesus to go into the city!**"

12. The next day, a great crowd of the caravan pilgrims, who had gone on into the city for the feast, when they heard that Jesus was coming into Jerusalem, 13. went out to meet Him. They seized palm branches as they went and waved them shouting, "Hosanna: Blessed is He who comes in the Name of the Lord, even the King of Israel!"

KING. It is now Sunday. Jesus, thronged about by the residents of the city, starts toward Jerusalem. The bulk of the caravan had gone on into the city to join the other early arrivals (John 11:55). Then word is flashed that Jesus' party is approaching. The city is almost emptied as the crowds rush forth. This time Jesus doesn't spurn the attempt to make Him King. And it has a magical effect on the Galileans, whom He before refused. A new excitement fills the air. The people are filled with tumultuous joy. The decrees of the council are now futile in the face of this frenzy. However, it seems that none but Mary suspected He was coming as the sacrificial Lamb for this Passover.

BRANCHES. The road from Bethany into the city was lined with date palms, regarded from ancient times as the emblem of Israel. Luke mentions the strewing of the branches before Him. But John reports the people's shouting, noting the resurrection excitement. It is a rapturous moment. The Hosannas (mean: "Deliver now!" — the people believe the hour of their freedom from the Romans is at hand) will increase as the cheering crowd gets closer to the city. This is the 10th of the Jewish month of Nisam and the Paschal Lamb was to be "kept up until the 14th day of the same month." And then the whole congregation is to kill it in the evening. Jesus will die on schedule.

14. For Jesus had found a young donkey and sat on it, precisely as the Scripture said He would:

15. "Do not be afraid any longer, daughter of Zion:
See! Your King is coming, riding a young donkey."

16. At the time His disciples didn't understand the meaning of this, but after Jesus had been raised in glory, they remembered that the Scripture had said this about Him, and how they had carried out certain prophetic acts for Him (Matt. 21:4-7).

SCRIPTURES. A prophetic moment has arrived. Jacob said He **would come,** Daniel told **when** (even to the day), Zechariah told **how,** even to the donkey. And Jesus' ministry suddenly shifts. No longer does He avoid public acclaim, no longer does He refuse to be identified as Messiah. But even His disciples fail to see prophecy converging that day, they think it all happens by accident. Once again they are swept up on the fervor of king-fever! John would have us see the CONTRAST between the great **homage** paid Jesus and His humble equipment—a **donkey.** It should have been obvious that a king entering Jerusalem in such low fashion HAD NOT come to expel the Romans. Great men and kings rode only horses in those times.

17. This amazing reception was brought about by the testimonies of the crowd which had been with Jesus when He called Lazarus from the tomb, raising him out of death. 18. This explains why so many rushed out to meet Him —they had heard how He had performed this amazing sign. 19. Consequently when the Pharisees saw all this, they began remarking to one another—"See? We're not getting anywhere! The whole world is running after Him!"

EXPLAINS. John insists the resurrection of Lazarus is the real reason for the crowd's behavior. The city is all but deserted as Jesus' cortege approaches the gates. No one is thinking straight. Even the Pharisees hopelessly think all is lost. Behind this sweeping reception of Christ is the nation's passion for a deliverer—a Savior from the Romans, not from sin. The miraculous power of Jesus as evidenced by Lazarus, leads the people to think they have their long awaited King at last! As the Sanhedrin looks out the window upon this sight, it would appear the entire nation has been moved from their grasp. But the treachery of Judas is to save the day for them.

"Will John relate anything of Jesus' public ministry in the city following the jubilant entry?"

20. Now among those who had come to Jerusalem to worship during the feast, were some Gentiles, God-fearing Greeks. 21. They approached Philip, who was from Bethsaida in Galilee, with a request. "Sir" they said, "we would like to see Jesus." 22. Philip consulted with Andrew and the two of them then went to Jesus with the request.

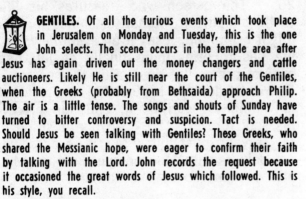

GENTILES. Of all the furious events which took place in Jerusalem on Monday and Tuesday, this is the one John selects. The scene occurs in the temple area after Jesus has again driven out the money changers and cattle auctioneers. Likely He is still near the court of the Gentiles, when the Greeks (probably from Bethsaida) approach Philip. The air is a little tense. The songs and shouts of Sunday have turned to bitter controversy and suspicion. Tact is needed. Should Jesus be seen talking with Gentiles? These Greeks, who shared the Messianic hope, were eager to confirm their faith by talking with the Lord. John records the request because it occasioned the great words of Jesus which followed. This is his style, you recall.

23. Then Jesus replied, "The time has now come for the Son of Man to enter into His glory. 24. In all truth I tell you: a grain of wheat will forever remain a grain of wheat unless it falls into the ground and dies. But if it does then it will bring forth a harvest of many more grains."

GLORY. Jesus answers the Greeks by addressing His disciples in their hearing. At this moment it is important that He withhold from His enemies every pretext for reproach. The Jews merely tolerated the converted Greeks. We know the Greeks hear Him for He answers with a miracle of nature well-suited to their philosophical ears. It was His custom to answer the Jews with their own Scriptures. The request of the Greeks stabbed the Lord with thoughts of His death. His spirit churns in agony as the hour seems to rush upon Him. Yet He sees beyond His death. These Greeks are a preview of the Gentile world which will come to Him as part of His glorification. Until the cross, Gentiles are isolated from the promises of God. The glory of a seed is the abundance it produces AFTER it dies. Thus Jesus is speaking **beyond** His death to picture His own glory as a harvest—a harvest of souls!

"How will Jesus apply this profound truth of dying to live!"

25. "The person who treasures his life on earth, clinging to human existence for what it might bring him, loses it all eventually. All this life has to offer must finally be left behind, everyone dies in time. But the person who learns to despise his earthly life, so that he is willing to sacrifice it, ends up preserving his soul forever. 26. Anyone desiring to be My servant must follow Me. If he does, he will not only be with Me wherever I am, but he will also be honored by The Father.

 LIFE. Man can look upon earthly life in two ways: as something to be prized desperately, or sacrificed for Christ. Those sacrificing their lives for the sake of the future, follow the example of Jesus and are trading human life for divine. The Greeks asked to see Jesus, but if they want to BE WITH Him, they must heed the grain-dying principle. Jesus will be surrounded in the future by those to whom His death gives divine life. It isn't a bad trade for it brings (1) eternal life (2) companionship with Christ (3) sharing in Christ's glory, honored by The Father. There is no shortcut. Death to self is required of all who expect to enjoy life after death. In its weakest sense it means the sacrificing of fame, family and fortune for Jesus. In its maximum sense, it means the loss of one's life in living for Christ.

"Surely all this talk of dying couldn't be pleasant for the Lord!"

27. "Now the anguish of My hour is upon

Me, My soul aches with the agony of temptation. 'Father, exempt Me from this hour!' That's what I feel like saying. But I can't. The very reason I came was to face this hour!"

ANGUISH. Jesus has been in death row for 3½ years. The cross is now 48 hours away. He has known exalted moments, also stabbing ones like this. The request of the Greeks reminds Him of the horror awaiting when He will "become sin for us," and "taste death for every man." The King of Glory is a sad figure, shuddering in anticipation of the moment when, as the Sinless One, He will have "laid on Him the iniquity of us all!" What is the alternative? Ask for exemption? Cancel the cross? Unthinkable! That's why He came. John, who omits the garden scene, gives us this little Gethsemene. The experience of Gethsemene was more than a garden to Jesus, it was the whole ROAD to Calvary. Yet the alternative is even worse. For unless Jesus died for us, God would remain an isolated "grain of wheat" forever!

28. "Father! Reveal the majesty of Your Name!" At that, a voice came from heaven . . . "I have revealed it and I will reveal it again!" 29. Thereupon the multitude which stood there listening declared that it had thundered. But some of them said, "An angel has spoken to Him!" 30. "This voice," explained Jesus, "spoke not for My sake, but for yours."

VOICE. Instead of a reprieve, Jesus asks the Father to proceed with the redemption plan. God replies, "I will." The people hear Him. When God speaks through a man, He uses that man's vocal chords. When He speaks through nature, He uses nature's vocal chords—thunder. According to the disposition of the people (their spiritual temperament), they would comprehend the sound. We observe 3 kinds of hearing (not sounds): (1) articulate speech by Jesus and His disciples, (2) the ring of angelic words, by those with somewhat susceptible hearts, (3) inarticulate thunderings by the insusceptible masses. Similar gradation can be noted in Paul's Damascus road experience.

REVEAL. When God says, "I have glorified it," He likely refers to the progressive revelation of Himself through **ancient Israel** first, then through the Person of Christ. When He says, "I will glorify it," He speaks of the future revelation of Himself through **the church** based on Jesus' death. Those hearing the angelic voices were probably the susceptible Greeks, with this becoming the confirmation they sought when they asked to see Jesus. The voice was not for Jesus or His disciples, they didn't need it. The thunderous sounds no doubt registered as the "voice of doom" upon the unbelieving Jews.

"Did Jesus interpret or explain the significance of this voice from heaven!"

31.   "Sentence is now passed upon this world, because the ruler of this world is destined to be cast out."

RULER. The fate of any kingdom rests with its ruler. With Satan consigned to perdition, the destiny of his followers is also determined. The "world" is the entire kingdom of Satan as the "god of this world" (2 Cor. 4:4), the unbelieving Jews included. Satan's expulsion is not a single event. He was first cast from God's presence (Luke 10:18), his hold on mankind broken at the cross (because Jesus provides a way out of his kingdom) (Col. 2:15), he is yet to be cast out of the spirit world and forced to operate in a body (Rev. 12:10). He will be cast into the bottomless pit for a time (Rev. 20:3), then finally cast into the lake of fire (Rev. 20:10). Getting Jesus to acknowledge him was his only hope of escape from perdition. He said, "Worship me and I'll give you the kingdoms of the world and you won't have to die."—Jesus says, "No!" His death on the cross seals Satan's fate (Gen. 3:15). The devil's last hope vanishes with the cross. Now Satan is in death row.

32.   "Now as for Myself, when I am lifted up from the earth, I shall draw all men unto Me."
33.   In saying this, He indicated the kind of death He was going to suffer.

LIFTED UP. The double-meaning of this verb continues, i.e., exalted to a throne or hoisted on a jibbet, though the Spirit now draws attention to the latter meaning. Yet the crucifixion is to be an exaltation for it dethrones the "god of this world." Thus, the Savior crucified is also the Savior glorified! The cross is not a defeat, but a victory. See also that it is Christ, HIMSELF, not the cross which draws men. The Greek indicates the EGO of the Lord attracts men. A corpse on a cross is hardly attractive, but a risen Lord is most inviting. As the Greek verb revealed Satan's casting out to be gradual, the Lord's drawing of all men is also gradual, rather than sudden.

DRAW. With the Lord's death providing a righteousness which makes it possible for sinners to fellowship with God, they can leave Satan's realm and live with God— **if they want to.** The Lord Himself means to woo the hearts of men personally. But how exactly? He plans to return in spirit form. People who return as spirits, after death, we call ghosts. It is as the Holy Ghost that Jesus will woo men and build His church (Matt. 16:18). **Outwardly,** His method will be men. That is, men will invite men. Yet **inwardly,** He Himself will bear witness to the invitation and take up residence in every willing heart. The Great Commission authorizes us to participate in that adventure. John will devote chapters 14, 15 and 16 to Jesus' ministry in the Spirit. The "Grain of Wheat" does not plan to live alone eternally.

"How did the Jews react to Jesus' forecast of His death by crucifixion!"

34.   Once more stumbling over His words, the multitude challenged, "Our Law says that Christ is supposed to live forever! What do you mean then by saying the Son of Man must be lifted up? If this is true, Who then is the Son of Man?"

WHO! Jesus has accepted public worship as Messiah. A voice from heaven confirmed it. It is hard to deny Him now. But then He says He is going to die violently. The crowd is shocked. Their Messianic tradition held that Messiah's arrival would be final and establish an eternal government (Psa. 110:4; Isa. 9:7). The hard-hearted ones who heard the thunder now have a way out, a loophole. Further, He has again shifted from the Messiah acclamation to the "Son of Man," expression for Himself. They can now take this as saying He is NOT Messiah. But Who then is He? They demand an explanation of this Son of Man. He ignores their theological problem, preferring instead to warn them.

35.   Jesus answered them, "The Light is still among you, but not for very long. You'd better do what you can while you still have light to see by. It will be too late once darkness comes upon you, for the man who walks in darkness has no idea of where he is going.   36a.   Trust in the Light while you still have It that you may become the sons of Light."

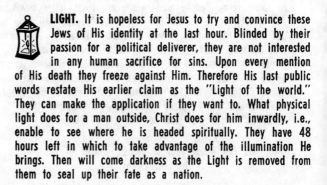

LIGHT. It is hopeless for Jesus to try and convince these Jews of His identity at the last hour. Blinded by their passion for a political deliverer, they are not interested in any human sacrifice for sins. Upon every mention of His death they freeze against Him. Therefore His last public words restate His earlier claim as the "Light of the world." They can make the application if they want to. What physical light does for a man outside, Christ does for him inwardly, i.e., enable to see where he is headed spiritually. They have 48 hours left in which to take advantage of the illumination He brings. Then will come darkness as the Light is removed from them to seal up their fate as a nation.

36b.   This was all Jesus would say to them. After that He went into hiding.

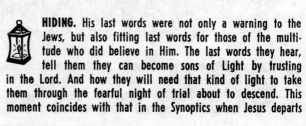

HIDING. His last words were not only a warning to the Jews, but also fitting last words for those of the multitude who did believe in Him. The last words they hear, tell them they can become sons of Light by trusting in the Lord. And how they will need that kind of light to take them through the fearful night of trial about to descend. This moment coincides with that in the Synoptics when Jesus departs from the temple to go to Bethany with His disciples. He will spend the last two days of His pre-cross life surrounded by His friends. It is now toward evening on Tuesday. Late Thursday afternoon He will return to Jerusalem to celebrate the Passover.

"Now that Jesus' public ministry has ended, how might one summarize the effect of all He said and did among the Jews!"

37. In spite of all the many signs which Jesus performed before the people, they would not believe in Him. 38. Their attitude toward Him was precisely as Isaiah prophesied it would be . . . when he said . . .

"Lord, is there anyone who has believed our message, among those to whom the power of God has been made known?" (Isa. 53:1).

SIGNS. From here to the end of the chapter, John summarizes the **public** ministry of the Lord and the results. No other evangelist does this. Looking backwards from the end of the century, John reflects on the claims and miracles of Jesus to consider how fruitless it all seemed to be. The condition of God's nation was no different in Jesus' time, than in the days of Isaiah. Isaiah's prediction of the hardness of Jewish hearts in the days of Messiah was correct. So far, John has listed eight great signs of the Lord and six of His claims to Deity. In spite of all that Jesus has said and done, the bulk of the Jewish people have refused to believe in Him. The cross and resurrection, the greatest of all, is yet to come.

39. The fact is, the people couldn't believe in Him. That too was as Isaiah said it would be . . .

40. **"He has blinded their eyes and clouded their minds, lest they should see with their eyes and perceive with their minds and turn to Me that I should heal them"** (Isa. 6:10).

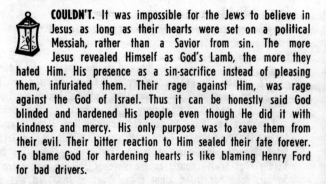

BLINDED. On the surface it sounds as if God performs spiritual surgery upon the eyes and hearts of people directly. But not so. God hardens hearts indirectly— by revelation. He reveals Himself in accordance with the faith-principle: supplying sufficient evidence for faith to operate but never enough to convince the unbelieving mind. Reaction to His revelation is determined by what is ALREADY in a person's heart, i.e., the predisposition to faith. The same revelation which hardens one heart, can tenderize another. As God's rain brings up either weeds or grain, depending on what is **already** in the soil, so His revelation brings out what is **already** in the soul. Pharaoh is the classic example of a heart hardened by revelation.

COULDN'T. It was impossible for the Jews to believe in Jesus as long as their hearts were set on a political Messiah, rather than a Savior from sin. The more Jesus revealed Himself as God's Lamb, the more they hated Him. His presence as a sin-sacrifice instead of pleasing them, infuriated them. Their rage against Him, was rage against the God of Israel. Thus it can be honestly said God blinded and hardened His people even though He did it with kindness and mercy. His only purpose was to save them from their evil. Their bitter reaction to Him sealed their fate forever. To blame God for hardening hearts is like blaming Henry Ford for bad drivers.

41. Isaiah was speaking of Christ when he said these things, for it was His glory he had seen.

GLORY. This is an incredible verse. When the ancient prophet had his vision of the Lord "sitting upon a throne, high and lifted up," and heard the angelic, "Holy Holy Holy," he was beholding the glory of Christ. The understanding of John the evangelist has been opened by the Holy Spirit to realize that the amazing passage of Isaiah 6:1-5 refers **directly** to Jesus. The blessed Trinity appeared to Isaiah. The glory of the Trinity is here called the glory of Christ. There is but ONE GLORY of the Trinity, therefore the glory of the Father is at once the glory of the Son and the glory of the Holy Ghost. Our souls stagger before the truth that the Carpenter of Galilee is King Jehovah of the Old Testament as well as the invisible Ruler in the sanctuary of the human heart in the New Testament.

"How about the educated rulers, who knew the Scriptures and saw how Christ fulfilled them, didn't any of them believe in Him!"

42.   Now there were many of the rulers who had come to believe in Him, that is, they were convinced of His identity. Even so they refused to acknowledge Him on account of the Pharisees. They feared to side with Jesus lest they be banned from the synagogue.   43.   They prized their standing in the eyes of men more than they desired the approval of God.

BELIEVED. We must not be deceived by the use of this word in the N.T. (John 7:47, 48). Here it represents the worst form of unbelief—**clear-sighted** refusal of Christ for carnal reasons. These leaders, and note the "many" of them, knew the Scriptures and understood how perfectly Christ fulfilled them. In spite of such conviction, they deliberately preferred the glory of man to the glory of God. Favor in the sight of their comrades meant more than favor in God's sight. This knowledgeable opposition to Jesus deserves the strongest indictment of all. These are worse than the "blind" Isaiah describes, for they "see." Passion does not obscure their vision. Their choice is willful. 48 hours earlier these "many rulers" were scheming and plotting Jesus' death. Had many of them truly believed, they would have overturned the decision of the council. Nicodemus is the only possible believer we know of so far.

"Should there have been any doubt as to Who Jesus claimed to be!"

44.   Jesus cried out, "The man who believes in Me, is actually believing in God rather than in Me.   45.   And the one who sees Me as I really am, is beholding the One Who sent Me!"

 CRIED OUT. John now summarizes the **claims** of Christ. The words "cried out," do not mean He made further appearances among the people, but indicate the urgency and emotion with which He has pleaded with Israel. Essentially He taught that faith in Himself was faith in God, as if there were no Christ. Jesus declared Himself a MEANS of revelation, just as a WORD is the means of transferring an idea. He is the Word of God. So perfectly is our Savior's HUMAN appearance a manifestation of God's glory, that faith in Him amounted to faith in the One Who sent Him. How crystal clear is our Lord's claim to Deity in these verses, yet how selfless was He in making the claim!

46.   "I have come as Light into the world, so that no one who believes in Me has to continue in darkness.   47.   However, if anyone hears My message and fails to heed it, I won't judge him for it. I didn't come as a Judge, I came to save the world.   48.   He who rejects Me, refusing My message, already has a judge. The very words which I have spoken will stand against him in that day, accusing and condemning him."

LIGHT. Jesus also warned Israel of the consequences of refusing Him. Inasmuch as He was a SHINING OF GOD and not a separate Light, men beholding Him were contemplating the very Source of spiritual light—GOD! As a shining of the true Light, Jesus was God's invitation to men to come and dwell in the Light. Put another way, it meant to come and be a member of the family of Light, God's Household. Yet there was nothing about the shining of Christ to **compel** people to leave the darkness. They can remain in darkness if they prefer and He won't judge them for it. He doesn't have to. Refusal of God's invitation amounts to self-exclusion from the divine family. In the Judgment Day, God's **spurned invitation** will stand as incriminating evidence against all unbelievers.

49. "And this is so because I have not spoken on My own authority. The words I have spoken did not originate with Me. The One Who sent Me, The Father Himself, gave commandment as to what I should say, even the very message I was to bring. 50. Therefore everything I have uttered, I have spoken precisely as The Father has bidden Me, and I know His command is—eternal life!"

WORDS. Jesus disclaims personal initiative for His words, declaring that His messages have proceeded from God via His lips. Thus, people hearing Him are really hearing the Father. This is why He is the Logos (Word) of God. John has now summed the **public** ministry of Jesus as a perfect revelation of The Father in the WORKS of Christ, the WORDS of Christ and the PERSON of Christ. Those embracing Jesus are actually embracing the Father. People shunning Him, spurn the Father. From now on Jesus' teaching will be confined to private sessions with His disciples. Israel as a nation has had 3½ years to receive her Messiah.

COMMAND. God sent Jesus to SAVE. He came for the sake of others, not Himself. God commanded Him to SAVE men. This was the **purpose** of His mission. Therefore God's commandment to Jesus meant eternal life for men. Inasmuch as Jesus is the perfect revelation of the Father, there is no way to approach God and by-pass Him. Those who don't want Jesus, don't want the Father. Those who love Jesus, already love the Father. How remarkable that so pure a revelation of God can be found in a being so purely human—Jesus Christ! Is this not a clue to the nature of man and his ability to participate in the Godhead? Indeed!

"With His public ministry over, will Jesus now concentrate on teaching deeper things to His disciples!"

13 1. Even before it was time for the Paschal feast, Jesus was fully aware the moment had arrived for Him to make the transition from this world to the Father. Yet, so completely did He love His own which were in the world, nothing could keep Him from going the limit for them, 2a. even though the devil had successfully planted the idea of betraying Jesus in the heart of Judas Iscariot, the son of Simon.

LIMIT. When Jesus leaves Bethany to keep the Passover at Jerusalem with His disciples, He knows death awaits. During the meal the betrayer will finalize his decision. Aware of this, Jesus goes anyway. Loving His disciples to the limit, He is ready to lay down His life for them. This last meal together will be expensive for Him, the price being the cross. Since there is "no greater love than this . . ." it amounts to a love-feast as well as a Passover celebration. Jesus and the Twelve gather in an upper room shortly before the Jewish Friday which begins at six o'clock Thursday evening. It will carry over into the night of the Passover.

2b. Now during the supper, 3. Jesus, knowing full well that the Father had committed the entire redemption program into His hands, and that He had come forth from God and was going back to God, 4. rose from the table. First He took off His outer garment. Then, taking a towel, He girded Himself with it.

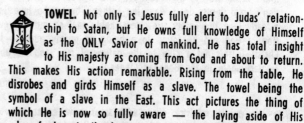

TOWEL. Not only is Jesus fully alert to Judas' relationship to Satan, but He owns full knowledge of Himself as the ONLY Savior of mankind. He has total insight to His majesty as coming from God and about to return. This makes His action remarkable. Rising from the table, He disrobes and girds Himself as a slave. The towel being the symbol of a slave in the East. This act pictures the thing of which He is now so fully aware — the laying aside of His robe of glory in the heavens to stoop to the depths of shame for those He loved to the limit. This dramatization of His spiritual humiliation is Part I of an amazing object lesson. The treachery brooding in Judas' breast doesn't deter Him a bit.

"Wow! That must have gotten their attention!"

5. Then He poured some water into a basin and began to wash the disciples' feet, drying them with the towel about His waist.

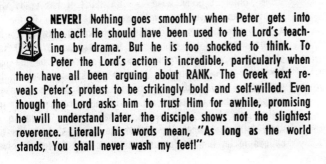

WASH. The washing of feet should have been cared for before the meal. Apparently there was no host to see that the disciples' feet were washed, neither were any slaves about. No disciple volunteered the job. Luke says they were too busy arguing who was the greatest among them since the lowest in rank would inherit the task (Luke 22:24). The absence of slaves no doubt kindled their struggle for preeminence. When their debate was the hottest, Jesus arose from the table to assume the role of a slave. The room was instantly silent. Then He brought Part II of His lesson, bending to the task they shunned. He washed their feet! How the disciples must have blushed! Likely He began with Judas.

6. Shortly it was Simon Peter's turn. "Lord," exclaimed Peter, "You would wash my feet?" 7. "Right now," answered Jesus, "you don't understand what I am doing, but later on you will." 8a. "Never, ever, will I let You wash my feet," avowed Peter.

NEVER! Nothing goes smoothly when Peter gets into the act! He should have been used to the Lord's teaching by drama. But he is too shocked to think. To Peter the Lord's action is incredible, particularly when they have all been arguing about RANK. The Greek text reveals Peter's protest to be strikingly bold and self-willed. Even though the Lord asks him to trust Him for awhile, promising he will understand later, the disciple shows not the slightest reverence. Literally his words mean, "As long as the world stands, You shall never wash my feet!"

"Surely the Lord didn't appreciate that!"

8b. "If I do not wash you," warned Jesus, "you cannot have fellowship with Me!" 9. "If that's the case, Lord," said Peter, "wash not only my feet, but my hands and face too!"

 FELLOWSHIP. Peter's continued refusal would have ended his disciple relationship with Jesus, for the Lord made it dependent upon this single point. First the idea of the Lord washing his feet was intolerable, but then the thought of broken fellowship with Christ was even more intolerable. So Peter goes to the other extreme, offering the Lord all the uncovered portions of his body. He is saying, "If washing my feet means fellowship with You, don't stop there. Wash the rest of me too!" Peter is still not tenderly submissive. He is dictatorial and the Lord must deal with him further.

10. But Jesus corrected him, "A man who is bathed is completely clean, with the exception of his feet. And all of you are so cleansed — that is, all except one." 11. The reason Jesus said, "all except one," was because He knew who His betrayer was.

 BATHED. The Lord now turns Peter's blustering mistake to good account and the result is a rich lesson in Christian fellowship with God. Jesus introduces a different Greek word — "BATHED." It has to do with washing the entire body with water. The picture is that of a man walking from the bathing pool (Roman custom) to the dressing room. After robing, his feet only are WASHED (another Greek word) to remove the dust contracted on the path from the pool. "Bathed," therefore speaks of salvation, the washing of regeneration. "Washed," speaks of the believer's frequent rinsing (by confession) of the sins accumulated in his daily walk. Jesus is therefore dramatizing the cleansing of daily defilement when He washed the disciples' feet. We are obliged to let Him do for us what we cannot do for ourselves.

EXCEPT. The Lord hints at His betrayer when He says, "except one." Judas is neither "bathed" nor "washed," even though Jesus applies water to his feet. External washings merely symbolize spiritual washings within the heart. Judas has NO spiritual washings of any kind. Peter was "bathed." "Bathed" Christians need daily "washings." There must be cleansing before communion. Saved sinners must exercise constant cleansing (via confession . . . 1st John 1:9), if they would fellowship with God. Jesus is teaching that truth when He warns Peter that continued fellowship with Him depends on His washing of his feet.

"Will Jesus go on to explain the two-fold object lesson He has just brought!"

12. After washing their feet and putting His garments back on, Jesus returned to His place at the table. Then He asked, "Do you understand what I have just done to you? 13. You call Me Teacher and Master, and rightly so, for that is precisely what I am."

UNDERSTAND. His question is calculated to summon their attention. He will give the answer. He begins by referring to their respect for Him as "Teacher" (the One from Whom they **learn**), and "Master" (the One Whom they must obey). Learning must precede obedience. In claiming these titles, Jesus again shows His awareness of His dignity. He has now laid aside the servant's towel to resume His place as "The Teacher" and "The Master." He is about to make an application of the humility and service He has demonstrated. But He first returns to a position of rank and authority before doing so. This adds great force to the words which follow.

14. "If I then, Who am The Teacher and The Master, washed your feet, you ought also to be willing to wash each other's feet. 15. I have given you an example which teaches you to do as I have done."

EXAMPLE. The real example of the Lord is NOT literal footwashing, but the humble service of one Christian to another. Judas would have been included in the blessing otherwise, for his feet were washed. The Lord did not say, do WHAT I have done, but "AS" I have done. If literalism were intended, it would have been pointless for Him to ask, "Do you understand what I have done to you?" He is demonstrating the duty of helping each other with respect to daily defilement and confession. When He says, "as I have done," He is pointing to: (1) the setting aside of **rank** (as He did), and (2) assuming even the lowest place of service for the sake of "one another" (as He did). The **example** they were to remember is that of a Christian serving his brethren — NOT a god stooping to wash his creatures.

 WASH. Literal foot-washing gained ground in the church at a time when **spiritual** foot-washing was disappearing due to the pride, lust and power which came to the leadership of the church. Then it was that popes and emperors began to wash the feet of commoners. It was a one-sided affair with superiors washing inferiors. The Lord clearly said . . . **"each other."** Literal foot-washing is climactic, often having more to do with shoes and socks and ceremonies than **spiritual** defilement. Jesus' example was that of **stooping** to the task of **cleansing** others (spiritual cleansing). The stooping to bring spiritual help to a brother in his daily walk is almost unknown today.

16. "Believe Me," said Jesus, "no servant is greater than his master, and no messenger is greater than the one who sends him. 17. If now you understand the meaning of what I have just taught you, put it into practice so as to enjoy the blessedness of it."

 PRACTICE. It is almost as if the Lord anticipated the establishment of foot-washing ceremonies as a substitute for the humble necessity of helping each other live holy lives. Well did the Master foresee the great error which would arise in the church with the elevation of the clergy. Thus He adds an axiom to reinforce His demand for humility, enjoining the disciples to remember they are not greater than He. If He can stoop to the task, so can they.

His admonition is forgotten ere two centuries pass. Today, doctrinal purity is exalted above personal purity. For reasons of pride entire denominations make doctrinal distinctions the basis of fellowship, rather than membership in the body of Christ. It was to teach humility that the Lord performed this act. Oh, that awful gap between KNOWING and DOING the Lord's commands.

"Did that same blessing also apply to Judas!"

18. "Inasmuch as I know intimately the ones I have chosen, I am not referring to all of you when I say that. It still remains for the Scripture to be fulfilled which says . . .

> **'He who eats bread with Me has stabbed Me in the back' "** (Psa. 41:9).

STABBED. A second time Jesus refers to a traitor in their midst. He is leading up to the announcement that one of their own number is going to betray Him. He quotes a Psalm of David in which he sang of the treachery he suffered at the hand of one of his intimates. Then He applies it to Himself and His betrayer, so that when it occurs, they will know it was prophesied. Surely Judas was staggered to learn a prophecy of Scripture applied specifically to him. "Eats bread with Me," bespeaks the closeness of friendship, while the phrase "stabbed Me in the back," is actually a Greek idiom "lifted his heel against Me" which has to do with delivering an unsuspecting kick against another person. Judas absorbs the meaning of these words.

19. "I am telling you this before it happens, so that when it occurs, you may believe that I AM. 20. Further, you must believe Me when I tell you that he who receives whomever I send, receives Me. And he who receives Me, receives Him that sent Me!"

BEFORE. Jesus pre-arms His disciples. In a few hours Judas' treachery will appear successful. By telling them of it in advance, they can more easily believe it was a part of the divine plan and not be overcome when it happens. Note also, that Jesus is quoting a Messianic Psalm, saying that it applies to Him. Thus He makes another claim to Messiahship. At this point the disciples have no idea who the traitor is, a testimony to Jesus' love for Judas and desire to give him every chance to repent of his evil.

WHOMEVER. Without this advance notice, Judas' treachery could easily crumble the confidence of the disciples. Judas, you recall, went on preaching missions and held healing meetings of his own. The question could be raised, what value was the work he did in Jesus' Name? Gospel effectiveness, Jesus is saying, has to do with the hearer, not the preacher. Does it matter if your mailman is pleasant or mean as long as you get the right letter? Anyone who receives a SENT worker is receiving the sender. Similarly, the sincerity of a servant is immaterial as long as a sinner receives the Word of God. It does its work regardless. In saying that they are sent from Him, as He was sent from the Father, He arms them with authority.

"Will the Lord tell them bluntly that one of them is a traitor!"

21. After He had said this, Jesus suffered convulsive agony deep in His spirit. "Believe Me," He said solemnly, "one of you will betray Me!" 22. Whereupon the disciples began to look at each other in complete mystification. They were at a loss to know which of them He meant.

AGONY. The agony of this moment is even greater than that Jesus suffered by Lazarus' tomb. It was painful for Him to say this. He has been hurt by the crowds, but to have one of His own plot so foully against Him, hurt worse. His eyes fall on the crafty Judas reclining there with the 30 pieces of silver already in his pouch. But the Lord doesn't identify him by name. He will make one last effort to redeem him. Luke tells us there follows a moment during which the mystified disciples inquire, "Lord, is it I?" Even Judas has to ask that so as not to appear suspicious. Matthew tells us that Jesus replied to him, "Thou hast said" (Matt. 26:25). You can imagine the distress piling up inside Judas about this time. It could tenderize his heart.

23. Now it happened that one of Jesus' disciples, whom He loved, was reclining so that his head was close to Jesus' shoulder. 24. So Simon Peter gestured to him, indicating he should ask the Lord which of the disciples He meant? 25. The disciple then leaned back closer to Jesus and whispered, "Lord, who is it?"

 LEANED. The ancients did not eat as we do, but reclined about a low table on couches or divans. They leaned on the left arm, their feet stretched out behind them, with the head of each near the breast of the person on the left. We can suppose that Jesus was between John and Judas, with John on the right. This way John would tilt his head back so as to whisper to Jesus. John never refers to himself directly, preferring to call himself "the disciple Jesus loved." Peter, who was further from the Lord must have caught John's eye, signalling him to inquire of the Lord whom He meant. Judas is taking this all in. What struggles must have occurred in his heart.

"Will Jesus now name His betrayer or will He give him a last chance to repent!"

26. Jesus answered, "It is the one for whom I will dip the bread before I give it to him." So when He had dipped a morsel He handed it to Judas, the son of Simon Iscariot.

 DIP. A dish on the table contained a sauce made of bitter herbs. After the second cup of the Paschal feast was passed, morsels of bread were distributed to all at the table so that they could dip together and recall the bitterness of that night in Egypt. The act of handing some-one a morsel that was **already dipped,** was a token of friend-ship. Thus in giving the betrayer the dipped bread, Jesus re-vealed two things: (1) that He knew the traitor's identity and (2) that Jesus still cared for him. Judas knows he is detected, yet loved. His heart could be melted by this — or hardened. Their eyes meet. Satan is standing by. The appeal to his heart fails. He accepts the bread without hesitation. His mind is made up. His heart is hardened.

27. As soon as Judas received the bread, Satan entered his heart. Then Jesus said to him, "Hurry, get on with what you have to do."

SATAN. The devil has no power to take over anyone without his permission. God has made the human will sovereign. Judas had resigned his WILL entirely to the WILL of Satan. In that moment (receiving the sop) his hardened heart became filled with the spirit of Satan to become his slave. The reverse occurs when a man submits to the Holy Spirit to become the bondslave of Christ. So, filled with the UNHOLY SPIRIT, Judas became the complete tool of the devil. We must not suppose he suddenly behaved as a demoniac, for not all filled with Satan's spirit so behave. He is also "an angel of light" (2 Cor. 11:14, 15). Note how the disciples felt his behavior was perfectly normal (vss. 28-29). Jesus must get rid of him. Not only would He separate Himself from the pain of his presence, but the sooner Judas is gone, the quicker He can open His heart to the confidential circle about Him.

28. Now none of those reclining about the table caught the drift of Jesus' words to Judas. 29. Inasmuch as Judas was in charge of their common treasury, some thought Jesus was tell-ing him to go and buy what they needed for the feast, or else that He was sending him on some alms mission for the poor.

BUY. John tacitly exempts himself as he speaks of the conjectures of his fellow disciples. He knew the intent of Jesus' words, but his remark is meant to show that the disciples didn't yet suspect Judas as a traitor. So they gave another turn to Jesus' words. Since Judas was the cashier, they supposed he was dispatched to buy supplies for the eight-day feast. But at night? Hardly. Nor yet that he would go at night on an alms mission to help needy families secure supplies for the festival. The truth is, they just didn't understand. John would have us see the holy way in which Jesus retained to Himself all knowledge of Judas' treachery. See how Jesus' attitude didn't change even after Judas was Satan-filled. Oh, that we could learn to silence our tongues so that none could learn from us the faults of our brethren.

30. So after taking the bread, Judas went out quickly — into the night!

NIGHT. Whoever goes out from the presence of Christ, goes into the night. Judas went into spiritual darkness to accomplish the work of darkness. But there is something awful about this separation. The hour sticks in John's mind. He wishes to remove any impression that Judas remained to participate in the feast, so he records his exit after the second cup. It is generally agreed by all commentators that Judas left before the Lord's supper. The Lord dispatches Judas on his evil errand so that He will be free to pour out His heart upon "His own." This will be the last moment of intimacy before the cross, and He would cuddle His beloved ones and relax completely with them without the pain of Judas' presence.

"With Judas gone, did Jesus immediately bare His soul to His disciples!"

31. Therefore as soon as Judas went out, Jesus said, "Now is the Son of Man glorified, and God was glorified in Him. 32. If therefore, God has been exalted by the Son's glory,

it remains for God to exalt the Son into Himself. And He will shortly."

NOW. Until Judas left, Jesus spoke under painful restraint. The presence of the betrayer prevented the outpouring of His heart. When Judas departs, the cross is as good as accomplished. The Satan-filled man will see it to the bitter end. Jesus is relieved. Not merely of Judas' presence, but He has triumphed (within His Spirit) over the consequences of the betrayal, His glory in the cross. Jesus glorified the Father by continuing to love Judas, refusing to betray him to the disciples. God's love was manifested when Jesus' heart didn't change, even though Judas yielded to Satan. See how Christian love has regard even for an enemy (Matt. 5:44). The Father, in return, exalts the Son by bringing Him back **into Himself,** i.e., restoring Him to His former glory. Thus Jesus returns to Spirit, since "God is Spirit" (John 4:24). There He resumes His majesty laid aside for the incarnation (Phil. 2:6-8).

SON OF MAN. For the 10th and last time, John records this **human** title of Jesus. This is amazing for the Lord now sees Himself beyond the cross and resurrection, crowned as the Head of the new creation! It was the SON OF GOD Who divested Himself of heaven's regality to enter the human stream **as a servant,** but it is the SON OF MAN Who returns! The Godhead has now acquired HUMAN EXPERIENCE. This truth offers the key to some deep passages ahead. It is also vital to understanding the richness of the life communicated to us by the Holy Spirit. When Jesus speaks of the Comforter (His Replacement) later on, He will have this in mind. By means of the incarnation of Jesus, the Comforter has already been a bondslave.

33. "My little children, I am only going to be with you for a very short time. You are going to miss Me, but I must tell you, even as I told the Jews, 'You cannot go where I am now going.'"

CHILDREN. With Judas gone, the Lord speaks as never before. He looks upon the circle of "His own," with deep affection. They have been together for 3½ years. Now He drops a bombshell of heartache as He tells them He must leave them to begin a different ministry. In the days to come He will be IN them, working THROUGH them. Therefore the little group has reached a time of sad farewell. Oh how they will miss Him after the flesh, so it is with tender pity He calls them "children." Remember how Thomas wished to go to Jerusalem to "die with Him!" (11:16). They prefer death with Him to being left behind — alone. But He cautions them as He did the Jews, "You cannot go where I am going." That, of course, is only a temporary restriction.

34. "So let Me give you a new commandment: love one another. I want you to love each other just as I have loved you. **35.** The distinguishing mark by which all men shall know you as My disciples is the love you show toward each other."

 NEW! Not exactly. The commandment to love one another is as old as the law of God. But HOW to fulfill it is as new as the example of Christ. Not only did the Eleven have the example of Jesus to imitate, soon they would be welded together into one body by the Spirit (I Cor. 12:13). The world cannot recognize disciples by their doctrines and denominations — particularly today when there are so many, but Christian love is unique among all men. None but Christians forgive and bless even their enemies. The world exacts an "eye for an eye." Among the early records of pagan observers, it is said again and again of the First Century Christians, "Behold how they love one another." The degree to which Christians manifest this love toward each other is the degree to which the world may recognize the disciples of Jesus.

"Did the disciples interpret these words as goodbye instructions!"

36. "Where are You going, Lord?" asked Simon Peter. "Where I am going you cannot follow Me now," answered Jesus, "though later on you will follow Me." 37. "Lord," said Peter, "why can't I follow You right now? I'm ready to lay down my life for You!"

232

FOLLOW. Peter gathers plainly from the Lord's words He meant He was going to die. It is to his credit that he is not staggered by the thought of following Him in death. But he scarcely realizes what he is saying. Little is he aware the Master is dying FOR HIM, afterwards to take up His wider ministry IN THE SPIRIT, also for him. The thought of separation from Jesus **in the flesh** is painful. The absence of Jesus' bodily presence from their midst seems more intolerable than death. So Peter offers to die WITH the Lord. Imagine the gloom which began to settle upon the disciples as Jesus spoke of His departure from them. Ahead lies the cross, burial, resurrection and finally the ascension when they see Him for the last time. Peter didn't get the rest of the statement, "Later on you will follow Me."

38. "Oh, so you think you are ready to lay down your life for Me, do you? Believe Me," answered Jesus, "before the rooster crows you will have denied all knowledge of Me three times!"

DENIED. Like the wild youth who says he would give his life for his mother, but won't even rake the leaves or clean up his room, Peter boasts of his willingness to die with Jesus. Before the morning rooster crows he will betray his Master three times. There is deep affection in Jesus' voice as He repeats Peter's words. Peter must have blushed, his bruised ego smarting. But Jesus knows him well. This specialized treatment is just what he needs and the Lord didn't hesitate to say it in front of the other disciples. Those words became a painful memory for Peter, for they were sealed to his soul by his thrice denial of the Lord that very night. The Lord gave them the last supper at this point.

"Jesus' words must have produced a sick feeling in all of them, especially Peter!"

14 1.   "Now don't let what I have just said to you cause your hearts to become overly distressed. Trust God and then you'll have complete confidence in Me."

JOHN
14

———

233

TRUST GOD. In a few hours their faith will meet the severest test. They will have to trust God that the arrest and execution of Jesus is part of the divine plan. Jesus says that trust in God is actually confidence in Him. Yet their hearts sag with the thought of His departure. He looks upon them with pity . . . if they only knew what was really happening, how glad they'd be. But alas, even today few understand what was taking place. Jesus will comfort them with words they won't understand, but they can feel the warmth of them. Thus we come to that portion of John which commentators call the "Holy of Holies." The disciples leave their places at the table to cuddle closer about Him as His words become loftier and more majestic.

2.   "My Father's house has accommodations for a multitude of people. If this were not so, do you think I would have told you on previous occasions, 'I go to prepare your room for you?' 3.   It's true, I am going to prepare places for all of you, but it is also true that I am coming again to take you to Myself — so that no matter where I am, you will be there too!"

TOLD YOU. In germ form, the Lord had already said to them that He was going before them to prepare the way for them. His "Good Shepherd" discourse was full of this truth (10:4, 11, 28, 29). He also hinted at it in Ch. 12:26. To comfort them in advance of His departure He means to develop this germ of revelation. Even if they don't comprehend the depths of meaning, they are to understand His going is for their sake. He is making some kind of spiritual preparation for them. As a result, they are never to be separated from Him again. Totally beyond them are the spiritual mechanics by which all this is accomplished. One thing is clear, the Father's house has room for them all and they are going to live there in the future.

 MYSELF. Observe how Jesus comforts them by saying He would come to THEM again. That word is in the present tense in Greek. It wasn't long before He did come to them — not to take them to heaven — but to HIMSELF! Don't miss that. How the Lord takes people to Himself is one of the sweet mysteries of the N.T. In a little over 50 days He returns to them, but not in a body. That part of the Lord's work was over. On the day of Pentecost He returned to take up the LARGER part of His ministry, that of building His church (Matt. 16:18). The process by which He would do this was by BAPTIZING people into His Spirit, so as to be eternally united with them. At this point the disciples have no hint that He means to indwell them, and that they will also be baptized into the body of Christ (I Cor. 12:13).

"Surely the Lord didn't expect them to grasp what He said, did He!"

4. "So, now you know not only where I am going, but you also know the way to get there."
5. "Lord," exploded Thomas, "we don't know where You are going, so how could we possibly know the way?"

 WHERE. Jesus made that statement to provoke such a question. Of course they didn't know. He was aware of that. But His masterful teaching is on display. Thomas is right. If a man doesn't know the destination, he certainly can't know the way there. A person must always know where he is going before he knows the way to any place. But that's the problem. Thomas is thinking of a PLACE. He can't picture God's house as anything but a huge hotel some place beyond the blue. Jesus is thinking of a PERSON — God! As long as Thomas pictures an outward place and wonders about a physical way to get there, it is impossible. Astronomers haven't found an edge to space, let alone a heaven beyond it. Thomas' thinking must shift from physical to spiritual if he is to grasp the meaning of Jesus' words. Jesus speaks of another realm (John 3:6). The O.T. idea was "down into sheol," saints included. Until Jesus came, nobody looked UP to heaven.

6.   "I Myself am the Way," replied Jesus, "for I am the Truth and the Life. No one is able to come to God except through Me.   7.   And if you had come to know Me for Who I really am, then you would have learned how to recognize My Father. From now on you do know Him — you've seen Him!"

WAY! They don't know it yet, but Jesus' death opens the way for them to come to God (Heb. 10:20). Thus Jesus Himself — a Person — is the way to God. Inasmuch as He is the perfect revelation of "The Father," He is also the TRUTH. There is no way to KNOW God apart from Him. Since it is His own Life which quickens men (Rom. 8:9, 10), He is also the Life. Since He is God, there is no way to CONTACT God apart from Him. Note, therefore, this is not speaking of religion, i.e., rituals, creeds, and denominations— but actual contact with God in Christ. To come to God, a person must MEET Christ. To have the LIFE of God, one must H-A-V-E Christ. His life cannot be separated from Him. This is why the indwelling of Christ in Person is necessary.

RECOGNIZE. The Lord answers Thomas by saying the WAY to God is NOT some kind of a road (religious process), but a PERSON — HIMSELF! Those who learn to recognize Jesus for Who He really is, have at the same time come to recognize the Father, for the Father indwells the Son. The shift to "My Father" (Vs. 7, etc.), is always used in speaking of His human relationship to the invisible God. What He hopes to teach them is that just as His Father indwells Him, as He stands before their eyes, so will He indwell them when He returns in the Spirit. Not until they are actually indwelt by His Spirit will they understand these words (Vs. 26).

"Could the disciples fathom anything of what He said!"

8. "Show us the Father," exclaimed Philip, "and we'll be satisfied." 9. "You, of all people, Philip!" answered Jesus. "All this time I have been with you and yet you still do not know Me? Anyone who has seen Me has seen the Father. How can you possibly say, 'Show us the Father?' "

SHOW. Peter and Thomas have asked their questions, now it's Philip's turn. The Greek indicates Jesus reacts to Philip. Recall how he ran to Nathanael exclaiming, "We have found Him!" But now we see he has harbored an error all these years. He never really learned to behold Jesus as God, but hoped He might somehow reveal the Father — **apart from Himself** — as if more could be found than revealed in Christ. Many today would like to discover God apart from Christ. They prefer some other form of revelation rather than His incarnation as the Carpenter. Jesus taught that He was the ONLY revelation of Deity, that we are NOT to look for anything or anyone beyond Himself. He reveals the **complete personality** of the Godhead (Col. 2:9).

SEEN. How do men see God in Christ? Did He mean His physical appearance? No. "God is Spirit" (John 4:24). No one has ever seen the INVISIBLE God (John 1:18, I John 4:12). When He put on the body of the Carpenter, His PERSONALITY was PROJECTED. Thus the word of Jesus is the Word of God, the love of Jesus, the love of God, the mercy of Jesus, the mercy of God, etc. God's nature was manifested in Jesus, because the OMNIPRESENT God was PRESENT TO the **incarnate** Christ. Think of Jesus as being linked to the Father by closed-circuit TV (Spirit-linked) so that God's own personality emanated from the Carpenter's body. Paul grasped this, expressing it simply, "To wit that God was in Christ reconciling the world unto Himself . . ." (2 Cor. 5:19). One day, when we are in the spirit, facing God The Spirit, we will see a PERSON no **different** from Jesus Christ.

10. "Don't you now believe that I am in the Father and the Father is in Me? And that the

words which I speak do not originate with Me, and that the works which I do, I do not perform by Myself? I tell you the Father is in Me and He communicates the words and does the works. 11. However, if you are not satisfied with My word for that, then consider the powerful works that I do. They are sufficient by themselves to convince anyone that the Father is in Me and that I am in the Father."

WORDS-WORKS. Philip doubts both that the Father is in Jesus and that Jesus is in the Father. So the Lord replies, as if to say, "If you can't take My word for it, then view My works and weigh them as independent evidence." He did this with the Jews earlier (John 10:37, 38). Even if Philip suspected Jesus invented the words, He couldn't have made up the works. They occurred **outside His being**, i.e., raising the dead, stilling the storm, multiplying the loaves, healing the sick and walking on the water, and clearly had to do with the government of God. Those works testify to the mutual indwelling of the Father and Son, being impossible otherwise. If they can believe that, He will then move on to the more amazing truth of His indwelling them. If God can indwell the Carpenter, the Carpenter can indwell them. This is the main point of His comforting counsel.

"Will Jesus now proceed to explain His new relationship to them when He comes to indwell them!"

12. "In all truth I tell you that whoever believes in Me will be able to do what I do — nay, he will be able to do even greater things, because I go to The Father."

GREATER. Jesus would comfort His saddened disciples by mentioning what He plans to do THROUGH them after He makes the transition to Spirit ("go to the Father"). A believer, due to his union with Christ in the Spirit, will be able to do works which ORIGINATE in Jesus, just as His works originated in His Father. They will be greater works inasmuch as the larger work of Christ lay BE-YOND His ministry in the flesh. In the days of His flesh Jesus came to reveal the Father and die as the sin-Sacrifice, but in the Spirit He will build His church (Matt. 16:18). Instead of just one Carpenter going about, there will be many "little Christs," due to His indwelling. A mere 120 souls gathered in the "upper room," prior to Pentecost, the total result of His preaching ministry. But through Peter, on the day of Pente-cost, He began His ministry as the Great Baptizer — something He couldn't do in the flesh. Since then a harvest of souls has been taken from the world as His greater work of building "the church which is His body."

13. "So that the Father may continue to be glorified in the Son, I will do whatever you ask in My Name. 14. I repeat, I will do anything provided you ask in My Name."

ASK. In the days of His flesh, Jesus was in constant communion with His Father, as if by closed-circuit TV. It was as if the Father thought and the Son acted. Notice that the Son will still be WORKING, though, through His disciples. Note how the disciples will be doing the work on an ASKING basis. They are to stay as close to Him (prayer) as He did to His Father. Inasmuch as Jesus will be building His church, He will still be working and glorifying His Father. The disciples are to take up the prayer ministry where He left off. Prayer will be the MEANS by which the Lord will execute His plans. There is no way to do the "greater things" and by-pass spiritual communion. The Lord simply will not be taken for granted.

MY NAME. The name of anyone is a revelation of that person. Jesus' Name is His character as revealed through the Carpenter. All prayer requests, therefore, must be consistent with the character of Christ. Consequently the Name of Jesus is NOT a blank check on the bank of heaven, it is a LIMITATION. This will shock readers who view "in My Name" as carte blanche. Every request must fit the plan and will of God and be fully in accord with the character of Christ. It does NOT mean the tacking of "in Jesus' Name" to the end of a supplication. The one who prays must be con-scious of the ambitions of Jesus and caught up in what He is doing, approaching Him even as He approached His Father. How do we know? Jesus is the One Who is going to do it. The Greek is emphatic about the Ego of Christ — "I will do it." And He won't do anything contrary to the divine plan or purpose (I John 5:14-15).

"Does He actually mean for the disciples to comprehend the truth of His spiritual return as the Holy Indweller?"

15. "If you love Me you will give heart-obedience to My commands, 16. and I will ask the Father to send My Replacement to befriend you and be with you forever. 17. I am referring to the Spirit of Truth Whom the world is unable to receive because it can't see Him and doesn't know Him. But you know Him, for He is with you right now and will be in you."

HEART-OBEDIENCE. Note that love for Christ is not expressed by gushiness or sentiment, but by embracing His commands and carrying them out because a person WANTS to. This is a different kind of obedience from slavish conformity to a set of rules or even a slave carrying out a master's commands. A different Greek word is used to express obedience to an order. The obedience spoken of here is done because a person **wants to,** not because he has to. It refers to the yearning within a believer to please the Lord. Jesus wants a cheerful response to His commands, which Paul says are "obeyed from the heart" (Rom. 6:17). The Greek indicates the commands of Christ are to be prized and treasured.

REPLACEMENT. The Greek reads "another paraclete." Literally it means someone called alongside to give aid. Observe the prepositions WITH and IN. The One Who is now WITH them is going to be IN them. We understand this to be the Holy Spirit, but NOT APART from Christ (John 7:39). It refers to the same Jesus Who is now WITH them but Who will be IN them as the GLORIFIED SPIRIT. His role is much greater than that of a "Comforter," as stated in the King James Version. By such words the Master teaches they will not be bereft of His presence, that He will return IN THE SPIRIT, thereupon to remain with them — forever! If they can believe that the Father is in Him as He stands before them, then it is not unthinkable that He can also return to be in them after He rejoins the Father in Spirit (John 4:24).

SPIRIT OF TRUTH. The Holy Spirit has several titles with each a description of His work in some way. As the "Spirit of Truth," He is the Teacher Who will recall all that Jesus has said to them and explain it. See now that it is vital NOT to separate the **personality** of the Holy Spirit from Christ. We Trinitarians err if we divide the Godhead too sharply, for there is but one God. The personality of Jesus is exactly that of the Father (John 14:9), even as it is also that of the Holy Spirit. There is but one personality in the Godhead (Col. 2:9). We will not see three separate Gods when we get to heaven, though for the purposes of revelation we observe the three distinct manifestations of the one God in human affairs (Mark 1:10-11).

"Can they grasp the idea of someone's presence apart
from a physical body?"

18. "I am not going to leave you bereft of My presence so that you are as orphans in the world. To the contrary, I am coming back to you. 19. Very shortly now, the world will see Me for the last time. But you will see Me, because I live on. And because I do live on, you shall live also."

ORPHANS. The Greek is "orphanos," and should not be translated "comfortless" as in the King James Version, even though He is seeking to comfort them with these words. It is not God's plan to make orphans of the disciples. Jesus will return to them by another means so that they can enjoy His presence in a way not possible in the flesh. The intimacy of spiritual union surpasses that of any physical union. Souls are joined rather than bodies. In less than 18 hours, death will remove Jesus from the world. When He is resurrected they will see Him temporarily with their physical eyes, but more important they will praise Him when their spiritual eyes are opened by the Spirit. The Apostle Paul speaks of this in 2 Corinthians 5:16. After His physical ministry is over, Jesus lives on to continue His "greater work" in the Spirit. They receive divine life through being joined to Him Who is the "Life-giving Spirit" (1 Cor. 15:45).

 COMING BACK. Some have taken Jesus' words here to refer prophetically to His second coming, which has been delayed 1900 years. The context does not support that interpretation. Such would be of little comfort to the broken-hearted disciples. His words are meant to dispel the gloom shrouding their spirits. "Let not your hearts be troubled," is specific counsel for them. "I am coming back," would be a deception if it didn't refer to His return to indwell in the Spirit. The truth of Jesus' physical return is so well established elsewhere, it is unnecessary to lift these words out of context to serve as proof texts. Succeeding generations can still draw comfort by implication without removing their force from the very ones He means to encourage.

20.   "In that day you shall know that I am in My Father and you in Me and I in you."

DAY. On the day of Pentecost He returned to indwell them and take up His "greater" ministry of building His church. Also on that day their understanding was opened to the truth of His indwelling. Further, they were to comprehend the whole range of spiritual indwelling. "You in Me" was a new idea. If they had grasped the idea of God in Christ, the next step was to fathom Christ in God, or **mutual indwelling.** The phrase "know that I am in the Father," means: know that I am ALIVE in the SPIRIT (God is Spirit). He says the same will be true of them, they will be IN HIM. How does one get "in Christ?" He is placed there (immersed). This is the "baptism in the Spirit" (1 Cor. 12:13). John the Baptist announced Jesus as the Great Baptizer. Yet Jesus never baptized anyone in the days of His flesh. The Holy Spirit carefully put into the record how only His disciples did that (John 4:2). Jesus' work as a baptizer lay beyond His cross, for that is how He builds His church. Summary: As the Father was in Christ, so will He be in them. As Christ was in the Father, so will they be IN HIM.

I IN YOU. Television unveils the mystery of Christ's in-dwelling. Consider how a man in a TV studio brings his presence to an audience. A studio transmitter sends his image to the surrounding area. By means of the carrier waves, he can enter every home with a TV set. Jesus, in heaven's studio, can reproduce His presence via the Holy Spirit (carrier waves) in every heart which will tune Him in. In a body, He could indwell no one. You can't stuff one body inside another. But in the Spirit, He can enter every heart which will tune in J-E-S-U-S. If men can infinitely reproduce their presence in homes by means of circuits and transistors, surely Jesus, by means of His Spirit, can infinitely reproduce His presence in hearts. (See under 7:39.)

21. "The man who truly loves Me embraces My commands and obeys them from the heart. Any man who loves Me in that fashion will simultaneously be loved by My Father. I will love him and reveal Myself to Him."

LOVE. Jesus could have billions of admirers and fans with a few demonstrations of power. The world loves that sort of thing. But obedient disciples are rare. See again that love for Jesus is not a matter of affection or sentimentality, but a heart yearning to obey Him. As Jesus gave **demonstrated** love to us, so are we to give **demonstrated** love to Him. It is not enough to say, "I believe, therefore I love." One should say, "I love therefore I obey." Recall how only the servants knew Jesus had turned water into wine? Those working closely with Him behold His power (John 2:9). It is heart-obedience that permits a man to know the presence and power of the Godhead in his life. With human hearts becoming the "temple of the Holy Ghost," it is unthinkable that the Lord could feel at home in anything but a heart which longed to obey Him.

"Now that must have provoked a question from someone!"

22. At this point, Judas — the other Judas, not Iscariot — asked, "Lord, how is it that

You are going to reveal Yourself only to us and not to the world?"

 HOW IS IT! This is Judas Thaddeus. We saw the other Judas leave the table to carry out his evil errand. His question is founded on what Jesus said in verse 19, that the world would see Him no more. Such a notion countered their Jewish idea of the Messiah. They expected the world to bow before a Jewish king. That He should henceforth minister to them **in secret,** is baffling to Judas. Even so, he did discern that the Lord was speaking of an entirely new kind of program which saw Him revealing Himself only to the elect — after His triumph over death.

23. "Whoever loves Me," answered Jesus, "will cherish My teachings and obey them heartily. Then My Father will love Him and We will come to him and make Ourselves at home within him. 24. But the man who does not love Me ignores My words. And does so in spite of the fact the teaching which you hear from Me is not Mine, but originates with the Father Who sent Me."

 WE. This is an amazing statement! When the Lord says "We" — it appears we are again instructed NOT to divide the Trinity too sharply. If Christ is IN the Father, and also IN the disciples, with Both present IN THE SPIRIT, we have at once a mysterious indwelling of the Godhead. Thus every believer individually, and all believers collectively, form a "HOUSE for God in the Spirit" (Eph. 2:22). Can this be anything less than the tabernacling of God IN His people — the true shekinah! In the days of Jesus' flesh, the shekinah was IN Him, but now in these days of the SPIRIT, the shekinah is IN US! Wonder of wonders! What then is the real dignity of man when the God of all glory is able to dwell within him! Note, however, the basis for this privilege is heart-obedience to the Word of God — the very thing the world refuses.

IGNORES. With the words of Christ originating in the Father, God speaks through Christ to the disciples and the world. Those who ignore His words cut themselves off from any possible revelation of the Deity. Jesus hereby announces that all future revelation will be only to those who show their love for Him by the way they lovingly obey His word (Vs. 21 above). Therefore there is now no way to know God or approach Him apart from the word of Christ. The pagan world is consigned to spiritual darkness. The only witness left to them is the testimony of nature. Nature indeed points to the FACT of God (for a world can't make itself), but it in no way REVEALS God. The creation is as yet unredeemed (Rom. 8:21-22). And the "god of this world" (2 Cor. 4:4) is the only one revealed in it, i.e., the fang, claw and floods and pestilence.

"Wow! What fabulous truth! No wonder we need the Holy Spirit to understand it!"

25. "Now I have told you all this while I am still here with you, **26.** but My Replacement, the Holy Spirit, Whom the Father will send in My behalf, will be your Teacher. He will recall to your minds all that I have said to you and make it plain."

TEACHER. Jesus promises that none of His words will be lost, but called to mind by the Spirit when He comes to indwell them. They do not grasp what He is saying now, but after Pentecost they will recall perfectly what He taught — and understand it. This accounts for the accuracy of the other Gospels written 20 to 25 years after Jesus' death. Christ, returning as the Holy Ghost, will expound His own words to their hearts. What a Comforter He is! Coming in the Spirit, He is able to bring the work of His cross with Him and apply it to our hearts. Thus His death becomes our death. This is why the Law cannot touch us. And His life becomes our life. This is why we will live with Him forever. By virtue of His indwelling, the atonement is accomplished IN us the moment we receive Him, whereas it was accomplished FOR us 2000 years ago.

27. "And here is My legacy to you — peace. The peace I give you is My own and therefore not at all like that which the world gives. So don't let your hearts be distressed or dismayed. 28. True, you did hear Me say, 'I am going away,' but you also heard Me say, 'I will come back to you.' Now if you really loved Me you'd be glad that I am going to My Father, for My Father is greater than I.''

 PEACE. "Peace!" This was the usual oriental greeting at parting. But Jesus is not simply saying goodbye. He is passing on to them His own peace as an **inheritance**. It is wholly unlike any other. Who dies and leaves his wealth and then comes back to give it to his heirs? Jesus not only LEAVES the peace-legacy as an estate, but returns to GIVE it to His heirs. He is the Executor of His own will. The disciples are sad as He speaks of leaving, but shortly He will return to fill their hearts with joy. In the interim they must trust Him by faith. During His earthly ministry Jesus was totally unruffled, tranquil because of His Father's care (Matt. 6:25-34). That's the same peace we inherit, and He brings it to our hearts **in Person.**

 GREATER. When Jesus stooped to participate in humanity, He emptied Himself of the **majestic attributes** of Deity (Phil. 2:6-8). Why? They can't be used in a body. A body, for example can only be in one place at a time, thus omnipresence is impossible. A baby's brain is totally blank, just the opposite of omniscience (Luke 2:52). Yet our Lord did NOT strip Himself of the divine PERSONALITY. For then He would have ceased to be. Personality has to do with BEING, and He came to reveal the personality of the Deity. As long as He occupies a HUMAN ROLE, the Father remains in a "greater" role, since a person working in SPIRIT, easily does greater things than one in a body. As a HUMAN, Jesus was "sent," therefore inferior to the Father in ROLE, though not in His being. For Him to become the first Christian and our example, it was necessary for Him to **descend** to our level, thereby subordinating Himself to the Father. Once

He is out of the body, indwelling us as the Glorified Ghost, those body-limitations no longer apply.

29. "I have told you of My going before it happens, so that when it occurs, your faith will not be shaken. 30. I don't have much time left to talk with you like this, for the ruler of this world approaches. Even so, be assured there is nothing in Me which allows him to exercise any dominion over Me. 31. But in order that the world may know that I love the Father and do exactly as He commands—let us now arise and be on our way."

 RULER. The disciples do not know that Satan had possessed Judas and preparations were going on against Jesus in Jerusalem. Intuitively the Lord sees the devil preparing his pawns. But He avows Satan has no power to take Him. Jesus' death is a voluntary submission to His Father's orders, NOT a successful plot of the devil. Satan can do nothing without the Lord's cooperation. For the devil to dominate anyone requires the victim have some desire for evil. Satan's power is limited to the evil content of a man, for he works by suggestion only. If a person will not respond to evil, Satan can't touch him. The sinlessness of Christ gave the devil nothing to work with, yet he tried hard enough (Matt. 4:1-11). Our Lord's death was a voluntary sacrifice. Proof of this is His statement to rise from the table. He is going to keep His appointment with death.

TOLD YOU. Prophecy is not a Christian toy. God does not give or preserve His Word to satisfy those curious about coming events. Prophecy contains a six-fold blessing: (1) It forewarns and forearms God's people, (2) glorifies God as fulfilled events vindicate His Word, (3) removes much sting from tribulation when it arrives as predicted, (4) motivates increased dedication and sacrifice, (5) causes rejoicing when His Word is proven steadfast, (6) strengthens Christians in the midst of trial. When the prophetic Word is adjusted to fit someone's ideas of the future, God's people are robbed of its sureness.

"As they leave the upper room to proceed toward the Mt. of Olives, will Jesus continue to teach the disciples?"

JOHN
15

247

15 1. "I am the real Vine and My Father owns the vineyard."

VINE. At this time of the year the vines have been harvested with the cuttings piled along the sides of the Kidron Valley and burned. The sight of the burning fires undoubtedly prompted this discussion. Likely the party stopped before a stripped vine as it lay bare and pruned back for the next crop. Jesus is ready to apply what He taught them in the preceding chapter. In saying He is the "real" Vine, He indicates the physical vine merely symbolizes the truth of fruit-bearing, and should not be pressed beyond that. All the particulars of the vineyard business should not be applied to Him and the disciples. The chief concern of any vineyard owner is the crop yield. That is the truth featured here.

2. "Any of My branches which do not bear fruit, He cuts away. Those which do bear fruit, He prunes back to increase their yield."

FRUIT. In the last chapter Jesus taught the truth of His indwelling and spoke of the "greater works" which would be possible because He would be working from WITHIN His disciples. The discussion here is NOT salvation, but fruit-bearing or the productivity of the Christian's life. Fruit-bearing has to do with WORKS. There is another kind of fruit which is borne by the Christian, that has to do with his PERSON. Paul mentions it in Galatians 5:22-23. Inasmuch as this entire chapter is speaking of WORKS, salvation is not in view here. Salvation is by faith alone. Even the Arminian tradition, which argues against the doctrine of eternal security, does not teach salvation by works. Arminians insist that salvation is by faith alone. This chapter is NOT dealing with salvation, therefore, when it speaks of branches being cut away, an explanation other than the loss of salvation is demanded.

BRANCHES. It is not the stalk which bears the fruit but the branches. The stalk supplies the energy and sustenance needed to cause the grapes to form and ripen. By this, the Lord teaches that the disciples will do the actual work in the "greater" ministry of building His church while He works in them supplying what they need (power) to accomplish it. They will bear fruit with Him in a marvelous partnership. But two kinds of branches are mentioned — productive and non-productive. As pretty branches are useless to a vineyard owner, so are fruitless disciples of no value to God. These have to be cut out, for they have no other value in the vineyard business. The Lord has only one thing in mind — building His church. Note the branches are NOT dead, just unproductive.

"Where did that leave the disciples!"

3. "By virtue of what I have taught you, you are already cleansed. 4. It will be your responsibility to abide in Me. For My part, I will abide in you. You know there is no way for a branch to bear any fruit by itself. It has to abide in the vine. Therefore you must abide in Me if you are to bear any fruit."

ABIDE. John's use of the word "abide" does not mean to exist in Christ. It goes beyond the idea of salvation to allowing one's life to be regulated and shaped by what Jesus taught. And following that, vigorous participation with Him in the fruit-bearing enterprise, i.e., building His church. The disciples are to abide in Jesus, exactly as He abode in the Father in the days of His flesh. To sit back, passively accepting what Christ did for us is NOT abiding. Bible study is not abiding. Until a man submits to His word and allows his life to be disciplined by what Jesus said, he does not even begin to abide. Beyond that, He must align his ambitions with those of the Lord so that they have one mind and one objective between them.

CLEANSED. When He was washing the disciples' feet, He told them "Ye are clean" (John 13:10). They were "bathed," He said. Every heart which receives His word has this experience. His word cleansed them as they submitted to it. It caused them to leave businesses, former companions, Israel's religion, immorality, and cling to His word when all others turned away from it (John 6:68). They stand cleansed, just like the ugly pruned vine before them. How it pictures them. As that vine is ready for the next crop, so are they ready to begin bearing fruit. However, they must wait some 50 days until they are baptized into the real Vine on the day of Pentecost. Then Jesus will work through His cleansed branches to produce fruit.

"Do they understand that Jesus is going to bear the fruit through them!"

5.   "I am the Vine and you are My branches. He who abides in Me and I in him bears much fruit. But apart from Me you can do absolutely nothing.   6.   He who does not abide in Me is thrown away like a cutoff branch which soon withers. When they have all dried out, the workers collect them and throw them on the fire where they are burned."

BURNED. As they talk, vineyard fires flicker along the slopes of the Kidron. A Passover moon bathes the stripped vineyard. The teaching is dramatic. What good is a life not invested in Christ? None. Jesus' arm may have swept toward the fires. The disciples felt it. They cared not to be in that category. This chapter speaks of reaching lost souls and bringing life to them as we move out in obedience to Jesus' word. That is how His church is to be built. Those who refuse to join with the Lord in His "greater" work, are of no value to "the Vine." He can't use leafy, showy Christians, who are without fruit. Fruit is all that counts in the grape business. If there is no fruit they cannot remain in the Vine, they are cut off.

CUTOFF. This discussion has to do with abiding, not salvation. If there is no abiding, there is no fruit-bearing. Non-productive Christians are cut off. If not from salvation, what then? From intimacy with Christ and the entire operation of the Vine. The Lord put it to Peter just like that when he refused to allow Him to wash his feet (John 13:8). It is impossible to enjoy close fellowship with Christ and be disobedient. Many today are churchy, but few are involved in the thrills of fruit-bearing. They are not abiding, hence they are cut off from the whole purpose of the Vine. Not only do they forfeit the great adventure of their own faith, but they will be sorry when they stand before Him in the judgment (2 Cor. 5:10). The non-productive Christian will regret his wasted life when he sees his works go up in smoke like a pile of dried-out cuttings (1 Cor. 3:12-15).

*"Jesus said these disciples would bear much fruit.
How is that to come about!"*

7. "If you abide in Me and allow My words to govern your prayer life, you can ask for anything you want and have it, 8. for this is how the glory of My Father is to be revealed. In so doing you will bear much fruit, thereby becoming My true disciples."

ASK. Earlier He cautioned that prayer requests must be limited to petitions in His Name, i.e., consistent with His character and ambition. Now He advises they can ask and receive anything provided it coincides with what He has taught them. A prayer life regulated by Jesus' word, asks of God only as Jesus would ask. Again, it is not a blank check, but the privilege of a prayer life such as He enjoyed in the days of His flesh. They will ask of Him — as He asked of the Father — so that Christ may do His greater work through them. The glory of God is also to be limited to the disciples, for they are all He has to work with. Disciples are MORE than mere believers, they are fruit-bearers. In fact, one cannot be a disciple until he bears fruit. He can be a Christian, but not a disciple. How solemn that God would depend on us for the display of His glory!

ANYTHING. The disciples must have been shocked at the judgment of the fruitless branches. Above all they didn't wish to be among the empty-handed. Those fires looked ominous. The Lord, sensing their fears, assures them they will bear fruit. But it will come through prayer, and only the proper kind. No request would be too bold provided they asked for things which tended to (1) the glory of Jesus, (2) the salvation of souls, (3) the spiritual prosperity of each other. They are to enjoy unlimited freedom within the framework of Jesus' teachings. Every such request is heard and answered, though we need to understand God is not impressed with the form of our words. Neither is His timing likely to match our short-sighted vision.

9. "I love you in precisely the same way in which the Father loves Me. If you would continue in this love, you will have to do as I have done. 10. You will abide in My love if you obey from the heart all of My commandments, even as I abide in My Father's love by keeping His commandments with all My heart."

COMMANDMENTS. Here is a warning for obedience. If they wish to continue in a real love-fellowship with Jesus, they will have to obey Him. The commandments of Jesus include all the precepts, warnings, promises and instructions He has given for the regulation of our lives. To abide in a love-fellowship with Him, these must be taken to heart. The Lord wants heart-obedience, a **joyous** submission to His word. Love obedience is NOT conformity to a set of rules. It is given because a man WANTS to, not because he HAS to. A different Greek word expresses the obedience of a slave to a ruler. Jesus doesn't want that kind. Our obedience to Him is to be like His to His Father, loving, voluntary and hearty (Col. 3:17, 23).

"Wow! That changes the quality of our obedience to Christ, doesn't it!"

11. "I have told you all this so that My joy can become your joy. In order that you might experience such joy to the limit of your capacity, 12. I give you a specific charge: love one another as I have loved you."

JOY. In spite of Jesus' tribulations, His joy in His Spirit was undiluted and exceeding. He reveled in the glory of His task and the eternities of fellowship ahead. He saw what was coming after we put off this mortal body to be with one another in heaven. Such a vision filled His heart with joy overflowing. He wants them to have the same experience. As if sharing a secret with them He says, "Love one another." Joy can never exist for its own sake, but must always be a by-product. Therefore the means for experiencing Jesus' joy is the mutuality of brotherly love. The fellowship of eternity is to begin — NOW! (1 John 1:3, 7).

13. "There is no greater love than the kind which makes a man willing to lay down his life for his friends."

NO GREATER. The Lord explains the kind of love He means for them to show toward each other. It is the kind ready to make the ultimate sacrifice for someone else. This love gives. The **most** anyone has to give is his life. A man might RISK his life for his country or to effect a rescue, but **deliberately** laying it down is another matter. See how it goes way beyond the idea of sentiment or affection. It involves the WILL. Such a love for Jesus means more than the passive acceptance of His love for us. It means we must be willing to serve Him to the death if necessary. For that is how He loved us — to the death (John 13:1). What then of the Christian who claims to love the Lord, but refuses to obey Him, let alone lay down his life for Him? Such claims have to be all talk.

"Isn't this love-obedience arrangement quite different from the usual disciple-master relationship!"

14. "You are My friends if you do as I command you. 15. No longer am I going to call you My slaves, for a slave does not share his master's confidence or his ambitions. I am calling you friends for I have disclosed to you everything that I have heard from the Father."

 FRIENDS. A common servant or legal slave does as he is told, no questions asked. He conforms to his master's wishes or else. He is not told WHY he does anything, he just does it. He is not privy to his master's plans or motives. Jesus now exalts His disciples to the level of friends, by confiding in them the fundamental concept behind His sacrificial death and making them "co-partners" in His plans for building His church. They are to be His servants in the same way in which He was the Servant of God — freely, joyously, vigorously. Such slavery is the highest form of friendship. Jesus loved us enough to die for us. When you love someone that much, you become a slave as well as a friend. Parents are often love slaves to their children. Bound to them by love, they serve them because they want to, not because they have to. Jesus has already served us to the utmost. Now it is our turn to serve Him that way.

 SLAVES. Are they not also His slaves? Indeed. And they will be, forever. Ah, but a very different sort. From now on they are not to consider themselves slaves in the legal or king-subject sense. They are free to serve Him or ignore His orders — as they choose. Of course, they are responsible for their choice. He wants them as His TRUE slaves only, i.e., from the heart. A man who makes himself a love slave of Christ is more closely bound to Him than one who merely takes orders from Him. A man is a slave to tobacco, for example, because he wants to be. He desires to be and therefore is a heart-slave to the habit. James, Peter, John, Paul and Jude all boasted of their titles as the "bond-slaves of Jesus Christ," even though they enjoyed the rank of apostles (Rom. 1:1, etc.). The name "Christian" was derived from the fact that the early disciples were all considered the slaves of Christ, bearing the name of their Master.

16. "It was not that you chose Me, it was that I chose you. And I have appointed you to the task of reaching forth and bearing fruit, the kind that lasts. I also appointed you to the privilege of prayer, with the Father giving you whatever you ask in My Name."

FRUIT. As branches reach forth from the stem, so are they now ordained to go forth and produce more disciples. Jesus speaks here as though Pentecost were an accomplished fact. Apart from His indwelling they can bear no fruit. The disciples thus receive their apostolic offices. This is their authority to go into action. Christianity is to GROW, not die with the death of its Founder. But see again how fruit-bearing is connected with prayer. Christ is to be their partner in action. This is a double ordination, both to go and to pray. The Lord makes prayer a part of the Commission, so that His disciples will not forget His presence is part of the fruit-bearing process. There can be no fruit without His working, but He will not participate without being asked. Jesus doesn't want to be left out of the fellowship of His greater ministry in the Spirit.

17. "This then is My charge to you: love one another."

CHARGE. All that Jesus told them in verses 11-17, He now sums in one fundamental utterance. Everything He said about the joy they were to have; their friendship with Him; His choosing of them and their appointment as apostles, is all bound up in the law of mutual love. The sweetest harmony, tenderness, concord and unity, is to weld them into a close knit band of His own. Soon He will be gone from their sight, after that to return and work through them in the Spirit. The outward expression of His presence will be as they love each other. They will need it. Shortly they will encounter the hatred of the world. Only as they stand together in this mutual love, which manifests His presence among them, will they be able to meet hatred and triumph over it. That charge has never been revoked. Christians may again face an hour when mutual love will be their only means of survival.

"Is He then preparing the disciples for persecution!"

18. "If the world hates you, bear in mind that it hated Me first. 19. If you belonged to the world, it would treat you as one of its own. But since I have chosen you out of the world so that you no longer belong to it, the world will hate you. 20. Remember how I said to you earlier, 'No servant is greater than his master?' Inasmuch as they have persecuted Me, you can be sure they will persecute you also. And they will pay the same attention to your words as they have to Mine."

 HATE. The world hates Christ, that's certain. Soon the disciples will see how much (the cross). He prepares them for the persecution which will come through their identification with Him. Since Christ represents godliness, He is a wet blanket on what the world calls fun and success. The world advocates ego-exaltation, condones greed and approves selfish ambition. The rich and powerful are always admired. But Jesus teaches a man must deny all that to follow Him. Therefore His way opposes that of the world. He is hated because of it. The extent to which the world hates us, is the extent to which it sees Christ in us. The Christian whom the world approves, cannot be like Christ. Since we are as He was in this world, we share the fellowship of suffering.

"You mean the world's hatred for Jesus is transferred to His disciples!"

21. "They will treat you this way since you are identified with Me as My disciples and because they do not know the One Who sent Me. 22. If I had not come and spoken to them as I have, they would not be guilty of sin. But as it is, they no longer have any excuse. 23. He who hates Me hates My Father also."

GUILTY. The Jews professed to love God, but actually they hated Him. This hatred was not exposed until God arrived as the Carpenter. Then they could examine His PERSON to decide what they really thought of Him. Their decision to kill Jesus was based on the perfect revelation of God as a Man. Concerning the **formal act** of rejecting God, they would have remained guiltless. They could always claim they didn't really know what He was like. But with the advent of Christ they got a good look at Him and didn't like what they saw or heard. The rulers especially hated His words which tore away their mask of hypocrisy. No longer could they play religion and hide behind the letter of the Law once He had expounded the spirit of it. The world, of course, has always rejected the truth of God clearly stamped on His creation (Rom. 1:20).

24.   "They would not have been guilty of sin had I not appeared among them doing the works which no one else has ever done. But now, with open eyes they have beheld My works and hated both Me and My Father. 25.   Even so, it has all come to pass in fulfillment of that which is written in their law, 'They hated Me without cause.'"

WORKS: If above the Jews hated Jesus for His words, His works stirred equal hatred. They saw the mighty things He did and were jealous because they couldn't match them. Because He healed, they wanted to hurt Him. Because they were proof He came from God, they became enraged and attributed them to the devil. With every work He performed, whether redemptive or healing, they "blinded" their eyes rather than see Him for Who He was. In their fury to disavow Him, they cast aside all fear of God and openly hated Him "without cause" (Psa. 35:19). The Greek for "without cause" means as a gift. God's gift to His people was that of love and light and life. They returned it with their gift of hatred, disownment and crucifixion.

26.   "But when My Replacement arrives from the Father, the Spirit of Truth Whom I will send

to you from the Father, He will bear witness to Who I really am. 27. And you are to be My witnesses also, for you have been with Me from the first."

 WITNESSES. Jesus will soon depart the world amidst shame and hate. The disciples appointed to the holy office of apostles will inherit the reputation of the despised and rejected Carpenter — not an enviable situation. But Jesus has an answer: His Replacement. He will return as the Holy Ghost to indwell the disciples, thus forming a blessed partnership. Notice how the Spirit's work is separate from that of the disciples. It will be His task to certify the words of witness uttered by the apostles. That is why He is called the Spirit of Truth. Men will hear words from the lips of Jesus' disciples, but they will know they are true because of the inner witness to their hearts. See the qualification of an apostle, "been with Me from the first," which in the case of the apostle Paul was made up by a direct call from the risen Lord.

SPIRIT. This passage is a fine proof text for the Trinity, yet we also have a remarkable indication of the oneness within the Godhead. In John 14:26 Jesus says it is the Father Who sends the Spirit. Here He says He will send the Spirit. This is not a contradiction, but a reminder that we must keep in mind the unity of the Godhead even as we are conscious of the distinct functions of each. The fact that both the Father and the Son are said to SEND the Spirit, is a testimony to the essential unity of God, whether we speak of the Son or the Father. In Chapter 14 He said He would send His Replacement in the same breath in which He said He would come to them. Dividing the Trinity too sharply would make this impossible.

"If the ministry of the disciples is destined to be rejected, wouldn't their persistent witnessing provoke fierce hatred against them!"

16 1. "I have told you all this in advance so that your faith in Me will not be shaken when these things come to pass. 2. They will excommunicate you from the synagogues, yea do even worse— for the time is coming when the man who kills you will think he is rendering God a real service. 3. And they will do these things because they have no true knowledge of either the Father or Me. 4a. I am telling you about these things now, because when they actually take place I want you to remember that I told you of them in advance."

KILL. The Lord's intuitive glance sees the events soon to befall the disciples. Knowing of them in advance is to safeguard them against the overthrow of their faith. Excommunication would come first then death. The apostle Paul, as Saul of Tarsus, was himself an example of the hatred and fanaticism which raged against the early church. He thought he was offering God a sacrifice of dead Christians. But in those days he lacked the true knowledge of God. The disciples were to draw consolation from the fact that the world's hatred was not due to their misconduct or deficiencies within themselves. In fact, any hatred for Christ coming against them, meant to share in His suffering — an honor. Remembering how He warned them in advance should help to sustain them in the critical hour. Even so, it doesn't sound like a joyful inheritance to them.

4b. "I didn't say these things to you earlier because I was still with you. 5. Now I am going back to Him Who sent Me and yet none of you asks Me, 'Where are you going?' 6. Instead you allow what I have told you to become a matter of intense sorrow."

SORROW. They have reason to be sorrowful. The future doesn't look a bit good. To follow a martyr isn't the most appealing prospect. Previously the Lord had spoken of persecution, but never this plainly. In those days they were blinded by their passion to see Him exalted as King. Words of warning escaped them. Now that He is going to die, they are again blinded — this time by sorrow. They are so pre-occupied with their loss and being left alone in the world, they haven't bothered to consider what His departure really means. He mildly rebukes them for lingering over His . . . "I go away," when they should have inquired into His . . . "Where I go." They have focused on the sad side, (the death and decay of the seed—John 12:24), neglecting to investigate the glad side. Apparently His statement about the Replacement went over their heads.

7. "Nevertheless you must believe Me when I tell you it is to your advantage for Me to go away, for it is the truth. If I do not go away, My Replacement will not come to you. But if I go, I will send Him to you."

ADVANTAGE. See how Jesus insists they "must believe" the truth of His Replacement. He could have easily summoned the Holy Spirit while He was in the world— but NOT as His Replacement. The GHOST aspect of the Spirit's ministry required the death of Christ (John 7:39). The Lord promised to return to them via the Spirit, for there is no other way for people to receive of the **fulness** of Christ. The disciples had to lose Jesus as a man on earth, in order to know Him as the exalted God on the throne of their hearts. No longer were they to know Him after the flesh, but behold Him with the eye of the spirit (2 Cor. 5:16). He had to withdraw from being WITH them in order to be IN them. They would soon experience a blessed communion with Him daily which would transcend any communion they had with Him on earth. The book of Acts shows what they gained in faith and strength by Jesus' physical withdrawal.

TO YOU. The Spirit will come to this sorrowful band tagging behind the Lord, not to the world. Little do they dream what it means. All the work of the Spirit described below will be done **through them.** When Jesus dies, the world thinks the "Jesus incident" is closed. But it has only started. This handful of beggarly fishermen inherit the task of shaking the world. They will be persecuted, but they will also rock the world because the Son of God dwells in them. It would have been the greatest calamity for Jesus to die and NOT return via the Spirit. The Jesus story would have ended at Calvary. As it is, emperors, kings and the nobles of the earth are condemned by the preaching of unknown and despised folks.

8. "When He comes He will convict the world of sin, righteousness and judgment."

 CONVICT. The pentecostal diffusion of Christ (Spirit baptism) is the crisis of the world. When the Holy Ghost arrives to indwell the disciples, the tables will be turned. The world may **persecute** Christians, but Christians will **prosecute** the world as sinners. The Spirit will work through God's people to smite the hearts of the unregenerate. Convicting power has to do with what happens in others when they hear the truth from the lips of Christians. Power has no effect on the believer himself, **it is not something he experiences.** It has only to do with the RESULTS taking place in others when Christians speak in Jesus' Name. It is the PRESENCE of the Spirit which affects us. The world is convicted ONLY as Christians speak. Why? Because the Spirit comes to believers only and not to the world. Note too, that the convicting power is based on the work Christ did in the flesh.

 SIN, ETC. The convicting issues in three specifics: (1) convicted of doing evil — sin, (2) convicted of what they should have done — righteousness, (3) convicted of the consequences — judgment. Christians moving in the power of Christ are like God's traffic cops. A policeman says, for example, (1) "You were speeding"— sin, (2) "there's the speed limit sign" — showing what you should have been doing — righteousness, (3) "and here's your traffic ticket" — judgment. The Holy Spirit is the Christian's badge of authority to make these arresting statements to sinners. The moment the truth is uttered by a Christian, a testifying witness of the Spirit occurs in the heart of the sinner. He knows it is true, regardless of any words to the contrary from his lips.

9. "He will convict the world of sin, because they do not believe in Me."

 SIN. Mention the Lord to the unsaved and they feel guilty. They cringe inside. Why? They ARE guilty. Yet the man who has Christ does not feel guilty. Why? He is NOT guilty. Christ has borne his guilt for him. But does all the world feel guilty like this? No. There is no guilt until they encounter the news of Christ which must come by way of a servant of the Lord. They are guilty because they do not believe in the Lord, but how can they believe in Whom they have not heard? They can't (Rom. 10:14). The Holy Ghost brings the conviction AFTER God's people have spoken of Jesus, not before. If God's people are silent, so is the Spirit. If we do not speak, there is no conviction. Without this conviction sinners feel no need for a Savior. This function is limited to the obedience of God's people. We do the speaking, He does the convicting. One is no good without the other.

10. "He will convict of righteousness, because I go to the Father and you no longer behold Me."

RIGHTEOUSNESS. The righteousness of God is now available if men want it (2 Cor. 5:21). By His obedient life and perfect keeping of the Law, Jesus did for us what we cannot do for ourselves — make ourselves righteous. His obedience took Him to the cross by which He went to the Father. Because He did go to the Father (to operate in the Spirit), this righteousness is available as a FREE GIFT in Christ. (O.T. saints had righteousness imputed to them only.) But since He cannot be seen . . . "no longer behold Me" . . . He must be received by faith. The Spirit convicts sinners they need this righteousness and that they can have it by receiving Jesus. Whenever a Christian speaks about righteousness, the sinner receives a simultaneous witness from the Spirit that there is no way to live with a Holy God apart from righteousness. (Righteousness is the same whether found in the O.T. or the N.T.) We can point to the cross like a policeman points to the traffic sign.

11. "He will convict the world of judgment, because the ruler of this world has already been judged."

JUDGMENT. If a man refuses Christ, we can pronounce his fate and the Holy Spirit will convict him of its certainty. He will know he is under sentence and headed for hell. Why does the Holy Spirit do this? If the ruler of this world is already sentenced to hell, how can his subjects hope to escape? Until a sinner learns that refusing Christ sends him to hell, he will not fear judgment. The Spirit must work THROUGH the disciples to certify such words. This conviction comes only as Christians WARN the unsaved of their condition. We are authorized to warn the wicked of their way. The Spirit then backs our words with convicting power. Those resisting God's command to repent and receive Christ are guilty of the same rebellion as Satan. Thus they earn the same fate.

"Do the disciples understand they will have this power as equipment for meeting the hostility and opposition of the world!"

12. "I still have a great deal to tell you, but it is all beyond you right now. 13. However, when My Replacement comes, He will guide you into all the truth for He is the Spirit of Truth. In no case, though, will He act independently of Me in any way, neither will He bring you any communications on His own. He will relate only that which has been given to Him. He will make plain to you the things which are to come, even as He hears them."

 MAKE PLAIN. Jesus would explain further, but it will have to keep until He comes to indwell them. Yet, they will not be new things. Much of what Jesus taught in the 3½ years was in germ form. When He returns in the Spirit He will expand and explain by the internal teaching process. There is but one voice and mind in the Godhead, thus no member of the Trinity can act independently of the other. As the world is **convicted** by the internal teaching process, so will the disciples be **taught** by it. Since Jesus is the Holy Ghost, there can be no other teaching by the internal process except His own. He has already said, "I have given you everything that I heard from My Father" (John 15:15). Much of it is yet to be explained by the internal process after Pentecost. At this point they do not have the faintest idea what most of His teaching means. He has given it, knowing He will expand and explain it all later.

THINGS. We know from the writers of the N.T. what are some of the "things" Jesus later expanded and made clear. By the inner teaching method, Paul comprehended the separation of Christianity from Judaism and the gatherings of various people into one body, the church. He understood the art of satanic warfare. John shares with us his understanding of end time events as set forth in his "Revelation of Jesus Christ." From these writers we learn the spiritual mechanics of regeneration, the background of Law and the wonder of grace, as well as how to witness in the power of the Spirit. Yet none is really new or in any way apart from the teaching of Christ. The inner counsel of the Holy Spirit is LIMITED to explaining the things of Christ as He taught them to His disciples. This verse strikes hard against all additions and pretended revelations beyond the teaching of the Lord.

14. "I am the One He will be glorifying when He makes these things plain to you, for He will be deriving them from Me. 15. I have a perfect right to say that everything He teaches is Mine, for everything that belongs to the Father is also Mine."

MINE. Here we gain a glimpse of the inner relation of the Trinity. Notice the inter-existence of the Father, Son and Holy Spirit. Jesus says He has a perfect right to say everything the Spirit teaches is His own property, because the fulness of God is His own possession. The "everything" belonging to the Father is unlimited in Greek, showing that Jesus was conscious of His essential unity with the Father. While the oneness of essence within the Godhead is clear, there also appear the different roles. Jesus distinguishes Himself from both the Father and the Spirit. He avows on the one hand that the fulness of the Father is His, on the other He says the Spirit cannot do anything apart from the fulness of the Son. Thus we observe: when it comes to essence, the Godhead cannot be divided, but when it comes to the functions or offices of the Godhead, we clearly see three personalities.

"Is all He says here meant to prepare them for carrying on the work after He departs!"

16. "In a very little while you will not behold Me any longer, yet again in a little while you will see Me." 17. This remark caused some of His disciples to confer with one another, "What does He mean by these words? On the one hand He says, 'In a little while you will not behold Me any longer,' then He turns around and says, 'In a little while you will see Me.' And listen to His reason, 'Because I go to the Father.' " 18. So they were asking, "What then is this 'little while,' He is talking about? What do you suppose He means by that?"

 LITTLE WHILE. This phrase is impossible for them to grasp. The answer lies in Jesus' use of two different Greek verbs for seeing. In a little while they will no longer BEHOLD Him (physically), but again in a little while they will SEE Him (comprehension by contemplation) fully and gloriously when He returns in the Spirit. He is saying, you will not **behold** Me any more walking with you. That is over. But you will **SEE** Me as you have never seen Me before. Because we are on this side of Pentecost we know what it is to have Christ unveiled before our spiritual eyes, but they knew nothing of that experience. They understand His words, "because I go to My Father" to mean physical death and nothing more. They don't see how they can contemplate Him once He is dead. This is an experience which cannot be explained in advance. They must wait for the actual event to occur.

"Does He intend to answer their puzzlement with a clear answer!"

19. Jesus, aware of their desire to question Him, said to them, "Are you trying to learn from each other what I meant when I said, 'In a little while you will not behold Me any longer, yet again in a little while you will see Me?' 20. In all truth I tell you, you are going to weep and mourn, but the world will be glad.

You are going to sink into despair, but your grief will be turned to joy."

 JOY. Jesus knows His statement "a little while," is a baffler. But like many of God's truths, this one must await the passing of time and fulfillment before they can understand it. In our own lives we sometimes face sorrow, asking God why it has come. He doesn't explain, but says, "My grace is sufficient for thee." When we ask how long we must suffer He replies, "I will never leave thee nor forsake thee." Afterwards we understand His purposes and are glad. So instead of expanding a statement which requires the Pente-costal experience to be understood, He comforts them with the promise of joy. He can't explain it now. He can only say, "I know your sorrow, but believe Me, it will all turn to joy when you see what it really means."

21. "When a woman is about to give birth to a child, she knows by the pains when her time has come. But as soon as her child is born, she forgets her agony. Her suffering is turned into the joy of maternity. 22. That is how it is to be with you. You will have your time of sorrow and pain, but I will see you again and your hearts will be filled with joy— and no one will be able to take this joy from you."

TURNED. To explain the joy the disciples are to know, the Master employs the exquisite example of a woman in labor. As soon as a new mother has her new baby nestled in her bosom, so great is the pleasure and delight she forgets the pain of giving birth. Without the pangs of travail, though, she could not know this joy. Jesus says the disciples' sorrow is like that. In time their grief will **give birth** to joy. Their pangs are the fears of losing Him and the death of all their hopes when they see Him crucified. Yet, out of that same death-hour arises a new program which finds HIM cuddled within the bosom of every Christian. The new fellowship with Christ is ETERNAL, hence it is inseparable and indestructible. The Pentecostal diffusion of Christ will bring them into intimate fellowship with Him as He lives within their hearts. No power on earth will be able to separate them from Him and the joy which results.

23.   "And when that day comes, you will not have to question Me about anything. Believe Me when I tell you, if you ask anything of the Father in My Name, He will give it to you. 24.   So far you have made no requests in My Name. Start asking and they will be granted, bringing you overflowing joy."

THAT DAY. The great day of their understanding is Pentecost. The Divine Witness will arrive in their hearts ending their ceaseless questionings. For 3½ years they have been trying to fathom His amazing personality. They were constantly startled and perplexed by what He said and did, hence full of questions. However, once the Holy Spirit is IN them, a new kind of SEEING will occur. They will discern a majesty of Jesus they could not begin to penetrate when He was with them in the flesh. But now they are baffled by His reference to a "little while." It is, as He said, beyond them. Yet in that day it will all be perfectly clear.

ASK. The new program will end the disciples' quizzing Jesus about anything. Their perplexity will be replaced with inner convictions. Once they see Him spiritually, their wonderings concerning Him will cease. They will then shift to a wholly different process of speaking directly to the Father themselves. This would be quite new to Jews reared in a tradition of going to a priest. It would be a new dimension of spiritual life to talk to God as Jesus did. After Pentecost they will be able to approach God directly and know the thrill of receiving answers to their requests. This experience is calculated to bring them overflowing joy. However, since it is in Jesus' Name, it will have to wait until He returns to indwell them as the Holy Ghost. Could they have known what awaited them, they would have begun rejoicing immediately. But alas, such knowledge requires the Holy Spirit. There was no shortcut to Pentecost.

25. "Until now I have been teaching you by way of figures of speech. But the time is coming when I will no longer use parables, but communicate to you directly and plainly about the Father. 26. When that day arrives, you will be able to make your requests directly to the Father. It will no longer be necessary for Me to make any requests of the Father on your behalf, 27. for the Father Himself adores and treasures you because you have loved Me and have believed that I came forth from the Father."

COMMUNICATE. The disciples are going to graduate from the external and symbolical method of instruction to a brand new communication method — **spirit to Spirit.** Not only will they be capable of direct contact with God after Pentecost, but Jesus will teach them **internally.** As long as the Lord was in a body, He used external figures such as a door, vine, sheep, water, etc. to teach spiritual truths. But once He lives inside them, He will employ internal counsel, His Spirit bearing witness with their spirits (Rom. 8:16; 1 John 2:27). Those times when He used plain truth, i.e., "I go to the Father," etc. no one understood what He meant. Because man is the "image of God," and therefore a spirit-being himself, he is capable of receiving spiritual communications. They are unconscious, of course, but nonetheless real. We call them convictions. The same process by which the world is convicted of sin, Christians are convinced of the truth.

DIRECTLY. The Lord then speaks of their direct approach to the Father without ANY intercession on His part. As God's sons (because they are IN CHRIST) they will be able to come to His throne without the aid of ANY mediaries, **Jesus included.** Pentecost changes the program. On that day they will be baptized INTO Christ. From then on they will enjoy the same access to God that Jesus had in the days of His flesh. Prior to Pentecost, He must pray for them.

But after Pentecost, they can contact God on their own, in Jesus' Name. Thus it is written, "He LIVES to make intercession for the saints" (Heb. 7:25). As long as Jesus LIVES, they will have this privilege. It is because we are IN CHRIST that the Father loves us as much as He loves the Son (John 17:23). We are in the family of God, therefore no intercessors are needed. Christ is our INTERCESSION because we are IN HIM.

"Wow! Do the disciples really fathom what He means by the direct-teaching method!"

28. "I came from the Father when I entered the world, and now I am going to leave the world and return to the Father." 29. "Say! You are speaking plainly," exclaimed His disciples, "You are not using parables now. 30. Now we can see that You really do know all things, for You don't even have to wait for us to ask You questions. This convinces us that You really have come from God."

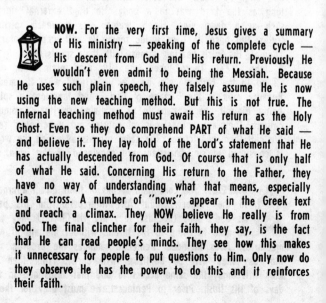

NOW. For the very first time, Jesus gives a summary of His ministry — speaking of the complete cycle — His descent from God and His return. Previously He wouldn't even admit to being the Messiah. Because He uses such plain speech, they falsely assume He is now using the new teaching method. But this is not true. The internal teaching method must await His return as the Holy Ghost. Even so they do comprehend PART of what He said — and believe it. They lay hold of the Lord's statement that He has actually descended from God. Of course that is only half of what He said. Concerning His return to the Father, they have no way of understanding what that means, especially via a cross. A number of "nows" appear in the Greek text and reach a climax. They NOW believe He really is from God. The final clincher for their faith, they say, is the fact that He can read people's minds. They see how this makes it unnecessary for people to put questions to Him. Only now do they observe He has the power to do this and it reinforces their faith.

GOING. The second half of Jesus' statement was beyond them. They didn't understand it, therefore they were unable to exercise faith in connection with it. The first part was easier to believe. It had already happened. Jesus had actually come and was there with them. But since He had not yet returned to the Father via the cross and ascension, it would have taken remarkable faith to apprehend such a thing. However, they are sincere in what they do believe and the Lord is pleased to accept it. It is on that basis He will commend them to the Father (John 17:8). The second half of His statement will be clear to them after He is resurrected and ascended. Then they will be able to believe it. Were they able to exercise such faith in advance, they would not have fled when Jesus was arrested and condemned.

31. "Well now, it appears that you do believe," answered Jesus. 32. "But listen, the time is coming, yea is already here, when all of you will be scattered, each to his own business interests, leaving Me all alone. Yet I am never really alone, for the Father is with Me."

 DO BELIEVE. When this is read as a question (King James), it ignores the fact He is truly proud of the faith they do have. At the same time, He lets them know that same faith is inadequate for the test ahead of them. They will break. Peter will deny Him three times before morning. Even so, what faith they do have is enough to make them true disciples. That faith has yet to grow, but it is sufficient for salvation. The Greek does not insist the disciples will flee to their homes, but rather to their business interests. When a man feels he has made a bad investment, he retreats to protect himself financially. These men had forsaken all to follow Jesus, depending on Him to provide for them. Upon His death, they returned "to their nets" sadly lamenting, "We trusted that it had been He which should have redeemed Israel" (Luke 24:21). It is that very trust which the Lord was pleased to accept.

NOT ALONE. These are some of the most profound and sublime words of the Lord. He is at perfect rest in the Father, though facing His darkest hour. The Master finds His comfort in the presence of God. His words,

"Leave Me alone," imply a loving rebuke, one which they will keenly feel later on. As a man, Jesus will feel their desertion of Him at a time when, humanly speaking, He needed it most. This must hurt. But the absence of their loyalty as friends, is more than made up by the clear consciousness of His Father's presence. He lived above the level of human loneliness, He reveled in the deep affection of the Father. Consider then the real pain of the cross, "My God why hast Thou forsaken Me!" That was the most stabbing moment of all! He **was** alone then!

33.   "I have said all these things to you, not to sadden you, but to make you look to Me for peace. The world can only bring you tribulation, so take heart and be cheerful — I have overcome the world."

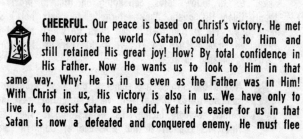

PEACE. This is His farewell discourse. The party has now reached the edge of the Kidron ravine. They will cross it to enter Gethsemane. Jesus pauses to speak about peace. Essentially He has told them: (1) He is going away only to return and be in them, (2) that His joy will be theirs upon His return in the Spirit, (3) that after that, they would be in direct contact with God. That will bring them great peace when it comes to pass. But He has just said they will all forsake Him in the desperate hour. How can such words bring peace? Ah, there is no finer peace than to learn that Jesus loves you though knowing the worst about you. It is this knowledge which makes it possible for them to return to Him after forsaking Him in the hour of trial. Then His eyes go heavenward. He speaks aloud to the Father, taking a last spiritual breath before entering the garden where He will wait for Judas and the soldiers. Even before His final conflict with Satan, He announces . . . "I have overcome the world!"

CHEERFUL. Our peace is based on Christ's victory. He met the worst the world (Satan) could do to Him and still retained His great joy! How? By total confidence in His Father. Now He wants us to look to Him in that same way. Why? He is in us even as the Father was in Him! With Christ in us, His victory is also in us. We have only to live it, to resist Satan as He did. Yet it is easier for us in that Satan is now a defeated and conquered enemy. He must flee from us when we command him to do so in Christ's Name. When a man is forgiven and heaven bound, his soul is peaceful. When he knows he can triumph over his worst enemy, he should relax. When he considers that every threat against him is only temporary, what can take away his joy? It is therefore the Christian's duty to be joyful. The peace of Christ which Christians know on the inside is to be completed on the outside by a cheery smile! Rejoice always!

"Do Jesus' tremendous words to His disciples trigger a yearning within His own soul!"

17 1. Thus Jesus spoke to them, and after He had finished, He looked toward heaven and said, "Father, the hour has come. Glorify your Son in order that your Son may glorify You!"

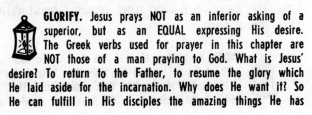

GLORIFY. Jesus prays NOT as an inferior asking of a superior, but as an EQUAL expressing His desire. The Greek verbs used for prayer in this chapter are NOT those of a man praying to God. What is Jesus' desire? To return to the Father, to resume the glory which He laid aside for the incarnation. Why does He want it? So He can fulfill in His disciples the amazing things He has just told them. His earthly task is done. He is ready to begin His greater work in the Spirit. Ah, but He can only do this via the cross. In effect, He is praying for the cross to take place. The cross is part of His glory, for the plans of heaven depend on His sacrificial death. No wonder Satan sought to dissuade Jesus from dying as the "Lamb of God," and offered an alternate method for accomplishing the same thing WITH- OUT the cross (Matt. 4:8-9). The future glory of God depends on the Pentecostal outpouring of Christ (as the Holy Ghost) by which the church will be formed and men gathered into the heavenly family.

2. "For You have given Him authority over all of humanity, that He might give eternal life to all those You have given to Him."

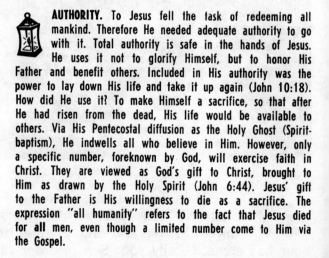

AUTHORITY. To Jesus fell the task of redeeming all mankind. Therefore He needed adequate authority to go with it. Total authority is safe in the hands of Jesus. He uses it not to glorify Himself, but to honor His Father and benefit others. Included in His authority was the power to lay down His life and take it up again (John 10:18). How did He use it? To make Himself a sacrifice, so that after He had risen from the dead, His life would be available to others. Via His Pentecostal diffusion as the Holy Ghost (Spirit-baptism), He indwells all who believe in Him. However, only a specific number, foreknown by God, will exercise faith in Christ. They are viewed as God's gift to Christ, brought to Him as drawn by the Holy Spirit (John 6:44). Jesus' gift to the Father is His willingness to die as a sacrifice. The expression "all humanity" refers to the fact that Jesus died for all men, even though a limited number come to Him via the Gospel.

3. "And this is eternal life: coming to know You, the only true God and Jesus Christ Whom You have sent."

KNOW. Knowledge of the true God is the distinctive truth of the O.T., while the distinctive truth of the N.T. is knowledge of the Sent One, Jesus Christ. The "true God," is in antithesis to the unreal or mythical gods of the heathen; also of Judaism, for her god (estranged as she was from Jehovah), was not the true one. Otherwise the Jews would have received Jesus. The personality of Christ is that of the Father, thus He could say, "He that hath seen Me hath seen the Father." It is striking that eternal life is here referred to as knowledge. However, the Greek word for "know" goes beyond mere intellectual knowledge to include the ideas of **seeing** and **understanding** as well as **meeting** the true God. Observe then how it is impossible to know the true God without seeing Him in Christ, yet they see Him only as the "Sent One" for that is the limit of their faith.

4.   "Having finished the work which You gave Me to do, I have glorified You on the earth.
5.   So now, O Father, exalt Me to Your side again, restoring to Me that glory which I had with You before the world was made."

 FINISHED. Jesus speaks in anticipation, one which sweeps past Gethsemane and looks down on Calvary where He sees Himself crying out, "It is finished!" Our Savior is so certain of His future He says without hesitation, "I have finished the work You gave Me to do." Again He is not asking, but expecting. His earthly ministry has now ended. He has perfectly revealed the Father in word and deed. He has flawlessly manifested Him in His life and teaching. That's what He came to do. Now it is done. He has reached the hour of His departure from the world. He is anxious to get on to the bigger ministry now that the foundation work has been completed. These words constitute a priestly offering of Himself as a sacrifice. He expects the Father to carry out the exaltation on the basis of His finished work.

 EXALT. Specifically, He is saying that He is ready to resume the glory which He laid aside for His descent into the world (Phil. 2:6; John 1:1). Yet He is doing more than taking on His old glory. To His former glory will now be added His HUMAN EXPERIENCE. He acquired this as He went about revealing the GRACE and TRUTH of God in human form. He is ready to shift to the Spirit so as to operate in the OMNIPOTENCE, OMNIPRESENCE and OMNISCIENCE of God as He works through His disciples. In order to do this greater work, the Lord will need those attributes. He cannot return as the Holy Ghost without being exalted to His former glory. Yet when He does return, it will be as "the MAN Christ Jesus" (1 Tim. 2:5), or God with human experience added to His other attributes (Heb. 4:15).

"So far Jesus' words speak of His desire for His own glorification. Does He not plan to mention His disciples to the Father?"

6. "I have manifested Your character and personality to the men You gave Me out of the world. They belonged to You and You gave them to Me because they have kept Your Word. 7. Now they have reached the point of knowing that everything I have presented as being from You, really is from You. 8. They believe that the message which I have given them, You first gave to Me. They have accepted it. Consequently they have come to know in their hearts that I Myself have come from You. Therefore they now fully believe that You did send Me."

GAVE ME. Before Jesus makes any requests, He makes recommendations. He presents the disciples to the Father as His very own. True, they have not yet been enlightened by Pentecost, but they have acted on the light they did have. They have gazed upon Jesus to behold the personality of God. They testified that He alone had the words of eternal life. Now they are finally convinced He has come from God. This has come because they responded to the inner witness of God to their hearts. They were drawn to Jesus because of His words. That's how God gave them to Christ. They belonged to God, i.e., they were Israelites. But unlike Judas and the nation, they didn't turn away from Jesus' words. Thus they were sifted out of Israel to join themselves to Him.

Because of this, the Lord considers them wonderfully victorious, having withstood the test. He is therefore pleased to present them to the Father as His own.

 FULLY BELIEVE. As the disciples acquired more information about Jesus, they proceeded toward a firm conviction about Him. His works led them to believe His words. From His words there sprang a true recognition of His divine nature. From this they came to believe in His mission as sent from God to bring life into the world. In addition, He committed to these men the very things He received from God, thus making them bearers of the Word of life. This, of course, puts them in need of the keeping power of God. The world hates that Word. When Jesus makes His request, it will be for God to KEEP them in the world. The ministry of Christ today stems from the fact that He gave the Word of life to His disciples; it is also the authority for the New Testament.

"Will His request be for His disciples only, since He plans to ask God for their safe-keeping?"

9. "I am making this request on behalf of My disciples only. I am not praying for the world, but only for those whom You gave Me, because they are Yours. 10. Inasmuch as everything that is Mine is also Yours, and they have glorified Me with their faith, they have also glorified You."

 NOT THE WORLD. On other occasions the Lord did pray for the world, but not this time. Only His disciples merit this kind of safe-keeping. The world will of course profit, for the end result is "that the world may believe." Since the Word of God has now been entrusted to these men, it must also be made secure in them. The world will never have a chance to know God and believe in Christ if these are not preserved. Therefore this request is limited to His disciples and those who later come out from the world to believe in Him. At this point, the world is regarded as a hostile force, against which the disciples need the protection of the Father. With Christ's property also the Father's property, Jesus' glory in His disciples is also the Father's glory. This too must be protected.

11. "Now I am no longer to remain in the world, but they will stay in the world even as I am on My way to You. Holy Father, guard them in Your Name, that Name which You gave Me, so that they may be one, just as We are one."

GUARD. This is the principal point of Jesus' prayer. He commits His disciples to the safe-keeping of the Father. He says HOLY Father for the world is utterly evil, with its prince (Satan) the real **unholy enemy.** Therefore this plea for protection transcends physical harm. The Greek for "guard," indicates day and night watchfulness as a personal guardian. The indwelling presence of the HOLY God is to attend their thoughts and actions. Jesus lived in the CONSCIOUSNESS of His Holy Father, so are we to live in the consciousness of the HOLY Ghost. But even beyond the moral keeping of God's holy presence, their souls are safe in Christ. They are joined in the Spirit to the one body, the invisible church. If anyone were ever snatched from the body of Christ, the glory of God's Name would be tarnished. Since He has a reputation for being faithful, Christians are safe in Christ to the same extent He will go to protect His glory.

12. "As long as I was with them, I kept them safe in Your Name, the same Name You gave Me; and I guarded them so that not a one of them was lost, except the one destined to be lost, even as the Scripture said he would be."

EXCEPT. Jesus didn't lose Judas. Judas lost himself. Jesus is satisfied He did all He could to save Judas. Even the moment Jesus is praying, Judas could repent and be saved. The fact that Scripture foretold Judas' fate does not mean that God predetermined his fate. In no way does God CAUSE anyone to perish. The Scripture would not have been written had not God foreseen Judas would perish. Why then was it written? In order that his perishing might be an evidence of God's foresight, so that the acts and end of even a traitor might be a witness to the truth. While Jesus was with the disciples, He served as their personal guardian. He was the means of their God-consciousness. He manifested the NAME (character) of the great I AM via His physical presence. Now that the program is shifting to a spiritual operation, they are to be kept by the SPIRITUAL PRESENCE of the Lord.

13. "And now I am coming to You. I am saying these things while I am still in the world so that My joy will also be fully in them.   14.   I have delivered Your message to them and the world has hated them because of it. It also hates them because they no longer belong to the world, any more than I belong to the world. 15.   Even so it is not My desire that You should take them out of the world, only that You should keep them from the evil one."

EVIL ONE. Jesus prays within the hearing of His disciples. His example is calculated to awaken the spirit of prayer within them. They will soon be speaking directly to the Father as they see Him do it. This will bring them great joy once they enter into personal consciousness of God through the Holy Ghost. Inasmuch as the work of God in the world is to be carried on by them, they must not be taken out of it, or even isolated from it by monkish practices. They are to charge into the world full steam, protected against over-temptation by the indwelling Lord (1 Cor. 10:13). If they will use the resources of their indwelling Guardian, they cannot be defeated. However, Christian victory is NOT automatic. The apostle James understood they were to use these resources to deal directly with Satan, their chief enemy (James 4:7). Thus, they could not only talk to God in prayer, they could also command the devil to depart from them.

"Did the Lord speak to the Father as to precisely how He wanted the disciples kept from Satan!"

16. "They are as foreign to this world as I am. 17. Set them apart from the world in truth. Your Word is the truth. 18. I have sent them into the world just as You sent Me into the world. 19. For their sakes I have sanctified Myself, that they may also be set apart for the truth."

SET APART. Jesus requests the double sanctification of His disciples. First they are to be set apart from the world in the truth. Then they are set apart as they go into the world with the truth. A building can be set apart as a holy sanctuary, but it is different with a man. Not only is his work holy, but he himself is to be holy. A foreign embassy in our country would be set apart from our land. But if we went inside that embassy we'd also find people with different customs, speech, affairs and origin. So with us. We're "born from above," citizens of another realm, therefore it is expected that we will live and act in accordance with the customs and practices of heaven. Our persons are set apart to LIVE the truth, even as our works are to declare the truth. Jesus' example shows how far a man should go in demonstrating his difference from the world—all the way to the cross if necessary. Our separation from the world is a protection from Satan.

20. "Not only do I pray for these, but also for those who will put their faith in Me because of their words, 21. that they may all be one. O', that they may be one in us, even as You Father are in Me and I in You. And by this enable the world to believe that You sent Me. 22. The glory which You gave to Me I have given them, that they may be one even as We are one. 23. In order that the world may know that You did send Me and have loved them even as You have loved Me, I pray that

they may be welded into a unit because I am in them and You are in Me."

 UNIT. The Lord now prays for all who will become believers as the Word of truth passes from the apostles to succeeding generations. He desires ALL believers to be WELDED into the one family of God. God answers this desire with the baptism of the Holy Ghost (1 Cor. 12:13). The fragmentation of the visible church must not be confused with the undeniable fact that every believer is instantly welded into the one body the moment he receives Christ. Jesus is asking for the **essential unity** of the one body. True He would like the inner unity of the Spirit to be outwardly manifested to the world, but that is up to the believers, not God. God can effect the inner bond, but Christians must effect the outward unity. With the spiritual unity of the saints an accomplished fact, it remains for them to recognize it and "love one another." We are as surely joined to one another as Jesus is to the Father. What a startling effect it could have on the world if it showed! Satan cannot touch the inner bond, even though he has devastated the outward unity of the saints.

"Did Jesus also pray for the future status of the saints?"

24. "Father, it is My decision that all these whom You have presented to Me as a gift, shall be with Me where I am. I desire that they behold My glory, the glory which You bestowed upon Me before the foundation of the world."

DECISION. Jesus is NOT making a prayer request here, for the Greek indicates an expression of His will. This is a tender communication to the Father that He is ready to assume possession of all the believers of all ages who have been given to Him as a gift by the Father. He does, at Pentecost. And once He does, they are sealed forever (Eph. 1:13, 14). His words guarantee His own will be with Him forever, for He wants them to share His ETERNAL estate. The central idea is that they will BE with Him wherever

He is—forever! The verse points to the consummation of things, for the glory they are to behold predates the creation of the world. It is the ETERNAL glory of Christ they will behold. To behold the eternal glory of Jesus requires that His disciples share in His eternal estate. With eternity guaranteed by Jesus' prayer, there is no way for Satan to threaten the safety of the souls of those in Christ. He, himself, will not be around to threaten them in eternity (Rev. 20:10).

25. "O, Righteous Father, it's true the world hasn't known You, but I have known You, and these men have come to know that You did send Me. 26. I have made Your Name known to them and I will continue to make it known to them, so that the love You bear Me will be in them, inasmuch as I am to be in them."

RIGHTEOUS. God's righteousness works in two ways: He is faithful to exalt those who come to know Him and to judge those who refuse to know Him. The world has not known God either in His natural revelation, or yet as revealed in Christ. Consequently the world rightly deserves judgment. The condemnation is that Christ, **as a man,** was able to know God and reach a complete understanding of Him. Those following Jesus were also able to know Him through Christ's words. Therefore they deserve to be exalted. They stand with Him against the world. Before, Jesus said "Holy Father," when desiring His disciples be preserved by the holy presence of God. Now He says, "Righteous Father," when appealing to the justice of God. The "world" and the believers are opposing forces. Jesus expects the Father to exalt believers and judge the world. It would be unjust of Him to do otherwise since Jesus has already paid the penalty for believers.

CONTINUE. Jesus has no thought of ever being separated from His own. From the moment He seals a man at salvation (the Pentecostal experience), He will abide in that man forever and be the eternal revelation of God to Him. The eternal safety of the disciples is sealed by this prayer. See how Jesus has made the Name (glory) of God the basis of their security. He is saying, if You don't love them, You don't love Me, for I am going to be in them forever. If a single saint could be separated from Christ, the glory of God would indeed be tarnished. We are as safe from Satan as the bond between the Father and the Son. We find the answer to this request in the experience of the apostle Paul, who avowed that nothing could separate us from the love of God which is in Christ Jesus (Rom. 8:39). God's love for us in Christ guarantees our participation with Him throughout eternity! This is why we were made in the first place.

"With the prayer for His disciples finished, does Jesus continue toward the garden of Gesthemane to keep His appointment with Judas?"

18 1. As soon as Jesus had spoken these words, He and His disciples continued on across the Kidron ravine. There was a garden there, and He and His disciples went into it together. 2. Now Judas, the Lord's betrayer, knew of this place for Jesus frequently met there with His disciples.

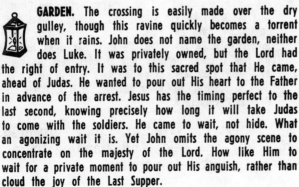 GARDEN. The crossing is easily made over the dry gulley, though this ravine quickly becomes a torrent when it rains. John does not name the garden, neither does Luke. It was privately owned, but the Lord had the right of entry. It was to this sacred spot that He came, ahead of Judas. He wanted to pour out His heart to the Father in advance of the arrest. Jesus has the timing perfect to the last second, knowing precisely how long it will take Judas to come with the soldiers. He came to wait, not hide. What an agonizing wait it is. Yet John omits the agony scene to concentrate on the majesty of the Lord. How like Him to wait for a private moment to pour out His anguish, rather than cloud the joy of the Last Supper.

3. So Judas, accompanied by a detachment of soldiers from the Roman cohort and temple

police provided by the chief priests and Pharisees, went to the garden. They were equipped with lanterns and torches and weapons.

 WEAPONS. What a story Judas must have told the temple authorities. They arrive ready to beat the bushes and encounter stiff resistance. See how the Sadducees (chief priests) and the Pharisees combine their efforts against the gentle unarmed Lord? The moon is out, lanterns are not needed except to chase someone trying to escape. They are prepared for a search among the trees. Roman soldiers (political powers) are needed, as well as temple police (ecclesiastical powers), for Jesus is to have both Jewish and Roman trials. The sanctity of the garden is broken by the rough tread of combined Roman and Jewish power. His prayer is finished just before the approaching band is heard (Luke 22:47).

4. Jesus, fully aware of all that was to happen to Him, stepped forth to meet them. "Who is it," He asked, "you are looking for?"

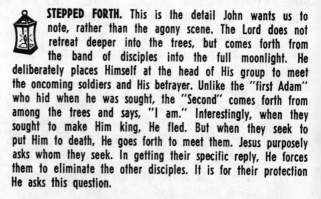 **STEPPED FORTH.** This is the detail John wants us to note, rather than the agony scene. The Lord does not retreat deeper into the trees, but comes forth from the band of disciples into the full moonlight. He deliberately places Himself at the head of His group to meet the oncoming soldiers and His betrayer. Unlike the "first Adam" who hid when he was sought, the "Second" comes forth from among the trees and says, "I am." Interestingly, when they sought to make Him king, He fled. But when they seek to put Him to death, He goes forth to meet them. Jesus purposely asks whom they seek. In getting their specific reply, He forces them to eliminate the other disciples. It is for their protection He asks this question.

5. "Jesus of Nazareth," they answered. "I am (He)," He said. And standing there with them was Judas the traitor.

 JUDAS. Judas had arranged to identify Jesus with a kiss. The Lord, of course, made it unnecessary by stepping forward. However Judas did kiss Him to fulfill his part of the bargain. In the face of Jesus'

Self-declaration this was a farce. John wants us to see how the Judas-kiss was frustrated by the Self-presentation of Christ. At the same time· he wants us to observe the Lord emerging from the ranks of His disciples to take His place before them. He had been deep inside the garden with the intimate three. The remaining eight were near the entrance. So it was necessary for Jesus to hasten out of the inner parts to meet the throng. He deliberately wanted to extract the statement from them as to whom they sought, before any other conversation was made. This also allowed Judas to stay with his group and among those falling to the ground because of Christ's word.

"Surely they weren't expecting that!"

6. As soon as Jesus said to them, "I am (He)," they shrank back and fell to the ground.
7. So again Jesus asked them, "Who are you looking for?" And they replied, "Jesus the Nazarene."

 FELL. The "I AM" was never uttered by the Lord without a most powerful effect. When walking on the waves He shouted "I AM" to comfort His amazed disciples, and settled a storm. It had a transforming effect on the woman at the well. Even the Sanhedrin came under such conviction with His testimony of "I am He!" the high priest tore his robes. Now an entire crowd of trained soldiers and religious officers stagger backwards, falling to the ground as if struck by an invisible blast of omnipotence. In a way we don't understand, this sudden Self-revelation of Jesus allowed His majesty to stream forth in a manner not hitherto revealed. Jesus could have easily walked away, leaving them in panic. They were completely at His mercy, powerless to seize Him. But He will **give** Himself to them **voluntarily.** His second question recovers them from the animating effect of His "I AM."

8. "I told you already that I am Jesus. If I am the One you are looking for, let these others

go.'' 9. Thus He made good on the words He had spoken earlier, ''I have not lost a one of those whom You gave Me.''

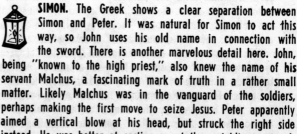

LET . . . GO. It was natural for the soldiers to arrest the eleven, but Jesus has forced them to say they seek Him only. Logically, the others should be exempted, but the meaning is deeper. His utterance is also a command, given in fulfillment of words He spoke earlier. In this case, however, they are preserved from physical captivity. But that does not exhaust the prophecy by any means. This present temporal deliverance is only a part of the great spiritual keeping from the evil one the Lord has in mind.

''Did the sight of Jesus' power over the Soldiers embolden His disciples!''

10. Simon, later called Peter, was wearing a sword. He drew it and struck the high priest's servant, cutting off his right ear. Malchus was the servant's name. 11. Whereupon Jesus said to Peter, ''Put your sword back into its sheath. Shall I not drink the cup which the Father has given Me?''

SIMON. The Greek shows a clear separation between Simon and Peter. It was natural for Simon to act this way, so John uses his old name in connection with the sword. There is another marvelous detail here. John, being ''known to the high priest,'' also knew the name of his servant Malchus, a fascinating mark of truth in a rather small matter. Likely Malchus was in the vanguard of the soldiers, perhaps making the first move to seize Jesus. Peter apparently aimed a vertical blow at his head, but struck the right side instead. He was better at casting a net than wielding a sword. The Lord instructed him to sheath his sword. In his zeal he again failed to understand the mission of the Lord. In rebuking him, the Lord condemned for all time the use of carnal weapons in defending the truth (Matt. 26:53).

CUP. The cup, of course, is the cross. Peter, one of the intimate three, heard the Master pray concerning the cup, "Let this cup pass from Me." The mention of "the cup" here is a striking allusion to His agony prayer. The Lord dreaded the cup (Luke 22:44). But viewed in the light of the **Father's will,** He is perfectly ready to drink it. Peter didn't understand this, so he acted out of zeal rather than knowledge. Sadly the Roman church has imitated Peter in his weakness rather than in his strength, when resorting to force to persecute the heretics. Jesus' words here speak of His voluntary surrender to His Father's will. He has bound Himself to "drink the cup." If force were needed to save them from this situation, He could summon **twelve** legions of angels, a legion for each of them (Matt. 26:53). Only one angel was all that was needed to strengthen Him after His final agonizing bout with Satan (Luke 22:43).

"Did the soldiers then proceed to arrest Jesus, even though they had been prostrated before His majesty!"

12. So then the detachment of Roman soldiers and their commander, along with the Jewish officers, arrested Jesus and bound Him. 13. First they took Him to Annas, for he was father-in-law to Caiaphas, who was high priest that year. 14. It was this same Caiaphas who had advised the Jews to let one man die for the sake of the people.

ARRESTED. The soldiers and temple police act in concert to arrest and bind Jesus. As soon as the crowd shakes off the effect of His words ("I AM"), which they no doubt attributed to demons, Jesus is led to Annas' house. Here He will face His bitterest enemy. Not only was Annas regarded by the people as the **true** high priest, he was the wealthiest man in Israel due to his control of the temple traffic (money changers and cattle mongers). In A.D. 7 he was brought from Egypt by Herod the Great to be the pontifex of Israel. But Rome replaced him with one of his sons seven years later. He was finally succeeded by five of his sons and now by his son-in-law, Caiaphas, so that the priesthood remained in his family. He was the power behind the religion of Israel. Annas will examine Jesus secretly, hoping to find something in His words worthy of a death charge. Then he will send Him to Caiaphas, who has already decided He must "die for the people." What kind of justice can one expect where the trial judge has already decreed he must die?

15. Simon Peter and another disciple followed after Jesus. The other disciple was acquainted with the high priest, so he went with Jesus into the high priest's court. 16. Peter had to stay outside on the street until the other disciple who was known to the high priest went out and spoke to the girl at the gate and brought Peter in.

FOLLOWED. The disciples fled as soon as Jesus was arrested (Matt. 26:56). But Peter and John, who were close companions, found enough courage to go to the place where Jesus was taken. Perhaps when John learned they had taken Jesus to Annas' house, he felt free to return, since he was known to this household. John is admitted at once, but Peter must stay outside until John can persuade the girl at the small gate, to let him in. Oriental houses were built on the street, with a gate admitting people into a courtyard which was surrounded by the main part of the house. A little gate, which was inside a large gate, would admit one person and was attended by a servant girl. Peter was admitted to the courtyard, whereas John, a family friend, was able to go further into the house to learn of the proceedings against Jesus. John was probably not present in the examination chamber, but surely close enough to hear what went on.

17. The girl on duty at the street-door challenged Peter, "Now you're sure you're not one of this man's disciples are you?" "I? Of course not," replied Peter. 18. It was cold, and the servants and officers had made themselves a charcoal fire. As they stood about it warming

themselves, Peter went over and stood with them to warm himself.

CHALLENGED. Even though John vouches for Peter, the girl wants to make sure she is doing right in admitting him. As Peter goes through the gate, the fire in the courtyard exposes him more clearly. She wouldn't like to admit a disciple of Jesus even if he is a friend of John. To play it safe, she asks her question. She expects him to say, "No," for the question is in the negative form. John she would admit for acquaintance sake though he were the Lord's disciple, but not Peter. This was Peter's first denial. Once inside the courtyard, Peter could go no further. His lie netted him nothing more than a place about the fire of His Master's enemies. John's friendship with the family allowed him to proceed into the house.

"While Peter was outside by the fire, what was taking place inside Annas' quarters!"

19. The high priest then questioned Jesus about His disciples and about His teaching. 20. "I have spoken openly before the world," answered Jesus, "I have always taught in the synagogue and in the temple and wherever Jews meet together. I have said nothing in secret. 21. Why do you question Me? Ask those who heard Me. They can tell you exactly what I said."

QUESTIONED. The Jews have been unable to trap Jesus in public debate. So now they resort to illegal arrest, hoping to extract from Him words which could be twisted into a charge worthy of death. If He could somehow be implicated in a plot against Rome, then He could be executed by the Romans as a political criminal. This idea had its roots in the Jew's passion to throw off the Roman yoke. They were continually plotting revolts against their oppressors. Annas is no doubt polite as he asks Jesus about His disciples and teachings, eager for a "slip" which might hint of a secret society. The Lord, aware of Annas' evil intent, speaks of His complete openness in all of His work. If you want information, He says, why don't you bring in witnesses? Plenty of people heard all I have said. Then He rebukes the high priest for this illegal and improper procedure in a life-death trial, "Why do you question Me?" The high priest feels the sting of Jesus' words. It shows, causing a security guard to strike the Lord.

22.   As He said this, one of the guards standing nearby slapped Him across the face and said, "How dare you answer the high priest that way!"   23.   "If I have said something evil," answered Jesus, "say so and bring forth the evidence of it. But if what I said was true, why do you strike Me?"   24.   Then Annas sent Him on, still bound, to Caiaphas the high priest.

ANSWER. This blow was delivered against Jesus' face to cover the embarrassment of the high priest. The guard was apparently rendering hypocritical eye-service to the pontiff. Now Jesus moves to act in His own defense. He demands they bring forth witnesses and evidence for the charges against Him as per their own law. By word and attitude, He protests the injustice of this evil and illegal treatment. His action here could be a shock to those who regard Matthew 5:39 to the letter. Unable to fix a charge, Annas sends Jesus still bound, to Caiaphas. The bonds are a sign that Jesus must be found guilty of some charge worthy of death. Then He is lead, perhaps across the courtyard, to Caiaphas' chambers where He will again be examined illegally. John does not report the examination by Caiaphas.

"Did Peter continue to stay in the courtyard, even though the girl asked that embarrassing question!"

25.   Meanwhile Peter remained standing by the fire keeping himself warm. Some of them asked, "You are one of His disciples, aren't you?" He denied it by saying, "Not I."

NOT I. We do not know whether Caiaphas occupied quarters in the palatial home of Annas, or whether Caiaphas had given up part of the official residence to his father-in-law. In any event, it seems clear both Annas and Caiaphas occupied the same house. To transfer Jesus from the room used by Annas to the place where Caiaphas would examine Him would take but minutes. When Jesus was led from Annas' quarters, He was taken through the courtyard where Peter was warming himself with the soldiers. Matthew tells us another maid became suspicious of Peter and prompted some men at the fire to question him. Thus his second denial came to his lips. He has to be very uncomfortable by now. What if someone recognized him as the one who struck Malchus? That was a criminal offense and here he is surrounded by police.

26.   Then one of the high priest's servants, a kinsman of the man whose ear Peter had cut off, remarked, "Say! Didn't I see you in the garden with Him!"   27.   Whereupon Peter denied it once more. And immediately the rooster crowed.

DENIED. What Peter feared might happen, did happen. His apparent nervousness no doubt invited suspicion. A kinsman of Malchus at least pretends to recognize him as one who was with Jesus in the garden. This time Peter resorts to foul language. By that they felt he couldn't belong to Jesus. Thus he had to sink low to escape from the enemies of His Master. As Jesus is being led from Caiaphas' quarters, His eyes meet Peter's right at the time of this last denial. Peter is crushed (Luke 22:61). John wants us to note how Peter's guilt intensifies with each denial. Surely he didn't intend to deny Jesus, but whenever a Christian allows himself to be in the wrong place with the wrong people, he finds his stand for Christ compromised.

"After Caiaphas examined Jesus where did they take Him!"

28.   From Caiaphas' house Jesus was led to the Governor's mansion. By now it was approaching daybreak, so the Jews remained out-

side the mansion for fear they would be defiled and thereby disqualified after eating the Passover.

DEFILED. John does not report the examinations of Jesus by Caiaphas and the Sanhedrin. All have judged Him worthy of death, yet they are unable to fix charges deserving the death penalty. Even if they did, the Jews have not the authority to punish by death. So Jesus is taken to Pilate the Governor. They plan to force Pilate to condemn Jesus on political charges worthy of a Roman execution. But they remain outside the Governor's mansion, letting Pilate come to them. A Jew who enters a Gentile's house is ceremonially unclean for the rest of the day (until 6 p.m.). They don't wish to become unholy while plotting a murder. Earlier Jesus had called these leaders "blind guides which strain at a gnat and swallow a camel." Now they demonstrate the truth of those words. They don't want their Passover feasting cancelled by uncleanness. Ceremonial uncleanness, that is, for their hearts are full of evil. They had eaten the Passover meal the evening before, as had the Lord and His disciples.

29. So Pilate went outside to them and asked, "What charge are you bringing against this man?" 30. They answered him by saying, "Do you think we'd be bringing him to you unless he had committed a crime?" 31. To which Pilate retorted, "If that's the case, you take him and judge him by your own Law." But the Jews protested, "We're not allowed to put anyone to death." 32. Thus they confirmed the Lord's own prophecy concerning the method of His death.

CRIME. The Jews are going to give Pilate a bad time. They don't want him to examine Jesus, just sentence Him so He can be executed under Roman Law. Religious authority has decided to kill Him, but they want political authority to do it for them. The Jews detested Pilate and he hated them. Their words to Pilate demanded he execute Jesus without delay. His reply has the force of, "Why are you bothering me with this?" A large crowd had been assembled outside the mansion for the purpose of intimidating the Governor, who was in town to insure against any Jewish rebellion. He faced the possibility of a riot and Rome wouldn't like that. This gave the chief priests some leverage over him. But they have something more vicious in mind. They will blackmail Pilate with the threat of impeachment before they will allow him to release Jesus.

 DEATH. The Jews were allowed to execute by stoning provided the Governor confirmed the Sanhedrin's death sentence. However, should the Governor decide to examine the prisoner himself, he then reserved the right to release or execute him, himself. The Roman method of executing political revolutionaries was crucifixion. So the Jews don't want Pilate to examine Jesus, just kill Him. Since they further know Pilate would not find their **religious** charges against Him as deserving of death, they plan to accuse Jesus of a **political** crime, i.e., establishing a kingdom opposed to Rome. That way the state would have to execute Him and their consciences would be clear. Normally Pilate would determine the guilt or innocence in such cases, but they say they have already found Jesus guilty and demand Pilate execute Him. In other words, murder with legal sanction. The key issue therefore is the KINGSHIP of Jesus, not what He taught.

"Surely Pilate saw through their scheme!"

33. Pilate went back into his mansion and summoned Jesus. "So—you are the King of the Jews?" he said. 34. "Is that something you have concluded on your own," replied Jesus, "or did someone else suggest the idea to you?" 35. "What!" Pilate reacted, "do you take me for a Jew!" Your own countrymen and their chief priests have turned you over to me. What exactly have you done?"

KING. On his first encounter with Jesus, Pilate calls Him a king. Jesus undoubtedly looked every inch a king as He stood there, His majestic attitude was not veiled. Certainly He didn't look like a wild-eyed revolutionary plotting against Rome. Pilate would have heard of it before this if He were. So Pilate's first words are as much as exclamation as a question. But he wasn't ready for Jesus' answer. It jarred his Gentile spirit to have Jesus suggest such a conclusion was his own. Only a Jew would acknowledge a **spiritual** king. Pilate was schooled in Jewish affairs. He knew of the coming Messiah who would also be King of Israel. From the first, Pilate sensed the Jews had twisted Jesus' claim as a spiritual king (John 12:13), to make Him appear a political revolutionary. Then the disturbed Pilate does a rare thing. He asks Jesus what He has done. From this we gather he knew the Jewish charge to be false. Suddenly it was Pilate who was on trial.

36.   "My kingdom is in no way connected with the world," said Jesus. "If My kingdom were of this world, My servants would this moment be fighting to keep Me out of the hands of the Jews. But as it is, My kingdom has no connection with this world at all."

KINGDOM. Jesus acknowledges that He has a kingdom, but His answer is negative. His kingdom lies outside the jurisdiction of Pilate or any worldly authority. The pronoun "MY" is emphatic in Greek. He emphasizes His kingship, but He hastens to add that it does not originate in this world, neither is He making any claims on the kingdoms of this world — therefore He cannot be a threat to the Roman Empire. As proof, Jesus observes that not one of His servants has lifted a hand to prevent His arrest and trial. If His kingdom were a worldly one, His fighters would even then by trying to liberate Him. Pilate considers this as striking proof of Jesus' innocence. No worldly king would voluntarily submit to a mock trial based on false charges. Besides, Jesus bears Himself as a king as He stands before this representative of the highest political power on earth.

37.   "So then you are a king," said Pilate. "You use the right word when you call Me a

king. However, the reason I was born and came into the world was to bear witness to the truth. All who respond to the truth recognize My voice." 38a. "And just what is truth?" asked Pilate.

TRUTH. The Lord reveals the nature of His kingdom. He is the King of Truth. He was "born" a king. He "came" into the world to establish a kingdom of truth. He says His kingdom grows as people hear and respond to His voice. Pilate now hears that voice. The Father is drawing Him by means of it. This is Pilate's moment for salvation. No such opportunity was given to Annas or Caiaphas, for they were immune to truth. But Pilate was capable of recognizing truth, even if he didn't have the courage to obey it. He was now confronted with salvation in the best form for a man in his position, the language of government. He understands perfectly. Jesus is saying to Pilate, if you are a man of truth then you will feel an impulse at work in you right now. You feel drawn to Me, because you hear the voice of the King of Truth. But Pilate's mind is too practical and too cowardly to face the truth. He makes no personal decision about this "King" before him. Still he is greatly bothered and tries to cover the matter with a philosophical question, the answer to which he doesn't really want.

"You mean he didn't want Jesus to answer him!"

38b. With those words, Pilate wheeled about and went back out to the Jews. "As far as I can see," said Pilate, "there is no reason to condemn this man."

NO REASON. Pilate turned his back on Jesus abruptly and went out to the Jews. His question, "What is truth," may have been sincere, but he didn't want the answer. He was afraid, perhaps, of what it might have cost him had he listened further. Pilate prized his job more than doing what he felt was right in his heart. But he is completely convinced of Jesus' innocence and gives the Jews his official verdict of acquittal. Luke says this enraged the priests and elders who stood in danger of losing their prey. So they stirred the mobs to shout charges of Jesus' conspiracy against Rome. Pilate who now wants to release Jesus, hits on a plan whereby he thinks he can appease the crowd and free the Lord at the same time.

39. "But you have a custom of demanding that I release to you a prisoner during the Passover. Would you like for me then to release the King of the Jews?" 40. This only served to stir a fresh outcry, "Not this man! We want Barabbas!" Now Barabbas was a militant revolutionary.

CUSTOM. Instead of carrying out his verdict of "not guilty," Pilate resorts to shrewdness. He thinks to get the people themselves to release the Lord. Matthew says Pilate placed Jesus and Barabbas side by side before the crowd and bid the people to choose between them. He was sure they'd release the gentle Christ before they'd unleash such a criminal and bring down the wrath of Rome. But the plan backfired. He was unwise in again referring to Jesus as the "King of the Jews," for it stirred their anger. The people (prompted by the priests), chose Barabbas and Pilate was caught in his own trap. From now on he will resort to desperate measures in trying to secure the release of the Lord, but it will be hopeless. He has compromised himself before the cunning Jews and they sense their advantage over him. Regardless of his next attempts, Pilate will not be able to release the Lord.

19 1. Then Pilate took Jesus and had Him scourged. 2. The soldiers put a crown on His head which they had woven of thorns and then they threw a purple military cape about His shoulders. 3. Repeatedly they would come up to Him, slap Him across the face and say, "Hail, King of the Jews!"

SCOURGED. Pilate had Jesus viciously flogged in the vain hope of satisfying the accusers. The Roman method of scourging was so cruel it was never inflicted on Roman citizens. The body was stripped, tied in a stooping position to a low block or pillar, then the bare back was lacerated with an unlimited number of lashes. The whip consisted of twisted leather thongs, often with bits of metal in them. Victims frequently fainted and died on the spot. Pilate had Jesus scourged in the sight of the people hoping to excite their compassion. In Pilate's eyes, Jesus was stripped of dignity and reduced to nothing. He felt the Jews might turn to pity after witnessing such a horrible beating and release Jesus. Even the soldiers were allowed to vent their feelings against Him.

4.   Then Pilate went outside and spoke to the crowd, "See, I am bringing Him out to you that you may know I find no guilt in Him whatsoever!"   5.   Then Jesus emerged wearing the crown of thorns and the purple cape. "Behold the Man!" said Pilate.

BEHOLD. Pilate felt sure Jesus' awful condition would stir pity within the crowd. The action has gone like this: (1) Jesus was beaten in the sight of the people, (2) then He was led in a mock procession into a hall inside the mansion where the soldiers made sport of Him, (3) now He is back outside. He stands there lacerated, bruised and bleeding. (No wonder He was unable to bear the cross all the way to Golgotha.) But Pilate blunders a second time. He underestimates the Jews' hatred for Jesus. Before they chose Barabbas over Christ, now they show no pity as he had expected. Alas, this was a case for justice, not pity. Pilate declared Jesus innocent of any charge. But he was right in one thing — "Behold the Man!" There never was a man like Jesus.

"Pilate seems to fare badly in trying to outfox the Jews."

6.   When the chief priests and the temple officers saw Him, they led the populace in loud shouts of "Crucify! Crucify!" But Pilate answered them, "You take Him and crucify

Him yourselves for I find no fault in Him at all." 7. With that the Jews protested, "We have a Law, and according to that Law He must die, for He claimed to be the Son of God."

YOU TAKE HIM. Pilate feels smug behind his authority. He is well aware the Jews have no power to crucify anyone. So his words are uttered in derision. "At last," he may have thought, "I have found a way out of this dilemma." But he wasn't ready for the next tactic of the Jews. They shifted their charges from the political accusation back to their true spiritual complaint against Him. . . . "He claimed to be the Son of God." That, of course, was now the truth and why they hated Him so, but it didn't merit a Roman death. This is why they didn't make the charge earlier. But now Pilate has compromised justice and acted in defiance of his own "not guilty" verdict for the third time. So they have him over a barrel. The Jews can make their charge stick for he is no longer in a position to deny them.

8. When Pilate heard them say this, he was more afraid than ever. 9. So he went back inside his mansion to speak to Jesus privately. "Where do you come from?" he asked. But Jesus gave no answer.

NO ANSWER. Pilate feared when the truth was finally spoken, for he was capable of recognizing truth. Word of Jesus' kingship angered the Jews, but it scared Pilate. He felt the truth of their statement. A religious fear of Jesus entered him. It may have been the fear of vengeance from Jehovah of the Jews. In any event, he suspects a super-terrestial Monarch may indeed be before him. But Jesus refuses to answer Pilate's second inquiry. He had already told him enough for a man ready to DO the truth. But for one who has turned his back on the "King of Truth," further testimony is useless. As He did before Herod and Caiaphas, Jesus remains silent. From now on Pilate will try to release Jesus out of mounting fear. When the King of Truth refuses to speak, that is the most emphatic answer of all—**silence!**

10. "What!" said Pilate, "You refuse to speak to me!" Don't you realize I have the authority

to release you and I also have the authority to crucify you!" 11. "The only authority you have over Me," answered Jesus, "is that which has been granted you from above. And for that reason the one who handed Me over to you is guilty of greater sin than yours."

AUTHORITY. Pilate is now full of fear. But Jesus has wounded his ego by refusing to answer his question, "Where do you come from?" Pilate should have remembered his duty and used his authority to release Jesus, but now he speaks from offended authority. The Lord answers that Pilate's authority has been derived from a higher authority, greater than that of any throne on earth. He says that Pilate's job is a sacred trust from heaven, not a gift from the emperor. There was enough spiritual susceptibility in Pilate to recognize the truth of what Jesus said. Because Pilate has misused this authority, he is guilty of sin against heaven. The Lord now speaks as Judge, with Pilate on trial as the accused.

GREATER SIN. Some say "Sin is sin," but the Lord here speaks of degrees of sin. Pilate has avoided pronouncing any sentence, yet he would deliver up an innocent man to be executed. He is guilty of weakness in his office, having been dominated by the crafty and determined Jews. The leaders of the plot against Christ are guilty of more than injustice, they have conspired against the truth. At least 3 degrees of sin appear in this scene: (1) the soldiers, apart from any convictions, crucify Jesus, (2) Pilate sins against his own conviction that Jesus is innocent, (3) the Jewish leaders, holding convictions opposed to the will of God, carry out their determined plot. There is some compassion in Jesus' last recorded words to Pilate, for the frightened governor now seems determined to release the Lord if he can.

12. When Pilate heard that, he became desperate to release Jesus, but the Jews kept shouting, "If you set this man free, you are no friend of Caesar, for anyone who sets himself up as a king, opposes Caesar!" 13. Upon

hearing those words, Pilate led Jesus outside and sat down in the judgment seat in a place called The Pavement. It's Hebrew name is Gabbatha.

FRIEND. "Friend of Caesar" was a prized title inaugurated under Caesar Augustus. Tiberius Caesar was now the emperor. It is not likely that Pilate had already received this honor, but surely he coveted it. Shouted threats of impeachment indicate that letters could be sent to Rome, accusing Pilate of befriending someone denounced as anti-Caesar. That would place him under suspicion himself. So Pilate is through playing with the matter. He capitulates at once. He goes to the judgment seat, an elevated area of mosaic pavement in front of the mansion. With his career threatened, the weak Pilate is ready to pass sentence, regardless of truth or justice.

"You mean he is going to sentence Jesus knowing full well He is innocent!"

14. It was now after sunrise of Passover-Friday. Pilate said to the Jews, "Here is your King!"

PASSOVER-FRIDAY. If Jewish time were reckoned, John's sixth hour would be noon. That is impossible since Jesus had already been on the cross hours before then. Writing after the destruction of Jerusalem and from Asia Minor, he was probably calculating the day from midnight as did the Greeks and Romans. The time would then be after 6 o'clock, which would be a little after sunrise. This view agrees best with the series of events as reported by the other evangelists. Jesus was arrested before dawn. Peter's denials occurred prior to the morning rooster. The "day of preparation" is a technical Jewish term for Friday. This is Paschal-Friday, even as we say Easter-Sunday. This is Friday of Passover week. John likely chose the technical term to expose the inconsistency of the Jews in slaying their Messiah on a day when they should have been preparing themselves for the Passover-Sabbath (Saturday).

15. Upon those words they shouted, "Away with him! Kill him! Crucify him!" "What!" said Pilate, "You want me to crucify your King!" The chief priests answered, "We have no king but Caesar." 16. Then it was that Pilate handed Jesus over to them to be crucified. 17a. The priests willingly took charge of Him.

YOUR KING. Inwardly Pilate is ashamed of his cowardice before the Jews. He would avenge himself with a bit of irony. He knew the words, "Your King!" would sting. Behind his words is perhaps the further thought, if your King is now to be killed, your own destruction can't be too far behind. In any event, he would place the guilt on their shoulders. To crucify Jesus as King of the Jews means He dies as a **religious** criminal. But this only prompts the priests to shuttle the responsibility back to Pilate. You have him, they are saying, you execute him! They want Him to die as a **political** revolutionary. Pilate's last' words extract a degrading confession from the priests of the very people of whom it is written . . . "The Lord your God is your King!" (1 Sam. 12:12).

HANDED OVER. Pilate crumbles in cowardly surrender. He fears the loss of his office more than he fears the wrath of God. He is fully responsible for the death of the Lord. But it is a compromise, the Jews are to take Him and execute Him. He is handed over **to them.** They gladly take charge, joyously escorting Him to the place of execution. True, Roman soldiers performed the actual deed as required by Roman law, but it is a Jewish deed. The guilt of the Sanhedrin in its demand for Jesus' blood is beyond dispute. While Pilate was washing his hands, which occurs at this point, the people are shouting, "His blood be on us and our children" (Matt. 27:25). Though Pilate outwardly disclaimed responsibility for Jesus' death by washing his hands, this act did not relieve him of any guilt in God's eyes. Many of these same people who proclaimed their loyalty to Caesar died miserably in their rebellion against him forty years later.

"Did the Jews then lead Him to the place of crucifixion!"

17b. Carrying the cross Himself, He went out to the place named after a skull. In Hebrew it is called Golgotha. 18. There they crucified Him, and with Him two others, one on each side of Him with Jesus in the middle.

CRUCIFIED. How little John says about it. What he notes is the majesty of Jesus. Jesus did carry His own cross. The N.T. writers give us no description of the crucifixion. They simply state the fact. The Jews received Jesus from the hands of Pilate, but they didn't lead Him. He **took** the cross and went forth with it. That is majesty! When at last He had no strength, due to the scourgings, and His pace had slowed to the point of annoying the soldiers, they drafted Simon "to bear the cross after Jesus" (Luke 23:26). Golgotha is the Aramaic word for "skull," Calvary the Latin word. The place is outside the city, yet near the city. Gordon's Calvary, a rise which is at the Northern end of the temple hill, with features which resemble a skull, best fits the condition of the text. The exact place is unknown. The "Church of the Holy Sepulchre," which is within the city walls, cannot be the true site, despite all claims to the contrary.

CROSS. This was one of the most painful modes of death. The method was detested by the Jews. Mongols actually impaled victims on sharpened stakes, but Greeks and Romans nailed their prisoners to crossbars. The practice continued until abolished by Constantine the Great, who declared it an insult to Christianity. The victim bore his own cross, at least the crossbar. He was compelled to carry it to the execution site. Romans scourged their victims to hasten death. Those simply tied to the cross were left to die of starvation. Those nailed, were given a stupefying drink to deaden the agony. A footrest was provided so the nails would not tear through the flesh. The suffering was intense. Traumatic fever occurred from the inflamation of the wounds, which had swollen around the nails thereby preventing any loss of infected blood. Arteries were surcharged with blood causing throbbing headaches. Exposure, thirst and tetanus went to work. Even so, death seldom came before two to three days. In some instances it has taken weeks. The sudden death of Jesus was therefore a matter of astonishment.

19. Pilate wrote an inscription on a placard and had it fastened to the cross. It read, "JESUS OF NAZARETH THE KING OF THE JEWS." 20. The notice was read by many of the Jews, because the place where Jesus was crucified was not far from the city. It was written in Hebrew, Greek and Latin.

 INSCRIPTION. Having acquitted Jesus three times, Pilate could post no crime over Jesus. This is the governor's last bit of irony against the Jews. He knew the inscription would gall them, providing an open taunt. The charge is purely **religious**, containing none of the **political** accusation the Jews wanted. Pilate has obviously sensed the kingliness of Jesus. Though he is too cowardly to act on the truth he comprehends, he uses this means to compensate for the terrible injustice he has wrought. Thus the people are forced to consider their treason against the Messianic idea. The inscription in its three-fold form, symbolized the kingship of Jesus over the world: In the language (1) of religion (Hebrew), (2) of wisdom and culture (Greek), (3) of power and government (Latin).

"Surely the Jews were upset over that!"

21. Then the chief priests said to Pilate, "Don't write 'The King of the Jews,' but that He claimed to be the king of the Jews." 22. "What I have written," retorted Pilate, "stands as I have written it."

 STANDS. Feeling the sting of the inscription, the priests demand Pilate alter it. To have a true King of Israel crucified in this fashion amounts to disgrace for the nation. But Pilate feels secure again. He stands firm with the air of a ruling Roman. The Greek shows his reply to them indicates the placard stands as is, complete, and unchangeable. Yet it is not a charge at all, but a dark riddle. The inscription is the truth. Jesus is **NOT** guilty of anything, even in the Jewish sense. The Jews have indeed crucified their true King. As the Holy Spirit used the mouth of Caiaphas to predict the death of Jesus, so now does He use the pen of Pilate to declare the truth.

"What details of the crucifixion does John select!"

23.   After the four soldiers had crucified Jesus, they divided His clothes among them, each taking a share. His tunic was left over. Now the tunic was seamless, woven in one piece from top to bottom.   24.   "Let's not tear it," they said to each other, "but draw lots to see who gets it." This was in fulfillment of the Scripture passage which says . . .

> They divided my clothes among
> them, they cast lots for my tunic.
> (Psalm 22:18)

25a.   So it was that the soldiers occupied themselves.

CLOTHES. Jesus' earthly possessions consisted of the clothes on His body. Even those did not go to His people. Roman law automatically gave them to the executioners. The four guards shared His upper garment, girdle, sandals and linen shirt. His tunic was worn next to the body as an inner garment. It had no sleeves and slipped over the head and extended to the knees. The soldiers, of course, had no idea that their actions fulfilled a word of prophecy. Neither are they aware that history's greatest tragedy and triumph was taking place within an arm's length as they gambled.

25b.   Meanwhile, Jesus' mother, His mother's sister, Mary the wife of Clopas, and Mary Magdalene, stationed themselves near the cross of Jesus.   26.   When Jesus saw His mother and the disciple whom He loved standing there beside her, He said to her, "Woman, behold your son!" 27. Then to the disciple He said, "Behold your mother!" From that moment the disciple took her into his own keeping.

 WOMAN! John, who was himself an extremely tender-hearted person, introduces a touching scene. The early tumult of the crucifixion, during which no friend or relative could approach the cross, has subsided. Things are quieter now. The crowds have withdrawn to sit and watch (Matt. 27:36). There is time for the soldiers to gamble for His clothes. Then four women are seen near the cross. A man is with them. Apparently John was the only disciple to remain within sight of Jesus throughout the night. Then, with the pain and weight of the world's sin rolling over Him, Jesus sees His friends. He is not alone! When He looks into that face which He saw first when He entered the world, He knows a sword is piercing her soul. The dreaded hour had finally come. Not forgetful of the price she is paying to be the "mother of our Lord," He gives her another son.

 MOTHER. The friend of Jesus was fitted to be the son of Mary. Their hearts were knit in their common grief. Even as Jesus was enduring the unfathomable things of the cross, He was concerned for her. John was well-to-do. He would provide for her for the rest of her life. And yet, He was also disengaging the human bond between Himself and this precious woman. He bade her look away from Himself to John. The beloved disciple would be her son from now on. Jesus was to be her Savior and her God — nothing more. The cross severed all earthly ties (2 Cor. 5:16). Jesus more readily entrusted His mother to John than His half-brothers, since they were as yet unbelievers.

"Will John comment on the death of Jesus to expose the real wonder of the cross!"

28. It was some time after that, when Jesus knew full well that everything He had gone to the cross to accomplish was over and done with, He said, just as the Scripture predicted

He would, "I am thirsty." 29. There was a jar of soldier's wine standing there, so they saturated a sponge with it, and using a hyssop reed to raise it, put it to His lips.

 THIRSTY. The six hours have gone by. John says nothing of the three hours of darkness which covered the earth or yet of the cry of desolation. Something happened in that interval which redeemed us. We cannot fathom it, but the atonement was accomplished while Jesus was ALIVE in the body. Now it is finished and He is ready for a drink. Earlier He refused such a drink, wanting nothing in His system which would deaden His senses. The spiritual task before Him required His total faculties. Whatever it was Jesus intended to do on the cross was now done, completely and fully. The atonement is accomplished BEFORE Jesus dies. The wages of sin (a spiritual matter) is NOT the physical death of the Carpenter. It is something far deeper and more mysterious than that. Why? The man inside any body never dies.

"You mean the atoning work of the Lord was completed before He died!"

30. As soon as the Lord had accepted the sour wine He said, "It is finished!" Then He bowed His head and dismissed His spirit.

 FINISHED. The accepting of the wine signified the atonement was over. Until He had done the will of the Father, He would not take anything (Matt. 27:34). What was finished? Everything He came to do in the flesh. He had revealed the Father perfectly in His words and personality, now He had executed the atonement. All commanded of Him by the counsel of God as set forth in the Scriptures was done. From here on it would be a matter of APPLYING the finished work to individuals (the actual redemption). For that, of course, He must transfer to the Spirit. There is no way to connect the cross with the souls of men **physically.** Neither can the work of the cross be separated from the Christ of the cross. People must therefore receive Christ if His death and life are to become theirs. Until He makes the transition to the spirit, He is NOT AVAILABLE. Phase I is now over and Jesus is still alive on the cross. He is ready to make the transition to begin Phase II. The veil of the temple is about to be rent.

DISMISSED. Then Jesus did an astonishing thing. He bowed His head (it didn't fall down) and gave a command to His own spirit. He dismissed Himself from His own body. He is Spirit! This is the miracle of the cross. The cross didn't kill Jesus. His death was miraculous. He had the power to do this and said so (John 10:18). He left His body of His own volition. Not one of the Synoptics says Jesus died. All say . . . "He gave up His spirit." Death had no power over Him. He had the power over death. He needed to get out of the body to get on with His greater work, now that the atonement was finished. So He made His exodus from the body to operate in the spirit. Physical death was but a stepping stone to His greater work.

"How did the Jews feel about crucifying people on one of their holiest days!"

31. Inasmuch as it was Passover-Friday, the Jews were most anxious that no bodies be on the crosses on the coming Sabbath, for that

particular Sabbath was extremely solemn. Therefore they asked Pilate to have the legs of the men broken and the bodies removed. 32.   And so the soldiers came and broke the legs of the first man who was crucified with Jesus and then of the other,   33.   but when they came to Jesus and saw that He was already dead, they did not break His legs.

SABBATH. With their thirst for blood satisfied, the Jews are again concerned for ceremonial holiness. They first avoided personal defilement by refusing to enter Pilate's mansion. Now they will not permit their holy day to be defiled with bodies on crosses. The Passover Sabbath was the principal holiday of the Jews. See how carefully they preserve the ritual of their religion even though they have violated the very essence of it. The Roman custom left bodies on the crosses to putrefy, so the Jews are obliged to ask Pilate to hasten the deaths and have the bodies taken down. Mark tells how shocked Pilate was to learn that Jesus was already dead, and called for his centurion to confirm the report (Mark 15:44).

LEGS. Pilate gives the order and immediately soldiers set out to break the legs of the three crucified men. Apparently they had no knowledge of Jesus' death until they made the discovery at the scene. Their failure to break Jesus' legs is added testimony to the fact that He was already dead. Without this action, the other men would have spent several days or more on their crosses. The custom called for shattering the legs with a club, a procedure as brutal as crucifixion itself. It was not a "coup de grace," but a way of hastening death without showing mercy. It is actually additional punishment. Some have felt the method was used to prevent the escape of such criminals, but here the intent is clearly to end the lives and remove the bodies. The Jews wish to bury these men before sundown.

'With Jesus' apparent death so astounding, wouldn't the soldiers want to make sure He was really dead!"

34. But one of the soldiers pierced His side with a spear and immediately blood and water flowed out.

 SPEAR. To make doubly sure Jesus is dead, a soldier pierces His side with a lance. He would not have dared to do this, were he not absolutely certain Jesus was already dead. Otherwise he would have befriended the Lord with a merciful end to His suffering. Thus the death of the Lord is attested to by: (1) the statement of the centurion, (2) recognition by the soldiers, (3) the mortal spear-thrust, (4) burial by His friends. That answers the docetic view that He merely swooned. Jesus is not in the body when this occurs. He made His supernatural exodus earlier, for it is now toward sundown. Hence the concern of the Jews. While we were privileged to observe the Lord's spiritual departure, we have yet to consider how death came to His body.

WATER & BLOOD. The soldier's spear performs a post-mortem to reveal the nature of Jesus' body-death. During the atonement, i.e., when He exclaimed "My God, etc.," Jesus suffered unbelievable anguish. Emminent pathologists have shown how the pericardium (membrane enveloping the heart) can be filled with a water-like serum in cases of extreme agony extended over a period of time. The Lord's agony was horrible, but that didn't kill Him. He was in fair shape when He cried, "It is finished," even asking for a drink. No, He didn't die of a broken heart. He broke His heart to bring death to His body. The broken heart spilled blood into the pericardium where it clotted and remained separated from the serum. The soldier's spear punctured the distended pericardium which was pressing against Jesus' side. The contents spilled out to reveal two things: (1) the extreme suffering of Christ for us, as indicated by the large amount of fluid, for only two teaspoonsful are found in a normal autopsy, (2) the means by which death came to His body, i.e., the ruptured heart. The veil in the temple was rent simultaneously with the rending of the heart in the temple of His body (Mark 15:38).

35. The one who vouches for these things is an eyewitness and his testimony is true. He has both spoken and written what he knows to be the truth, so that you, like him, may also believe, 36. for these things occurred just as the Scripture said they would . . .

"Not a bone of Him shall be broken,"

37. And again another passage says,

"They shall look on Him Whom they pierced."

SCRIPTURE. Writing at the end of the century John recalls two Scriptures which bear on the event. Of all that happened that day on Calvary, two things burn brightly in John's mind: (1) the failure to break Jesus' legs, (2) the piercing of His side. The first Scripture relates to the Passover Lamb, with the command of Exodus 12:46 that not a bone of Him should be broken. The second Scripture relates to Zechariah 12:10 where the pierced Messiah is seen as Jehovah Himself. However, this Scripture is only partly ful-filled by the spear thrust. In the day when the Lord Jesus is revealed in glory, the world will be consternated to learn that its last act against the body of Jesus was an attack on God. John envisions the day when the world will finally realize what it has done (Rev. 1:7). The Scriptures merely foretold these events, they did not cause them.

"What then of the body of Jesus, who would be responsible for it!"

38. Later, when it was all over, Joseph of Arimathea, a disciple of Jesus, but who kept it a secret for fear of the Jews, went to Pilate asking permission to take away the body of Jesus. Pilate gave the permission so Joseph went and took down the body. 39. He was accompanied by Nicodemus, the same person whose first visit to Jesus was made at night. Nicodemus brought with him a mixture of spices consisting of nearly one hundred pounds of myrrh and aloes.

FEAR. Who ever dreamed two members of the Sanhedrin would emerge as such fearless servants of Christ. In this crisis they refused to allow Jesus' body to suffer a criminal burial. In the past, fear had kept the wealthy Joseph from identifying with the Lord. But that is over. He broke with the leaders of his day, daring to approach Pilate openly for the body of Christ. His actions were in outright defiance of the Sanhedrin, and touching a corpse made him ceremonially unclean. Joseph arrives at the cross at precisely the right moment to take down the corpse which had been accorded him. Nicodemus abandons his fear also and joins Joseph to become an outcast for Christ, even when the rest of His followers had fled. Both men throw caution and expense to the winds in caring for their beloved Lord, giving up everything men count dear. Will they be sorry? In a little over 48 hours they will shout for joy! How different from the disciples who fled in fear!

40.   And so they took the body of Jesus and wrapped it in winding cloths with the spices, for that is the way the Jews prepare a body for burial.   41.   In the vicinity where Jesus was crucified, there was a garden with a new tomb in it. It was one in which no man had as yet been buried.   42.   So, since the tomb was close at hand and also since it was the eve of the Jewish Sabbath, they laid Jesus there.

LAID. The tomb was an emergency decision. At sundown the Sabbath begins. They had to move fast in order to fulfill Pilate's instructions. Had it not been for the necessary haste, some other burial place, more honorable, might have been provided. Apparently Joseph eagerly gave up his own tomb as a willing sacrifice. Jews anointed bodies for the transition from death to **corruption,** which they took to begin on the 4th day (John 11:39). The Egyptians embalmed bodies to **preserve** them as mummies. The rock-hewn tomb could have been chosen by God for security reasons, i.e., to insure against later denials of the resurrection truth, but another significant feature is seen too. Since it was a "new sepulchre," it made it possible for Him Who was born from a virgin-womb to rise from a virgin-tomb.

20 1. Early Sunday morning, Mary Magdalene arrived at the tomb while it was still dark. Upon seeing the stone taken away from the entrance of the tomb, 2. she ran to Simon Peter and the other disciple Whom Jesus loved and said, "They have taken the Lord out of the tomb, and we don't know where they have laid Him!"

TAKEN. Jesus' tomb may be conceived of as a walk-in excavation in a rocky elevation with a huge stone fitted into the mouth. Mary and two other women arrive in the pre-dawn light and find the heavy stone removed. To them it appears a task force has rifled the tomb. John doesn't report what the angels said to them and how they fled in terror (Mark 16:7, 8). Mary ran to John's house with her alarm. Peter was there. We learn now where he went after his denial of Jesus. "Someone's stolen the Lord!" she cries. But she jumped to two false conclusions: (1) that the Lord was still in that dead body, (2) that it was stolen rather than resurrected. It should be noted that no one remains in his body when it dies, not even Jesus. A resurrection, therefore, should always be thought of in terms of a body, never of a person (2 Timothy 1:10).

SUNDAY. The Greek text reads "day one of the week." The first day has since been called the "Lord's day," not simply because He rose that day, but because the NEW CREATION based on His redemption work also began on Sunday. Seven Sundays later (Pentecost), Jesus returned in the spirit to begin the WORK of building His church. Modern Sundays are an extension of that first Pentecostal Sunday. Sunday then is not merely a day of **physical rest** (per the Jewish Sabbath, Saturday), but a day of **spiritual work** for Christ — the true rest. The Jewish Sabbath provided physical rest for the physical creation (bodies included) and speaks of a coming Sabbath for the earth. The Christian's Sabbath (Sunday) provides spiritual rest for souls (hard work for Christ). It is for those belonging to the new creation, those alive in the Spirit. Christians are delivered from the bondage of days (Rom. 14:5). They should shun those seeking to enslave them with any kind of Sabbath keeping (Col. 2:16; Gal. 5:1).

311

"Did Peter and John then rush to investigate Mary's report!"

3.   Peter and the other disciple set out at once for the tomb,   4.   the two of them running together. For a time they ran side by side, but then the other disciple ran ahead of Peter to reach the tomb first.   5.   Stooping down so that he could look inside, he saw the linen wrappings lying there, but he didn't go in.

RUNNING. Surely the detail of John beating Peter to the tomb is the word of an eye-witness. Such things are not invented. The pace no doubt accelerated as they came within sight of the tomb, with John the younger (?) getting there first. The sight of the tomb could have slowed Peter a bit, if he had guilt feelings. However, fear halts John outside the tomb, perhaps the fear of what he might find. Then his feelings turn to awe as he beholds the orderly arrangement of the wrappings lying in their place. The body had not been stolen as Mary had announced. That would be impossible and still leave the wrappings intact. These first facts have John transfixed with astonishment. He seems rooted to the spot.

"Was Peter affected that way!"

6.   Close behind came Simon Peter who went directly into the tomb, where he beheld the linen wrappings lying there,   7.   and the face-cloth which had been about His head, not lying with the other wrappings, but rolled together in a place by itself.

FACE-CLOTH. From where John was stooping and peering into the tomb, he may not have seen the face-cloth (napkin) lying just where it would be if a body were yet in its windings. But Peter saw it. He didn't know what to make of it. Before him was unmistakable evidence that the Lord's body had not been disturbed at all, but simply vanished from WITHIN the folds of the wrappings. The spices, all 100 pounds of them, were still lying inside the folds, undisturbed except as they sag for the lack of support from a body. There is no way to remove a body from the Jewish method of winding a corpse without disturbing the folds. The face-cloth lying intact is overwhelming evidence, for it was just as it had been about Jesus' head. The napkin was always separate from the wrappings of the body. So far, all Peter sees is that the body is gone and the grave cloths are undisturbed.

8. Then the disciple who reached the tomb first also went in. And when he saw the evidence, he believed, 9. for at this point they had not yet understood the Scripture which said He must rise again from the dead. 10. Then the disciples went home.

SAW. No one saw the Lord's body rise. But the evidence of it was plain enough. Three different Greek verbs are used in this incident to show how the two disciples reacted to the evidence. When John first looked into the tomb he "saw" the linens by **casual** inspection. When Peter "saw" the linens, he beheld them **critically,** carefully, but he didn't understand. But when John entered the tomb he "saw" and **understood** what had happened. He concluded ("believed") the Lord had risen as He said He would. John reaches this conviction on the basis of what Jesus had said (John 2:21; 12:24), not because he understood the O.T. passages which referred to the literal resurrection of Messiah (Psalms 16:10, etc.). His understanding of those passages was not yet sufficient for him to deduce such a thing. So the disciples returned home to await further developments. John, the first person to believe in the resurrection of Jesus, hurried home to tell Mary, His mother.

11. Now Mary remained outside the tomb weeping. In the process of pouring out her grief, she bent down and looked into the tomb. 12. There she beheld two angels in white, sitting one at the head, the other at the feet, where the body of Jesus had lain.

ANGELS. Shortly after Peter and John leave the tomb, Mary returns. She just misses them, else they might have shared their conclusions with her. Mary stations herself near the entrance. This is the only place on earth she cares to be. Here she can sob out her grief for the One Who delivered her from the seven demons to become the Lord of her life. As yet she doesn't understand the significance of the removed stone. Convulsed with crying she glances toward the tomb. Then on impulse takes a look inside. So great is her grief, she is unimpressed with the angels there. Though she fled from them in terror on her first visit, she is in no mood for their talk just now.

13. "Woman, why are you weeping?" they asked. "Because they have taken away my Lord and I do not know where they have laid Him," she answered. 14. As soon as she said this, she turned away. Then she saw Jesus standing there without realizing it was He.

WHY! Angels have a right to ask this. They are shocked that people do not believe what the Lord tells them. He has done exactly as He said he would — risen. A little faith in His words would make Mary's grief altogether unnecessary. But as far as she is concerned, all that is left to her is the dead body of her precious Rabbi. And now with that gone, her grief seems unbearable. She feels that only the sight of His dead body can bring her the comfort she seeks. So occupied is she with this grief, the presence of supernatural beings is no comfort. Any living person, no matter who, is not as important to her right now as that dead body.

Then she turns. Someone is standing there. But it can't be Jesus. He's dead. That's all her grief-stricken mind will accept at the moment.

"You mean she didn't recognize the Lord even though He stood right in front of her!"

15. Then Jesus spoke to her, "Woman, why are you weeping? Whom are you seeking?" Supposing Him to be the gardener, she said, "Sir, if you have carried Him away, tell me where you have laid Him, and I will take Him away."

GARDENER. Angels couldn't answer the longing in Mary's heart, so she turns from them. Someone else is present Whom she supposes to be Joseph's gardener. Jesus speaks first, not to identify Himself, but to test her. She should have been expecting a risen Lord, it was the third day. He has a right to ask why she is weeping. If she had truly believed Him concerning His resurrection, no tears would be needed. But she is too obsessed with that dead body for recognition of any living person. The Lord may have been clothed with only the loin cloth which crucified persons wore. Then it would correspond to the dress of field hands and gardeners. Regardless how much the Man before her might look and sound like Jesus, she is convinced He is dead. Her eyes and ears are blinded by grief. In no way has her faith prepared her to expect an appearance of the Lord. All that grips her now is an obsession for His body. She is in funeral shock.

16. Jesus said to her, "Mary!" She turned to move toward Him and as she did, she exclaimed in Hebrew, "Rabboni!" which means my Teacher.

RABBONI. The sound of her name on Jesus' lips shatters Mary's fog of grief. Recognition is instant. We can assume she fell at His feet immediately upon uttering these words, perhaps, as she had done before (Luke 7:38). She has her Rabbi back, never to be parted again — she thinks. She is unaware how the cross has changed everything. The old relationship is over. Jesus is not Mary's Rabboni, but her Savior and her God, as Thomas will later exclaim. Jesus will end this old relationship with her with penetrating words, just as He ended it for His mother at the cross. For Mary to address Jesus as "my Rabbi," is like the other Mary calling Him, "my son!" At this point Mary has no knowledge of Jesus' planned return in the spirit to live within her as the Holy Indweller. But He will speak of it.

"Wasn't the Lord pleased to have Mary excited about His return in the flesh!"

17. "Stop clinging to Me," said Jesus, "for I have not yet ascended to My Father; but go to My brethren and say to them, I ascend to My Father and your Father, My God and your God." 18. So Mary Magdalene went to the disciples with the news: "I have seen the Lord!" Then she gave them the message.

STOP CLINGING. If Jesus' mention of her name shattered Mary's grief, His next words blasted her mistaken idea about Him. Her preoccupation with His body has to be corrected. Besides, nothing can be as it was before the cross. A new relationship exists between Jesus and His disciples, He is now their Lord and their God, not the Carpenter-Rabbi. So Jesus breaks off the physical relationship with Mary by saying, "Stop clinging to Me (physically)." Then He adds, wait until after I have ascended and then you can cling (spiritually) all you want. This is Mary's initiation to the truth of touching Jesus spiritually (2 Cor. 5:16). The disciples had already been taught this truth. Mary now learns it is far more blessed to cling to Jesus by faith, than to embrace His feet as a Rabbi. Thus Jesus prepares Mary for the moment when the privilege of physical touch ends and the spiritual touching of Him will begin at Pentecost. Note how a woman was the first to herald the resurrection news.

MY BRETHREN. Though Jesus is not yet glorified (ascended), He uses the language of Pentecost as though it had already occurred. For the first time He uses the word "brethren" even though the disciples are not truly His "born-again" brethren until He returns to beget them "from above" (John 3:3). They have yet to be "sired" by the Holy Spirit (John 3:5) even as Jesus was sired by the Holy Spirit (Luke 1:35). Only then will they have the same Father **by birth.** Since nothing can now prevent that, He greets them in the dignity of their new life. Inasmuch as they deserted Him in that critical hour, these comforting words will bring them peace. See how Jesus' resurrection does not change His ROLE with respect to God. He will ascend as God's SON and return that way at Pentecost. Thus He will truly be a BROTHER to the disciples, while they will at the same time become true SONS of God. These words to them should bring amazing comfort. So far Jesus has completed only Phase I of His ministry for man. He has yet to apply His atonement to the individual heart—Phase II.

"What other resurrection incident does John select to show that Jesus is the Christ!"

19.   Late that same Sunday evening, when the disciples had met together behind closed doors for fear of the Jews, Jesus came and stood in the midst of them. "Peace be with you," He said.   20.   Then He showed them His hands and His side. When the disciples saw the Lord, they were overjoyed.

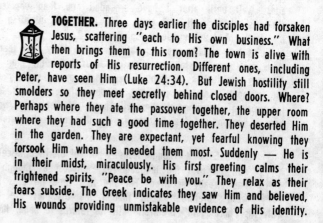

TOGETHER. Three days earlier the disciples had forsaken Jesus, scattering "each to His own business." What then brings them to this room? The town is alive with reports of His resurrection. Different ones, including Peter, have seen Him (Luke 24:34). But Jewish hostility still smolders so they meet secretly behind closed doors. Where? Perhaps where they ate the passover together, the upper room where they had such a good time together. They deserted Him in the garden. They are expectant, yet fearful knowing they forsook Him when He needed them most. Suddenly — He is in their midst, miraculously. His first greeting calms their frightened spirits, "Peace be with you." They relax as their fears subside. The Greek indicates they saw Him and believed, His wounds providing unmistakable evidence of His identity.

CLOSED DOORS. Jesus' entrance into this closed room after His resurrection was no greater miracle than His walking on the water before His resurrection. As He crossed the waves to enter the boat that night, so here He passes through the walls to enter this room. His miraculous entry was sufficient to identify Him, but His wounds dispelled any doubt that may have lingered. A different body was NOT needed for this appearance. Jesus was able to disappear before the cross (Luke 4:30). Appearing is no more difficult. He always had this power. Besides, it was God's plan for Jesus to appear in the SAME BODY after the resurrection. It was the one sign promised an "evil generation" (Matt. 12:39, 40). Jesus promised He would rise in the same body (John 2:19-21). Now He shows it off to His disciples as full proof of His majesty and power.

BREATHED. To dramatize what He has said about power and authority coming directly from Him, Jesus breathes on His disciples. This act pictures the forthcoming Pentecostal diffusion of Himself (Spirit-baptism). As He used bread and wine BEFORE the cross to symbolize His body and blood, so AFTER the cross He breathes in their faces to symbolize receiving the Spirit. As bread and wine are not His actual body and blood, so neither is His physical breath the Holy Ghost. This teaching method paid off big, for when the actual experience took place at Pentecost, the disciples were ready for it. There is no evidence they were amazed at what happened that day. The crowds were shocked, but Jesus' disciples were fully prepared for it. So much so, Peter could rise and explain it beautifully (Acts 2:38).

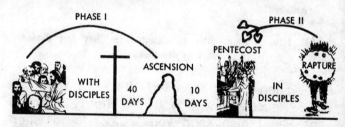

PHASE I — WITH DISCIPLES — 40 DAYS — ASCENSION — 10 DAYS — PENTECOST — PHASE II — IN DISCIPLES — RAPTURE

"What is the nature of the authority they are to receive via the Spirit at Pentecost!"

23.   "If you forgive any man's sins, they will have already been forgiven him; if you do not forgive them, they will not have been forgiven."

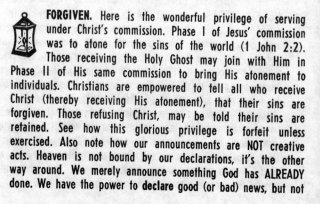

FORGIVEN. Here is the wonderful privilege of serving under Christ's commission. Phase I of Jesus' commission was to atone for the sins of the world (1 John 2:2). Those receiving the Holy Ghost may join with Him in Phase II of His same commission to bring His atonement to individuals. Christians are empowered to tell all who receive Christ (thereby receiving His atonement), that their sins are forgiven. Those refusing Christ, may be told their sins are retained. See how this glorious privilege is forfeit unless exercised. Also note how our announcements are NOT creative acts. Heaven is not bound by our declarations, it's the other way around. We merely announce something God has ALREADY done. We have the power to **declare good** (or bad) news, but not the power to **make** it. God is the One sinned against, not us. He alone can forgive. But since He is faithful to forgive, we have the privilege of declaring it in His Name.

"Were all the disciples present when Jesus did and said these things!"

24. Thomas the Twin, who was one of the Twelve, was not with them when Jesus came. 25. When the other disciples told him, "We have seen the Lord," Thomas replied, "Unless I see the nail marks in His hands and can put my fingers into the very nail holes themselves, and shove my hand into His side, you'll never get me to believe it."

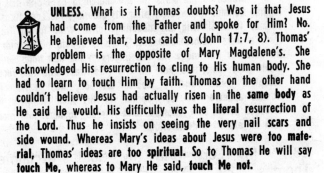

THOMAS. Why wasn't Thomas with the others when Jesus came? Perhaps he was ill. He didn't stay away out of cowardice, for he was ready to die with Him (John 11:16). Likely he was off someplace drowning in despair. Despondency can make a person ill. The other disciples refuse to abandon him. They do their best to convince him Jesus is risen. Honest, intellectual, truth-loving skeptic that he is, he stands his ground. He states the terms under which he will believe Jesus has risen. Since the Lord has already said "None is lost except the son of perdition," we can expect Him to rescue Thomas from his doubting condition. The disciples are still in Jerusalem. The Passover holidays will continue for the rest of the week.

UNLESS. What is it Thomas doubts? Was it that Jesus had come from the Father and spoke for Him? No. He believed that, Jesus said so (John 17:7, 8). Thomas' problem is the opposite of Mary Magdalene's. She acknowledged His resurrection to cling to His human body. She had to learn to touch Him by faith. Thomas on the other hand couldn't believe Jesus had actually risen in the **same body** as He said He would. His difficulty was the **literal** resurrection of the Lord. Thus he insists on seeing the very nail scars and side wound. Whereas Mary's ideas about Jesus were too **material**, Thomas' ideas are too **spiritual**. So to Thomas He will say **touch Me**, whereas to Mary He said, **touch Me not.**

"Surely the Lord is aware of Thomas' demand for proof. Will He meet that demand!"

26. A week later the disciples gathered once more inside the room. This time Thomas was with them. Again, though the doors were locked, Jesus came and stood in their midst. "Peace be with you," He said. 27. Then He called to Thomas, "Put your finger here! See — here are my hands! Now take your hand and put it in My side. Stop this doubting and believe."

 WEEK LATER. The disciples had already begun to make Sunday the important day. Here we have the beginning of the "Lord's day" in history. The Master honored it by His special appearances. It will likely remain as such until the end of time, for the Lord has a way of establishing days (vis. the Jewish Sabbath), even as He does His word. Thomas is willing to be convinced, his presence in the room proves that. They are in the same place they were a week before. Since this is now their new feast day, instead of Saturday, they do not set out immediately upon their homeward journey. They were reluctant to depart until Thomas is settled in faith, and confirmed in his apostleship.

FINGER. Jesus has immediate knowledge of Thomas' attitude. He comes to the disciples this second time specifically to deal with Thomas. It would be a hindrance to His plans for His church to have one disciple lagging behind. Immediately after His greeting, the Lord turns to Thomas to deal with his doubting spirit. With loving irony, Jesus accepts Thomas' demands. There is a note of triumph in His voice as He guides Thomas' fingers to the nail holes in His hands. Apparently the hole in His side was large enough to accept a man's hand. Of course His body was healed. The wounds appeared as scars, proofs of His identity. With this evidence before him, Thomas' faith is ready to burst into bloom with an explosive declaration.

28. "My Lord and my God!" exclaimed Thomas. 29. "You have become settled in

your faith because you have seen Me," said Jesus. "Blessed are those who are equally settled in faith and yet have never seen Me."

SETTLED. Jesus does not say Thomas' faith rests on what he saw, only that it was **settled** by what he saw. The Lord does not accept faith BASED on miracles (John 2:23, 24). Thomas had faith, as evidenced by his presence in the room. The Lord appeared to firm up his faith even as He did the other ten a week before. So that now Thomas has looked upon a Man to acknowledge Him as God in the flesh. Jesus' words are not meant to cast doubt on what faith Thomas did have, but to point up the **new method** for settling faith after Pentecost. Christians of the future, says Jesus, will not need **outward evidence** to confirm their faith, for the Holy Ghost will present convincing evidence **internally.** His words "Blessed, etc." do not indicate a higher faith, but a higher method of being secured in faith. After Pentecost believers will cry, "My Lord and my God" with exactly the same conviction as Thomas did on the basis of physical evidence. Not only is the evidence internal, it is present continually. The next forty days will prepare them for the transition of believing without seeing (1 Peter 1:8).

"Now that John has written what he believes will secure the faith of his readers, how does he close his Gospel?"

30. There are many other signs which Jesus did in the presence of His disciples which are not written in this book. 31. But these have been selected and recorded in order that you may learn to believe that Jesus is the Messiah, the Son of God, and being settled in your faith, possess eternal life through His Name.

RECORDED. John closes his Gospel telling HOW and WHY he has written what he has. He has selected certain events, all of which occurred in the presence of the disciples, and are sufficient not only to bring people to the faith, but settle them in it. To Christians he is speaking in the same manner in which Jesus addressed Thomas . . .

"Stop this doubting and believe!" He feels the Holy Spirit will certify what he has written so he is not bothered with having to prove anything. He insists that faith is to be deposited in Jesus Himself and in nothing else. We understand "eternal life," to be the equivalent of "in Christ," aware that the baptism of the Holy Spirit places us there (1 Cor. 12:13). The settled Christian then is one whose life is integrated with the person and character of Jesus. The next chapter, a postscript, was written sometime after John had completed the scheme of ideas set forth in the 20 chapters above.

21 1. Sometime afterwards Jesus again showed Himself to His disciples at the shore of Lake Tiberias. Here is the way He did it. 2. Simon Peter along with Thomas the Twin, Nathanael of Cana of Galilee, the sons of Zebedee and two others of Jesus' disciples were there together.

SHOWED. The Greek indicates this is an unusual appearance of the Lord. Not merely because of His instant-travel methods, but in that He reveals something new about Himself. The disciples are to see a new side of the Lord at this meeting. A few days have passed since He saw them last in Jerusalem. They have returned to Galilee per His word (Matt. 28:10, 16). Some weeks will go by before they return to Jerusalem for the feast of Pentecost. Also, the Lord has scheduled a big meeting to take place in Galilee (1 Cor. 15:6). Before this big rally occurs, He appears to these seven disciples at the Lake. His command to tarry at Jerusalem does not apply to this interval, but the time between His ascension and return at Pentecost.

"How will the disciples spend their time while waiting for the Lord to show up in Galilee!"

3. "I'm going fishing," said Simon Peter. "We'll go with you," joined the others. So they

went out and embarked in their boat. But all that night they caught nothing.

FISHING. With Jesus delaying His appearance in Galilee, the disciples are restless. Peter can't sit long. He decides to go fishing. The others elect to join him. They have forgotten an earlier time when the Lord called them from this very boat (perhaps?) to be "fishers of men" (Luke 5:10, 11). Ever since He said "Follow Me," this kind of fishing was no longer their business. Thus His delay was a test. They may have thought they were waiting for Him, but He was waiting for them to do this very thing. Well, it only brought them a new form of discontent. They toiled all night (the best time) and caught nothing. Into this futile situation the Lord will appear and use it as a teaching device. He won't rebuke them for returning to their old occupation. Instead, He will **work with them** to dramatize the other side (spiritual side) of their commission. So far the disciples haven't started to think of themselves as fishers of men, but the Lord will change that.

4. Jesus stood on the shore line as dawn was breaking. The disciples, of course, had no idea that it was He. 5. Therefore Jesus called out to them, "Boys! Haven't you caught your breakfast yet?" "No," they replied. 6. "Cast your net starboard," said Jesus, "and you'll get some fish." So they cast the net and couldn't haul it back on board because it was so full of fish.

BOYS! Streaks of light are breaking in the Eastern sky. Yet it is still very dark and hard to see. The Lord calls from the shore. They make out His form without recognizing Him. He purposely calls to them as might a stranger, but it is a disguise. He wants to reveal Himself by a means other than His voice. The disciples are to recognize Him **by what He does.** He calls out a term familiar to fishermen . . . "Boys!" (Lads! Young men!) No clue to His identity in that. We assume the net had been drawn up on the left side of the boat and they were giving up, ready to head for shore. With typical fisherman hopefulness they act on the word of Jesus and the net is instantly filled. It had happened before (Luke 5:6). This illustrates, perhaps, the futility of fishing for men without Christ, and the abundant success which comes from working with Him. The net is so full it cannot be taken aboard. It must be towed ashore.

"Wow! Doesn't that make them suspect it could be the Lord!"

7.   Whereupon the disciple whom Jesus loved said to Peter, "It is the Lord!" The moment Simon Peter heard it was the Lord he put on his sea-tunic, for he was stripped for work, and jumped into the water.

STRIPPED. Peter was not naked, for the Greek does not exclude the possibility of a loincloth, the characteristic dress of the fisherman at work. As was Adam, so here it is a guilty Peter who dons his sea-tunic, a sleeveless fisherman's garment which extends to the knees. He could swim in it easily, besides he has less than 100 yards to go. It is John who recognizes the Lord even though Peter is the first to act, reminding us of their actions at the tomb. Each is ahead of the other; John with his ability to perceive, Peter with his nervous readiness to act. What a combination for Christian work.

8.   The rest of the disciples came ashore in the boat, towing the net bulging with fish. They were not far from the shore, only about a hundred yards.   9.   When they get ashore they see a charcoal fire glowing, with fish and bread already cooking on it.   10.   Jesus said to them, "Bring Me some of the fish you have just caught."   11.   So Simon Peter returned to the boat and hauled the net ashore. Though the total in the net was as many as one hun-

dred and fifty three large fish, still the net was not torn.

 FIRE. The Lord has breakfast cooking when they arrive at the fire. But it is a charcoal fire, one not easily lit. May we not presume then some mysterious preparation —a miraculous fire? Why not? It is prepared for miraculously caught fish. The disciples see the bread and fish already on the coals. Then Jesus asks them to bring some of their newly caught fish to add to His. Again it is a nervous Peter who hastens to the boat and returns dragging the net behind him. The disciples take this all in. In a similar situation under similar circumstances, He told them they should become fishers of men if they would follow Him (Matt. 4:18, 19). The Lord's fish, already on the fire, likely picture His own ingathering of the O.T. saints to which are added those the disciples will gather as they work with Him after Pentecost (Heb. 11:39, 40).

 FISH. When Jesus first called them to be "fishers of men," He dramatized His orders by providing a miraculous draught of fish which broke their nets (Luke 5:6). Now that His resurrection has validated their ministry, they get another dramatization. This time the fish are numbered, and the net does not break. The real miracle is the size of the fish—153 is actually very few for their large nets. How do we understand this? The numbering (not the actual count) represents the numbering of the elect, with each person known to God. The net is the church. Though bulging with souls, it remains intact so that not one is lost (John 10:28). Peter, seen here dragging the net ashore, will again be pulling the net on the day of Pentecost when a catch of 3000 souls will be taken. Everything happening on the beach this morning is to be understood as having to do with Jesus' promise to make them "fishers of men." The new revelation of Himself is in the way **He helps them do it.**

"Is the Lord therefore teaching them about His part in working with them!"

12. Then Jesus gave the invitation, "Come, have breakfast." None of the disciples ventured to ask, "Who are you?" for they were fairly well

convinced it was the Lord. 13. Jesus then approached the fire. He took the bread, which He gave to them, and the fish as well. 14. Thus, for the third time, Jesus appeared to His disciples after His resurrection from the dead.

 CONVINCED. How do the disciples know it is Jesus? By what He does. The results, which followed their doing things as per His word, prove His identity. The disciples couldn't see Him in the darkness so as to recognize Him by sight. A charcoal fire gives off no such light. John wants us to feel their struggle in recognizing Him by His works. The new method has them uneasy, yet none is unsure enough of His identity to ask Who He is. This is precisely what Jesus wants. They will have to recognize Him after His ascension the very same way. Then He approaches the fire. As He bends low over the charcoal to get the food, the glow reveals Him by sight. Just as He washed their feet in the upper room, so He now serves them as a waiter. The lesson: if they will do as He commands, He will provide for their needs.

APPEARED. Jesus has made other appearances, but this is only the third time to His disciples as a group. He must have been standing away from the charcoal fire purposely so that His features were not recognizable. Thus the disciples had only His WORKS for identification. On a previous occasion, Jesus had miraculously provided bread and fish (John 6:11), but this time He does not give thanks as He broke the bread. Why? Because He didn't wish to make Himself positively known as yet. Giving thanks would have been an unmistakable identification. Only Jesus talked directly to God as a Son to His Father. This was one of the most awesome things they beheld in Him. However, it was something they themselves would be doing after Pentecost (John 16:26).

"Can Peter be comfortable served by his thrice denied Lord! Won't his denial have to be dealt with somehow!"

15. After they had eaten breakfast, Jesus said to Simon Peter, "Simon, son of John, do

you love Me more than these others?" "Yes Lord," he replied, "You know that I am fond of You." "Then feed My lambs," said Jesus.

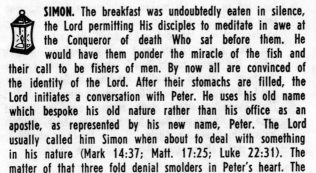

SIMON. The breakfast was undoubtedly eaten in silence, the Lord permitting His disciples to meditate in awe at the Conqueror of death Who sat before them. He would have them ponder the miracle of the fish and their call to be fishers of men. By now all are convinced of the identity of the Lord. After their stomachs are filled, the Lord initiates a conversation with Peter. He uses his old name which bespoke his old nature rather than his office as an apostle, as represented by his new name, Peter. The Lord usually called him Simon when about to deal with something in his nature (Mark 14:37; Matt. 17:25; Luke 22:31). The matter of that three fold denial smolders in Peter's heart. The Lord will use three questions in soul-surgery to cut the ache from Peter's heart.

LOVE. When Jesus said, "more than these," Peter's heart was cut to the quick. Just before he denied the Lord, Peter boasted, "though all forsake Thee, I will never . . . !" The Lord now raises the matter in front of the other disciples. The conversation turns on two different Greek words for love. Jesus asks, are you 100% devoted (agapao) to Me? A blushing Peter dares not use that noble word. Red-faced he replies, You know that I am fond (philo) of You. With his heart laid open, he would no more boast of his superiority over others. He drops the phrase, "more than these," thereby confessing his sin and foolishness in stating them before. Rather than vain announcements of his love, he will depend on the Master's knowledge of his heart. The Lord accepts Peter's statement, charging him to feed His lambs. "Lambs," would be new babes in Christ. See how it is not the lovableness of lambs that motivates Christian care, but affection for Jesus.

16.   A second time Jesus said to him, "Simon, son of John, do you love Me?" "Yes, Lord," returned Peter, "You know that I am fond of You." "Then shepherd My sheep," said Jesus.

SHEEP. Peter was shaken when the Lord asked the question a second time. But the Master would extract that word which means 100% devotion, if Peter is still inclined to big talk. But Peter sees himself honestly. He can't use that word. He is almost pleading with the Lord not to press his broken spirit further by demanding that lofty word "love" from him. Peter's denials have shown him that he does not love the Lord as he should. He cannot speak vainly now. How carelessly that word love is employed by Christians today. The Lord accepts Peter's statement and lays on him the heavier task of protecting the flock of God. The reference has to do with "guarding" God's people from the wolf, Satan. The "sheep" reference is an advance over the "lambs" of verse 15. He doesn't have to "love" the sheep, fondness for Jesus is basis enough. Again, affection for Christ should compel us to serve others, even if we don't love them.

17. Then for the third time Jesus spoke to Peter and said, "Simon, son of John, are you really fond of Me?" Peter was crushed when the Lord said the third time, "Are you really fond of Me?" "Lord," he replied, "You know everything. You know that I am truly fond of You." "Then feed My sheep," said Jesus.

THIRD TIME. This last question hurt most. The Lord used Peter's word (philo, not agapao) as if to question even his affection. The divine scalpel cut deeply. Peter protests: You know that I am fond of You. You can read my heart! Peter appeals to Jesus' perfect knowledge of his heart, as if to say, You must know that I am deeply fond of You. For every denial he had uttered, Peter has now given account. Three statements of fondness for His Master, balance the account for his three denials. Surely the Lord smiled His approval to Peter this last time. He did know His disciple's heart. Now the last speck of hidden feeling is out. The surgery hurt, but it was worth it. Peter can now serve Jesus as though the denials had never occurred. See how food for Christ's sheep is the first and last need, while shepherding (guarding) the sheep is the central action.

"With Peter restored to joy, will the Lord explain his future role and service!"

18.   "Believe Me Peter, when I tell you this. When you were a lot younger than you are now, you would dress yourself and go wherever you pleased. But when you are an old man, you will stretch forth your hands and another will gird you and take you where you do not want to go."

YOUNGER. The Lord discloses to Peter the manner of life awaiting him. He does so by contrasting his youth against his life as an old man. His youthful ways speak of his old nature. As Simon, he is independent and self-willed. As Peter, he shall mature to become subject to the will of God, denying himself for others. The Lord is speaking of Christian maturity when the needs and desires of others will dictate Peter's way of life rather than his own self-will. However, Jesus' words also contain a dark prophecy of Peter's destiny. Tradition has it that he finally submitted himself to Roman authority which bound him and crucified him.

"Was this a promise that Peter would reach old age or was Jesus referring to his certain martyrdom!"

19.   He said this to indicate the kind of death by which Peter was to glorify God. And with that, said to him, "Follow Me!"

GLORIFY. Writing these words at the end of the century, John has the advantage of looking back on what was already a historical event and well known to the churches. According to Tertullian and Eusebius, Peter was crucified, his death taking place 67 or 68 A.D. Had Peter still been living, John would not have publically written of his death in this fashion. The term "glorify God" was a customary expression for a martyr's death. To die for Christ soon became synonymous with glorifying God.

FOLLOW ME! If Jesus' prophecy of Peter's ministry and death were dark words, this "follow Me" is even darker. The Lord actually withdraws from the group of disciples and bids Peter follow Him — literally. Why? The Lord is obviously removing Himself, preparing to vanish from sight back into the spirit-realm. Does He wish Peter to see this? Is it to strengthen him for leadership and martyrdom? The command "follow Me" goes beyond the idea of Peter's following Him in a self-sacrificing life that leads to crucifixion. That has already been established. Apparently Peter is being taught by a dramatic device that even martyrdom is but a door to greater things in the spirit. Surely this was a mysterious moment in the resurrection history.

20.   Turning around, Peter noticed the disciple whom Jesus loved following them. He was the same one who had leaned against Jesus' shoulder at supper and asked "Who is it that is going to betray You?"   21.   When Peter saw him he asked Jesus, "What about this man?"

FOLLOWING. That Jesus and Peter took a mysterious walk is hereby confirmed. John indeed was following them. John, who considered himself a confidant of Jesus (as at the last supper) didn't feel the Lord's summons to Peter excluded him. So he tags along to see what happens. Peter looks backward and sees John following them. He loves John, and so far the Lord has not assigned a task or future to him. He inquires of the Lord's plans for John. Is Peter already turning his eyes from himself to show concern for another? Peter may have believed he was going to instant martyrdom, in which case this walk was a real test. His concern then might be that John was needlessly exposing himself to danger.

22.   "If I want him to remain until I come," said Jesus, "is it any of your business? You follow Me!"   23.   This statement of the Lord

gave rise to the rumor which circulated among the brethren to the effect that this disciple would not die. Yet Jesus didn't say, "He will not die," but instead, "if I want him to remain until I come, is it any of your business?"

REMAIN. The Lord mildly rebukes Peter, reminding him that each man has his own call and place in the church. What Jesus does say about John contains a prophecy of his future, and it is just the OPPOSITE of martyrdom. The opposite of martyrdom is natural death. Jesus' words, "until I come," most likely mean that John should remain alive until the Lord comes for him in **natural death.** It can hardly mean the parousia (the Lord's coming at the rapture), the destruction of Jerusalem, or the Lord's appearing at the end of the age, for none of those is the opposite of a martyr's death. Since the chapter is symbolical of the church, the coming of the Lord for John at the end of his life pictures the Lord's coming for His church at the end of the age.

RUMOR. A rumor arose that John was not to die but remain alive until the glorious return of Christ. It is important to see how John writes to kill the rumor. Obviously this epilogue was written by him, for another author would not have dared to speak so positively against the interpretation of the brethren. We note, too, that John makes no speculation as to what the Lord meant by "until I come," but limits himself to spiking the rumor. He wishes to make it clear the Lord didn't say he wouldn't die. The real meaning of the Lord's words remain dark. It is interesting how the Lord asks some to die as martyrs, yet not all. The beloved disciple was not asked to meet such a death, yet Peter was. We conclude it is Jesus' will for His servants to mind their own duty and not be concerned about future events as they relate to themselves or others.

"Does John reaffirm he has selected only a few things from the life of the Lord to prove that He is the Christ, the Logos of God!"

24. The disciple of which Jesus spoke is the same who has written these things and attests to their truth. We know that what he says is

true.   25.   Of course, there is much else that Jesus did. But, if it were all written down, item for item, I don't think the world itself could contain all the books which would be written.

BOOKS. After identifying himself as the author of this work, John reminds readers that he has not written as a historian, but has selected and arranged things consistent with his plan to prove that Jesus is the Christ. John never wrote in the first person. However, when it says, "We know that what he says is true," that "we know" is generally attributed to a copyist's addition made possibly at Ephesus. John's reference to the world being unable to hold the volumes which could be written, is his way of letting readers know it is impossible to exhaust the subject no matter how many books might be written. He is convinced he has written enough. He knows the Holy Spirit can use what he has recorded to satisfy any heart willing to be persuaded by the Word of God. John is himself abiding by the faith principle: God supplies sufficient evidence for faith to operate, but never enough to convince the unbelieving doubter.

DR. LOVETT is pastor of PC

Brother Lovett was saved through his "accidental" attendance at a minister's conference where he eavesdropped the conversation of a group of nationally known Christian leaders. There he overheard a discussion on the mechanics of salvation. For years he had been under conviction, yet no one troubled to introduce him to Christ. Armed with the necessary insight for the salvation experience, he hurried home to share it with his wife, Marjorie.

Together they knelt and invited Christ to come into their hearts.

A graduate of California Baptist Theological Seminary, he holds the M.A. and B.D. degrees conferred Magna Cum Laude. He has completed graduate work in Psychology at Los Angeles State College and holds an honorary doctorate from the Protestant Episcopal University in London. He is a retired Air Force Chaplain with the rank of Lt. Colonel.

Pastor Lovett is the author of the books and tools produced by Personal Christianity. The advent of his "Soul-Winning Made Easy," has dramatically changed evangelism methods in America, while the anti-satan skill offered in his "Dealing with the Devil," has alerted multitudes to their authority over our enemy through Christ. Dr. Lovett's experience as an editor of the Amplified New Testament and a director of the foundation which produced it, prompted him to begin work on "Lovett's Lights on the New Testament." His ability to explain the deep things of God in simple language, allows readers to understand their Bibles as the Holy Spirit intends they should.